Dear len,

Hope this helps —

love, len Anne

SCREENWRITING

Raymond G Frensham

TEACH YOURSELF BOOKS

For UK orders: please contact Bookpoint Ltd, 130 Milton Park, Abingdon, Oxon OX14 4SB. Telephone: (44) 01235 827720, Fax: (44) 01235 400454. Lines are open from 09.00–18.00, Monday to Saturday, with a 24-hour message answering service. Email address: orders@bookpoint.co.uk

For U.S.A. order enquiries: please contact McGraw-Hill Customer Services, P.O. Box 545, Blacklick, OH 43004-0545, U.S.A. Telephone 1-800-722-4726. Fax: 1-614-755-5645.

For Canada order enquiries: please contact McGraw-Hill Ryerson Ltd., 300 Water St, Whitby, Ontario L1N 9B6, Canada. Telephone: 905 430 5000. Fax: 905 430 5020.

Long renowned as the authoritative source for self-guided learning – with more than 30 million copies sold worldwide – the *Teach Yourself* series includes over 300 titles in the fields of languages, crafts, hobbies, business and education.

British Library Cataloguing in Publication Data
A catalogue record for this title is available from The British Library

Library of Congress Catalog Card Number: 93–85120

First published in UK 1996 by Hodder Headline Plc, 338 Euston Road, London NW1 3BH.

First published in US 1996 by Contemporary Books, A Division of The McGraw-Hill Companies, 4255 West Touhy Avenue, Lincolnwood (Chicago), Illinois 60712-1975 U.S.A.

The 'Teach Yourself' name and logo are registered trade marks of Hodder & Stoughton Ltd.

Copyright © 1996 Raymond G. Frensham

Typeset by Transet Limited, Coventry, England.
Printed in Great Britain for Hodder & Stoughton Educational, a division of Hodder Headline Ltd, 338 Euston Road, London NW1 3BH by Cox & Wyman Ltd, Reading, Berkshire.

Impression number	20	19	18	17	16	15	14	13	12	11
Year		2007	2006	2005	2004	2003	2002	2001		

CONTENTS

Acknowledgements

Copyright Permission and Rights Acknowledgements to: Richard Curtis for the extract from *Four Weddings And A Funeral*; Rob Grant & Doug Naylor for the extract from *Red Dwarf VI*; Jurgen Wolff for the flowcharts on pages 95 and 142; M&A Film Corporation Pty. Ltd., for the *Strictly Ballroom* synopsis; Writer's Monthly (ed: Alan Williams) and The Stage And Television Today for permission to quote from my articles.

There are many people to thank: to various members of the London Screenwriters' Workshop who have, in some measure, contributed: Mike Belbin, Colin Clements, Barbara Cox, Lawrence Gray, Melanie Heard-White, Peter Hogan, Henri Kleiman, Roddy MacLennan, Joanne Maguire, Susan Mundy, Margaret Ousby, Mark Parker, Phil Parker, William Sargent, Gary Seabrook and Allan Sutherland.

Industry figures who have assisted: Peter Ansorge and Allon Reich (Channel 4), Mike Bolland, Roger Bolton, Graham Clayworth, Stephen Cleary (British Screen), Dick Clouser, Andrew Curry, Richard Curtis, Andrew Davies, Tony Dinner, Nick Doff (TSI), Shaun Duggan, Charles Elton (First Choice), Barbara Emile, Julian Friedmann (Blake Friedmann), Malcolm Gerrie and Eileen Quinn (Initial), Michael Hauge, Richard Holmes, Anton Hume, Paul Jackson, Linda James and Lisa Paré (Red Rooster), John Kaye Cooper, Duncan Kenworthy, Lynda La Plante, David Liddiment, Adrian Mourby, Sue Nott, Jack Rosenthal, Gary Sinyor, Barry Smith and Laurence Brown (Richards Butler), Nick Symons (Carlton), William G. Stewart, Paul de Vos, Larry de Waay, Colin Welland, Ronald Wolfe and those interviewees whose quotes got cut.

To my typists: Yvonne Dickinson and Julia Humphries.

To the following for their support and encouragement: Simon Hill, Niraj Kapur, Patricia Madden, Dugal Muller, Olga Ruocco–Daley, Mike Shelton and Alan Smith; and to those friends whose social circles I had to withdraw from during the writing of this book – no doubt their lives improved immeasurably as a consequence!

Special thanks to my agent, Emma Darrell, of Roger Hancock Ltd., for services above and beyond the call of professional duty.

Finally, this book is dedicated to my parents, May and George, for everything – and more.

1

INTRODUCTION

❝ To make a great movie, you need just three things: a great script, a great script, and a great script. ❞

Alfred Hitchcock,
director

Why read this book?

This book is written for the starting-out screenwriter. The aim is not just to guide you through the intricacies and craft of writing for the screen (film, television and video), but also to give you guidance on how to approach the industry. Of all the different forms of writing, screenwriting is where creativity interfaces with business the most and you need to feel comfortable and confident when dealing with both. The media like to create a mystique about themselves and their working methods; I prefer to demystify the process.

You may already have a story you want to tell but don't know how to structure it into a screenplay. Or you may only have the enthusiasm to write, but no idea what to say. However, before you write scene one, there is still a tremendous amount of work to be done.

The book covers the techniques and specialist skills used in writing for the visual medium. It covers the practical questions I and many members of the London Screenwriters' Workshop have been asked over and over again: how do you get your ideas? what questions should I ask about my script or characters? how do I get an agent? how can I protect my copyright? and many more.

Many books on screenwriting approach the subject by laying down rigid rules that *must* be followed, particularly in regard to screenplay structure. This one is different. Here, when any guidelines are set out, I am not declaring 'this must be done'. What I *am* saying is two-fold:

- As a starting-out writer submitting your work to a producer, director or commissioning editor (i.e. those with the power to make decisions), your script will not be read by them. It will go to one of their Readers for assessment. It is their job, at the lower end of the production hierarchy, to sort through the 'slush pile' of unsolicited manuscripts (those not submitted by an agent). These professional readers are the people you and your script have to get past and impress. And any 'rules' this book outlines are the sort of points Readers have been taught and trained to look for in script submissions. And . . .
- You, the writer, need to know the rules of the game before you can begin to bend and stretch them to your own design.

❝ Writing a script is so much like writing a sonnet: you have very specific boundaries in which to shape a story.❞

Caroline Thompson,
screenwriter:
Edward Scissorhands, Black
Beauty, The Secret Garden

Basically, 90% of all scripts submitted are rubbish (for reasons you will discover in this book) and rejected outright. Approximately 10% are worth reading to the end. Of those, 2% are worth following up and calling the writer in for 'a chat', and only 1% are worth further serious consideration. (In Hollywood they say it's one script in every 100–130, but it's nearer one in 200, and rising.) Your script needs to get into that top 2%. This book will help you get there.

It is a distillation of accumulated knowledge and *experience* gained in the Workshop since it began in 1983, and from my own experiences in the industry as writer, script reader, teacher, film finance broker and producer, and as chair of the LSW. Most of what I teach is based on good films or television I've seen and bad scripts I've read. You will find it regularly illustrated with comments and experiences from writers who have made it or are now breaking through into the world of film and television.

There has never been a greater time for the industry. Audiences for film and broadcast entertainment are growing, demanding more, new and different experiences. The development of digital technology has meant a potentially limitless expansion of television, cable and satellite channels with the consequent air-time that needs to be filled. The opportunities are there to be grasped.

Finally, this book also supplies checklists (many gained from industry sources) and regular exercises you can use to analyse and assess your own efforts – 'interactive' in the truest sense of the word. What it is *not* is a substitute for your actually writing something – that's up to you.

❝ Never cross the road without a good script. ❞

Stephen Frears,
director

Original vs. Adapted

There are two types of screenplay: original and adapted. An original screenplay is one written directly for the screen and not based on any previously produced or published work (e.g. *Witness, Ghost, Tootsie, Heat, Speed, Rain Man, Home Alone, Four Weddings And A Funeral, The Singing Detective, Twister, Independence Day*).

An adapted screenplay is based on source material: a book, play, historical incident, true-life story (e.g. *Babe, Sense And Sensibility, Trainspotting, Field Of Dreams, Richard III, Quiz Show, Out Of Africa, Batman*) or, in films, a TV series (*The Addams Family, The Fugitive, Mission: Impossible*).

Over 60% of all produced screenplays are adapted, but nearly all first-produced scripts are original. Why? Because screen adaptation is a specialised skill (see Chapter 18) and because prior to starting a serious adaptation you need to obtain/buy the rights to the source material.

The rules of good screenwriting, however, apply to both forms.

Now list five other examples of each type of screenplay. Look at the films listed in your local paper. From what you know about them, work out what you think the screenplay credit will be for each film. Then check with the credit block on the film's poster. Were you right? You may find some posters carry only a simple 'screenplay by ...' with no reference to whether it is original or adapted. Why do you think this is?

Screenwriting: a collaborative process

The first thing you should realise is that *screenwriting is a collaborative process* – often painfully so, and it's simply a part of the beast you're going to have to deal with. You may be the sole author of your script, but from the moment you put that final full stop in place and send it to someone, the writer becomes part of a team. If you want total control over every word and image, write a novel or stageplay – the only way you'll achieve it in this game is to direct and produce your own work.

If your script is 'optioned' by a producer – where they buy the rights to exploit that property for a set period of time – it will go into 'development'. Here the producer will discuss the script with you and probably give you 'notes' asking you to rewrite or change certain parts to their suggestions (if amicably agreed) or demands (if not). Once a script goes into pre-production it is subject to input from the director, actors, set designers, special effects people and technicians. The script will be shaped further during actual shooting (making screen drama is the art of the possible, and budget is the bottom line) and the whole thing can change again in post-production when it is edited.

Why do you think that filmmakers do not settle for the writer's original vision? Do you agree that collaboration breeds creativity or do too many cooks spoil the broth?

If the thought of making changes simply to appease others bewilders, upsets or angers you, congratulations: you are on your way to being a screenwriter!

❦ It is the writer's screenplay, but the director's film – get used to it.❦

William Goldman,
screenwriter/author

Writer/director Wolf Rilla called the script a blueprint, and that's exactly what it is: a diagram of possibilities, used by the production cast and crew to realise the drama. It is created many months, sometimes years before the production appears on the screen. So at the start of your journey it is important to understand some of the technical parameters and visual possibilities in the screen media.

Defining the screenplay

They say film is the major art form of the twentieth century. Certainly other forms cannot reproduce the camera's controlled ability to enlarge and focus on what an audience sees, making it seem more real than real. This enlargement and focused intensity generates a level of *emotional realism* and *emotional identification* which is incomparable: it is to have this experience that audiences flock to watch the screen.

However, this experience takes place *in the mind of the audience* – and that is the area you must inhabit. The territory of the screenwriter is the *emotional experience of the audience*.

But to say that a screenplay is an emotional experience is not enough. a screenplay *structures* that emotional experience, giving it *direction* and *meaning* and a final climatic moment of catharsis.

The modern mainstream film screenplay may be defined thus: the story of a *character* who is *emotionally engaging* and who, at the beginning of the screenplay, is confronted with a *problem* which creates an *inescapable need* to reach a *specific goal*. The attempt to do so *inevitably* generates *almost overwhelming obstacles* which are finally overcome by the *transformation and growth* of the character.

The 'snapshot' nature of screen drama

Every story ever told is a collection of fragments. We don't recount every scene or detail that happened along the way, we select what we choose to tell (and leave out) and structure it into a good tale – even when we tell a joke.

Screen storytelling – and the screenplay – is the most fragmentary form of storytelling there is (after comic books). A film's story may take place over several days (or, as in *Driving Miss Daisy*, several decades) but you only have two hours of screen time to tell it in. So you select those fragments which create something that maintains the illusion of being a coherent and cohesive whole story.

If a novel or stage play – with its capacity to digress, address the audience directly, examine psychological insights, etc. – may be equated to making a home video, then screen drama can be seen as a series of snapshot photographs (i.e. scenes) brought together to create a larger overall picture. It is your job to choose the right snapshots – and learn what to *omit* – and assemble them in the order that is the most dramatically effective, drawing out the maximum emotional impact.

How do you decide what to omit? You leave out anything that the audience can *deduce* for itself. If a woman in an office says she is hungry and is going out to get a sandwich, what are the possible scenes? Let's consider the obvious ones:

1 Office. Pam says she's hungry and is going to get a sandwich.

2 Office, near door. Pam puts on her coat and exits.

3 Stairs. Pam descends the stairs and reaches the street door. She exits.

4 Street. Pam emerges from the door and crosses the street to the sandwich bar.

5 Sandwich bar. Pam enters from the street and queues at the counter.

6 Queue. Pam moves slowly in the queue and finally reaches the counter.

7 Counter. Pam orders a sandwich, waits as it is being made, and is given it in a bag.

8 Shop. Pam takes the bag to a nearby table and sits down.

9 Table. Pam opens the bag, takes out the sandwich and lifts it to her mouth.

10 Mouth. Pam takes a huge bite out of the sandwich. Now she's happy.

Now *you* decide which are the most meaningful steps in the above story. Choose the smallest necessary ones to tell this story coherently (answers: Chapter 22). Leave out the steps you think the audience can deduce. To leave steps in, ask yourself: is this meaningful to the story? does this move the story forward? would it damage the sense of the story if it were left out?

Film and Television: similarities and differences

Although both film and television deal in the same visual language and devices, there are a number of purely technical differences that should be initially appreciated.

Film	**Television**
Mainly shot on location with interior scenes shot either in a studio or on location.	Shot exclusively in a studio. Nearly all scenes are interiors (with occasional filmed exterior inserts).
A one-camera shoot, with the same scene filmed a number of times: firstly a master shot (a general all-encompassing shot), then separate takes for each of the main characters speaking, followed by any specific close-ups required.	Usually a three-camera shoot (a general shot including all the main characters and the set, plus one camera each for the main speakers).
Script format (see page 19) fills the entire page. Dialogue central, description runs across the page.	Script format (see page 20) uses the right-hand half of the page only. The left-hand is blank, i.e. everything on the right side of the page happens in front of the camera, the left side of the page is what happens behind the camera (this space will be filled in later with camera directions – the technical shooting script).

| Dialogue and (especially) visuals share the task of conveying the story and action. | Dialogue tends to carry the story and action. |
| Can carry numerous characters (possibly from ten upwards) but we focus on one of two specific people. | Can carry only a few characters (between five and seven). In series and soaps characters appear consistently. |

Also, remember the size of the screen – it matters. Film is much larger, demands a more visual kind of storytelling, and writers' and directors' ambitions are bigger. Television, although still a visual medium, is more intimate, and because it is more dialogue-driven, there is more reliance on 'talking heads' cutting and showing each character as they speak their lines. Moreover, if writing for a commercial TV channel, be aware there will be advertisement breaks and structure it into your script, building into each segment a climax or cliff-hanger that will hook your audience into returning after the break.

It is generally agreed that American films are more visual than their British and European counterparts, which are considered more literary (due to the tradition of the country) and more dialogue based. However, things are changing. But when an audience wants a truly moving, exciting, escapist or emotional experience, they still turn to the movies first.

Generally, the industry still considers film the highest attainment – it is 'art'; television is all that popular nonsense that gets shoved into people's homes (and if you write for the theatre or novels, you are considered a 'proper writer'). But the fact remains that with cinema, people have to make a conscious decision to see it, to travel and pay money to experience it. And being in a cinema is what they call a 'total experience' – even if that experience includes rustling sweet papers and the chattering voices behind you.

An old actors' maxim that might well be applied to writers is: they do theatre for the love of it, do television for the exposure and films for the money. Certainly money is in inverse proportion to the artistic fulfilment involved, but it also increases the more collaborative the process. And screenwriting is a *collaborative* craft.

❝ I am proud to say that twenty-three people contributed to the script for *A Fish Called Wanda*. ❞

John Cleese

Starting out

It is so easy for writers to spend all their time thinking or talking about writing rather than actually doing it. When you sit down and face that blank piece of paper there are thousands of reasons for not doing it (making the tea, reading the newspaper, watching TV). Of course you should ruminate on your ideas and script, but it's easy to do this at the expense of actually getting something written down. It's a good excuse, but it's still an excuse. So:

❋❋❋❋❋❋❋❋❋❋❋❋❋❋❋❋❋❋❋❋❋❋❋❋❋
❋   WRITE – Or Be Written Off   ❋
❋   ❋
❋❋❋❋❋❋❋❋❋❋❋❋❋❋❋❋❋❋❋❋❋❋❋❋❋

Think of it this way: writing is like a muscle that you need to keep exercising every day, even if it's for only thirty minutes.

> ❛ However raw the script, the voice should be apparent and still excite. Speak in your own voice and your originality will shine through. The craft can always develop later. ❜
>
> *Tony Marchant,*
> screenwriter

Don't expect a fully formed script to be delivered from the very start, or expect your own style to emerge directly onto the page at first effort. It really is a case of: write and write and keep on writing until you have written all the rubbish out of your system. It takes a while for you to discover your own voice. Often you will find other people telling you what your style is, which is why professional writers always recommend joining a writers' group for informed, constructive feedback. Remember:

❋❋❋❋❋❋❋❋❋❋❋❋❋❋❋❋❋❋❋❋❋❋❋❋❋
❋   Writers Train By Writing   ❋
❋   ❋
❋❋❋❋❋❋❋❋❋❋❋❋❋❋❋❋❋❋❋❋❋❋❋❋❋

It is also very easy for the writer to keep exerting energies on the same scene or sequence, writing and rewriting over and over again attempting to get it just right. In reality all you do is plough the same furrow, digging deeper and deeper while never actually reaching the end of your story.

So give yourself permission to write rubbish: don't set out to write it, but don't get hung up on it either. Get it written down first, then move on to the next scene until you reach the end. The time to revise is *after* you've got something on paper. In Art Arthurs' famous words:

❋❋❋❋❋❋❋❋❋❋❋❋❋❋❋❋❋❋❋❋❋❋❋❋❋❋❋❋
❋   **Don't Get It Right – Get It Written**   ❋
❋   ❋
❋❋❋❋❋❋❋❋❋❋❋❋❋❋❋❋❋❋❋❋❋❋❋❋❋❋❋❋

Writing a screenplay is a process of moving step by step towards your vision of how it should be. Accept those steps. Don't try to rush them. Relax and enjoy the process. And whatever you do, don't even attempt a rewrite until you have finished your first exploratory draft.

❋❋❋❋❋❋❋❋❋❋❋❋❋❋❋❋❋❋❋❋❋❋❋❋❋❋❋❋
❋   **Think Visual**   ❋
❋   ❋
❋❋❋❋❋❋❋❋❋❋❋❋❋❋❋❋❋❋❋❋❋❋❋❋❋❋❋❋

The screen is primarily a visual medium, so learn to think like a camera. The standard maxim states: "Show – Don't Tell". Remember this always. But never forget that *the territory of the screenwriter is the page*; it is your job to translate those images into words and the job of your script to *create the movie in the mind of the reader* – hook them, engage them, tell a great story that keeps them turning those pages until the end. Start to change the nature of your thinking processes: think visually and you will start to write visually.

❛ The one thing Corolco did say when they bought *Basic Instinct* off me was: it was superbly crafted and they paid that amount of money because the script conjured the movie from the page. ❜

> · *Joe Eszterhas,*
> screenwriter

❈❈❈❈❈❈❈❈❈❈❈❈❈❈❈❈❈❈❈❈❈❈❈❈❈❈❈❈
❈   **Look And Learn**   ❈
❈   ❈
❈❈❈❈❈❈❈❈❈❈❈❈❈❈❈❈❈❈❈❈❈❈❈❈❈❈❈❈

Finally, immersing yourself in the medium is *essential*. Screenwriters are mostly self-taught by way of reading published scripts, analysing videos and attending the occasional course. Indeed, much of it needs to be self-taught: a process of trial and error. So watch as much of it as possible. Read all the scripts you can lay your hands on. However, make sure they are original script drafts and not ones specially 'adapted' for book publication, as some are – see Chapter 22 for suppliers. But look and read with a critical eye. Use the points covered in this book to analyse the productions. Why does one film work and another fall flat? Look for the Acts, character development, plots and subplots, scenes and sequences, dialogue and subtext, etc. What made you keep turning one script's pages while another was a plodding read? Did the script *create the movie in your mind*? How did it achieve this? Was the style of writing particularly lively, gripping or funny? Did that translate to the screen version? What effect did it have on you – the audience? Learn from others, both those who have succeeded and those who have produced turkeys.

❈❈❈❈❈❈❈❈❈❈❈❈❈❈❈❈❈❈❈❈❈❈❈❈❈❈❈❈
❈   **IMPORTANT NOTE: The Audience**   ❈
❈   ❈
❈   **Throughout this book, whenever the term *audience* is**   ❈
❈   **used, it means TWO things:**   ❈
❈   **(i) the people watching the screen**   ❈
❈ **and (ii) the person reading your script for the first time.** ❈
❈   ❈
❈ **Bear this in mind at all times – not just when reading this** ❈
❈   **book, but every time you sit down to write your script.**   ❈
❈   ❈
❈❈❈❈❈❈❈❈❈❈❈❈❈❈❈❈❈❈❈❈❈❈❈❈❈❈❈❈

Your writing day: self-discipline and time management

❝ You need commitment to write a good screenplay. To succeed you must be willing to discipline yourself and put in the work. ❞

> *Joe Eszterhas,*
> screenwriter: *Basic*
> *Instinct, Jagged Edge*

❝ I just treat it as a job, like any other job, except it's better paid. I get to work by 10 and, apart from lunch, work through till about 6 or 7, then I knock off. ❞

> *Paul Attanasio,*
> screenwriter: *Quiz*
> *Show, Disclosure,*
> *Donnie Brasco*

The first step is possibly your toughest: learn self-discipline. Remember that this muscle needs daily exercise: the more you do it, the stronger it becomes. If you have limited time, set yourself a daily minimum word target (like Kingsely Amis' 500 words a day). Don't worry so much about the quality, the idea is to get into the habit. The secret is to know yourself, how and at which times of the day you function best, and under what ideal circumstances. We are all different. You need to discover that best time within yourself, and exploit that period to the fullest – *regularly*. Make an appointment with yourself.

❝ I try to give myself deadlines and write in my calendar 'First draft due one month from now'; I plan that out and try to meet those deadlines. I need a deadline because it is so easy to do something else. ❞

> *Tom Schulman,*
> screenwriter *Dead*
> *Poets Society, Honey,*
> *I Shrunk the Kids*

It's all down to self discipline and learning how to manage your time. There is no 'wrong' way of going about creativity. Just because nobody else has done it your way before or you know of no-one working in this way, does not make it wrong or any less valid. Your rule should be: Whatever You Feel Works Best For You – Do It.

❛ You've got a screenplay, 120 pages, there's a lot of white spaces, and it's full of double-spacing. There's no reason why you can't write three pages a day; it's not like writing three pages a day of a novel. Not many words, not many words. ❜

William Goldman

—— The role of the Script Reader ——

As already mentioned, the Script Reader (Hollywood now calls them 'Story Analysts') is the industry's first line of defence against the writer. They work alone, unseen, are poorly paid and they wield a huge amount of power over the new writer. Few writers have a good word to say about them, but Readers are considered a necessary evil by the industry. Production executives simply don't have the time to read through the vast numbers of screenplays submitted to them. Many are so badly written or poorly conceived they need to be sifted out before anything with the slightest potential is found. Script Readers are the screening process that filters out most of the rubbish. Once a screenplay has been read, the Reader will present a one or two page review (called 'coverage') to the producer or head of development. This assessment will give a brief plot summary followed by the reader's personal comments and conclude with two recommendations: one for the script and one for the writer. This recommendation will usually take the form of one word: Pass, Consider or Recommend. A sample blank Reader's report sheet is shown on page 14.

It is possible that the recommendation for the writer will be different to that for the script. You may have a great hook and an interesting story (Recommend) but it may be badly written (Pass).

If a Reader does not recommend a script by an unknown writer, it will be rejected automatically. If they do recommend the script it will be passed onto the people who count. So your first task is to get past the reader with a positive recommendation – for both you and your script.

Before reading a script, the Reader will first pick it up and feel the weight – does it *feel* like the right length? Then they will look at the last page number – shorter scripts are read first, the longer ones left till last. For feature films, a script of 90–100 pages will put a smile on the Reader's face; even up to 110 pages is acceptable. The *maximum*

SCRIPTS/FORMAT NOTES

TITLE:

AUTHOR:

AGENT: TEL:

READER: DATE:

OUTLINE:

COMMENT:

RATING: 1   2   3   4   5   6   7   8   9   10

Figure 1.2 Sample Coverage (Reader's Report) Sheet

acceptable is *120 pages*. I know it sounds silly – ideally a script is as long as a script is – but there are good reasons, and it is important to keep the Reader on the writer's side. If a Reader is put off by a heavy script, they will approach it with a negative attitude.

Next, the Reader will run their thumb over the page edges and fan the script briefly, gauging the ratio of black print to white paper on the page (they want to see lots of white): is it written to the right layout and does it look like a proper screenplay? Layout and presentation are important (Chapter 2).

Then they will read the first ten (nowadays possibly just five) pages, skip to read the last five pages, followed by reading a couple of randomly chosen scenes from the middle of the script. If they are satisfied and impressed, they will then read the complete screenplay from page one to the end.

You get them to do this by making your script interesting, engaging and easy to read. It has to work on screen, in the mind of the reader and on the page too. So many scripts, although they may be structurally perfect and may make great movies, are incredibly boring on paper. Your job is to *seduce the Reader*.

Getting past the Reader is just your first step, but as with all first steps, it could be the one that trips you up. This book will help you get through that barrier. The journey starts here.

❛ Why did Miramax pick up *The English Patient*? Because it was the best script I'd read all year. ❜

> *Harvey Weinstein,*
> M.D., Miramix Films
> (distributors)

❛ The script (*The Full Monty*) was so good that we gave it the green light within a few weeks of receiving it. ❜

> *Jim Wilson,*
> Director of Production,
> *Fox Searchlight,* L.A.

2

SCREENPLAY LAYOUT: YOUR VISUAL LANGUAGE

❢ Get hold of a professionally formatted script and note everything; from simple instructions like INT. and EXT. to the exact length, and *never stray from that format*. You might submit a masterpiece but if it's not properly laid out, the reader may give up after scene one. ❞

Lynda La Plante,
writer: *Prime Suspect,*
Widows, She's Out, etc

Before starting the creative journey it is important to establish some basic details about how scripts are laid out on the page and the technical language used.

The first thing to understand is:

❋ ❋
❋   Correct Presentation And Layout (Format)   ❋
❋   Are The First Essential Steps   ❋
❋   To Selling Your Screenplay   ❋
❋ ❋

So play by the format rules – some are flexible, many are not. Their purpose is *clarity* and *communication*, to make your script an easy read for the Reader. Don't fight them – use them.

All scripts submitted must be typed, on white A4 sized paper and on one side of each sheet. Any which are not are always returned unread. If sending to the USA, remember they prefer 8 ½" x 11" paper. They should also be typed using 10 characters per inch. Why?

- it's an easy read
- it helps the Reader time a script. Film format: 1 page of script = 1 minute of screen time. TV format: (generally) 1 page = 30 –40 seconds of screen time
- it allows other readers in the production process to understand quickly the content of the scripts and the intent of the writer.

Many novice screenwriters put enormous energy into perfecting their story, structure, characters and dialogue, yet forget the packaging. In this business, both content and packaging are critical. Producers and agents feel: a writer professional enough to get the packaging right is also professional enough to script a strong story. Hence, it is essential you get hold of some properly formatted scripts (both film and TV) – Chapter 22 lists source addresses. Reading them will soon show you what you can and can't change. Your aim is a *professional* and *readable* script.

Pages

Covers and title pages will be covered in Chapter 14. Page one is your first page of text. Pages are numbered in the top right-hand corner. Also on page one:

- **Feature film format:**
  You do not place the title at the top of the page. The first information to appear is FADE IN: in the top left-hand corner (FADE OUT. appears in the bottom right-hand corner of the last page, at the end of your script).

- **Television format:**
  UK (taped/studio) scripts have their own specialised layout (see Fig: 2.3, p 20). Commercial TV scripts have a break (for the ads) and are labelled Part One and Part Two.

All TV shot on film, TV films and mini-series use film format. All American teleplays (including sitcoms) use film format and are written

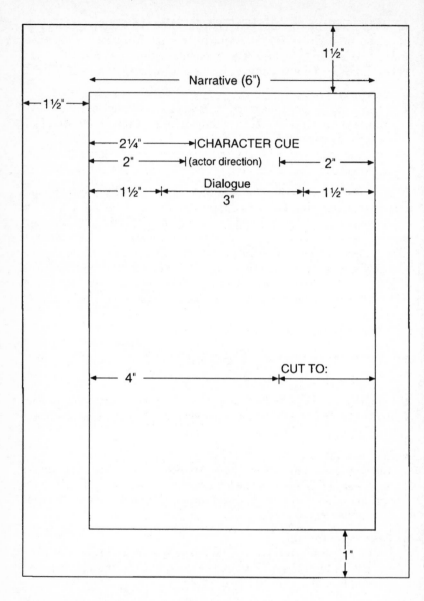

Figure 2.1 Film Screenplay Format Dimensions

63

INT. BEDROOM. MATTHEW & GARETH'S HOUSE - NIGHT

GARETH and MATTHEW, asleep, cuddled.

INT. CARRIE'S FLAT. BEDROOM - NIGHT

CHARLES and CARRIE are in bed.

>   CARRIE
>   I kind of knew this would happen.
>   The moment I said 'yes' to Hamish,
>   I had an awful suspicion there'd be
>   one final fling.

INT. FIONA'S BEDROOM. TOM & FIONA'S HOUSE - NIGHT

FIONA, awake, in bed reading.

INT. TOM'S BEDROOM. TOM & FIONA'S HOUSE - NIGHT

TOM, asleep, flat on his back, pyjamas buttoned to his chin.

INT. KITCHEN. CHARLES AND SCARLETT'S HOUSE - NIGHT

SCARLETT, drunk and asleep under the kitchen table.

INT. CARRIE'S FLAT. BEDROOM - DAWN

>   CARRIE
>   I think it's time you went.

>   CHARLES
>   But it's 5 in the morning.

>   CARRIE
>   And at nine in the morning my
>   sister-in-law comes round. We're
>   discussing bridesmaids.

>   CHARLES
>   You're right. I've got very little
>   to contribute on that one.

Silently CHARLES dresses.

>   CHARLES (cont)
>   Would you like to go out
>   sometime....

>   CARRIE
>   (not lifting her head
>   from the pillow)
>   No thanks.

>   CHARLES
>   Why?

Figure 2.2 Sample Film Script Layout Source:
Four Weddings And A Funeral © Richard Curtis

40. EXT. (OB)   <u>**STREET OF LAREDO**   **DAY**</u>
THE **APOCALYPSE BOYS** WALK SLOWLY
THROUGH THE SWIRLING MIST AND STOP.
KRYTEN STEPS OUT TO FACE THEM.
LISTER, **RIMMER** AND **CAT** FILE OUT
AFTER HIM, AND THEY FAN OUT ACROSS
THE STREET.

<u>DEATH</u>
Got yourself a little help, Sheriff?

<u>KRYTEN</u>
Now I remember. You're a computer virus. You
travel from machine to machine, overwriting the
core program.

<u>DEATH</u>
Have infection will travel, that's me. Let's see if
we can't tip the balance a little, here.

DEATH HOLDS UP HIS ARMS. A BOLT OF
BLUE ELECTRIC SHOOTS UP INTO THE SKY.
MIX TO:

41. INT.   <u>**OPS. ROOM**</u>
A BLUE SPARK SHOOTS OUT OF **KRYTEN'S**
HEAD AND TRAVELS UP THE WIRE
CONNECTING HIM TO THE A/R CONSOLE.
THE CONSOLE FIZZLES LIKE THE
NAVICOMP DID BEFORE, AND WE SEE THE
MONITOR SCREEN.
"SPECIAL SKILLS" AND FLASHING BESIDE
IT: "ERASE".

42. EXT. (OB)   <u>**STREET OF LAREDO**   **DAY**</u>
AS BEFORE.

<u>CAT</u>
What's he doing?

<u>RIMMER</u>
He's stalling. He spotted us for what we are: a
bunch of mean, macho, bad-ass desperados who are
about to kick his boney butt clean across the Pecos.
(THROWS TOOTHPICK TO THE GROUND)
Enjoy the show.

- 35 -

Figure 2.3 Sample Television Script Layout
Source: Red Dwarf VI (Episode 3: Gunmen Of The Apocalypse)
© Rob Grant & Doug Naylor

in Acts (two acts for half-hour, four Acts for one-hour) and this is typed at the top of the page above FADE IN: Each Act begins on a new page. Note that with filmed or taped series the series name is also included. Each Act begins with FADE IN: and ends with FADE OUT.

Note: the most notable thing about the first page of most film scripts is they contain little, if any, dialogue: you are trying to set the scene and atmosphere, establish your main character, intrigue us, draw the audience in, and get the Reader to read the full screenplay, not just the dialogue (they easily do!)

Scene headings

Scene headings, or slug lines, provide the basic where-and-when information for the scene that follows. Each new scene has its own slug line and they are always written in capitals. The information is set out in a very specific order, e.g.

> INT. CHURCH. REGISTRY ROOM – NIGHT
> EXT. MANOR HOUSE – DAY

Where

(a) Stated first is whether the scene takes place:

> INT. (interior – e.g. in a room)
> EXT. (exterior – e.g. in the street)

(b) then the general location is given, (c) followed by the specific location, e.g.

> INT. CASTLE. BED CHAMBER – DAY

You may often find (b) and (c) reversed, e.g.

> INT. BEDROOM. CHARLES'S HOUSE – NIGHT
> EXT. SCARLETT'S CAR. MOTORWAY – DAY

This is fine, as is:

> EXT. STREET. DOWNTOWN NEW YORK – DAY

The object is clarity for the reader. You decide, but if in doubt, stick to (b) then (c).

Note: If your scene takes place inside a car or train compartment, this is still an INT. scene, even though the car or train is outdoors, e.g.

INT. CAR – EVENING

INT. MOVING CAR LONDON STREET – DAY

You may also find INT./EXT. – this is where the camera's POV (point of view) is placed inside filming or watching an event outside (e.g. a scene happening out in the street being seen by someone inside a car), as in:

INT/EXT. CHARLES'S CAR/STREET – DAY

or EXT/INT. where the scene is happening inside (e.g. a house) being shot from outside (e.g. the garden), as in:

EXT/INT. GARDEN/HOUSE – EVENING

When

Usually, DAY or NIGHT is sufficient. You may find DAWN, MORN-ING, AFTERNOON, LATE AFTERNOON, DUSK, LATER, SAME TIME, or A FEW MOMENTS LATER, if there is sufficient reason for using these. You may sometimes need to use FOLLOWING or CON-TINUOUS if the scene or (particularly) conversation continues unhindered from the previous scene but shifts location. Generally, stick to the simple DAY or NIGHT.

The rule is: a new scene occurs whenever there is a change of either *location* or *time*.

NOTE:

- Scenes are never numbered in writers' scripts in film format. They only get numbered in later production drafts. However, UK TV scripts generally do have numbered scenes (check the series format first). American TV is as per film format.
- Scene headings are generally not underlined, though this is sometimes practised in UK television formats.
- Always double-space between the heading and the text and between scenes.

Scene direction

Also called 'the business', this is the text which contains all the descriptions (i.e. non-dialogue) of the characters' actions and natural events relevant to the story. Mostly written in lower case, clear, concise and uncluttered, not justified, it should be written in the *present tense*, e.g.

> Mr. Blonde closes the door after them. He then slowly
> turns his head towards the cop.

Characters names are always in lower case except for the first time they enter your script, when they are in upper case or capitals. If the weather is important to your scene, write it here in the business at the start, and in capitals.

All camera directions (if you must use them) are done in upper case throughout, although be careful and very sparing with these technical directions. Remember, you are not directing this film – and Readers can soon tell if you secretly harbour these ambitions by their overuse. Some scene directions, however, you will find commonly in scripts:

v.o.	(voice-over)
o.s.	(off screen)
M.O.S.	(without sound)
P.O.V.	(point of view)
f.g.	(foreground)
m.g.	(mid-ground)
b.g.	(background)

The last three are self-explanatory. Voice-over refers to dialogue that runs over the top of the scene, as in *Blade Runner*, *The Wonder Years*, and the opening of *Field Of Dreams*, *Maverick* and *Out Of Africa*, etc. It is (usually) narrated by the main character and tells part of the story. It is never heard by the other characters and may reveal the thoughts of the character speaking. It should be minimised. If used, it is placed where the dialogue goes and written out in full. For example:

KAREN (v.o.)
I had a farm in Africa.

o.s. refers to dialogue actually heard by the other characters (and the audience) but spoken by a character who cannot presently be seen on screen.

M.O.S. is used when you have people talking on camera but the audience does not hear the dialogue. For example:

> In the b.g. Charles and David talk together M.O.S.
> They both use sign language. Charles is very deft and
> comfortable with it.

Try to minimise your use of M.O.S.

P.O.V. (i.e. the camera is seeing things through one particular character's eyes) is used a little more often.

Camera angles

Leave them out! A sure sign of an amateur is an abundance of camera angles (pans, dollies, zooms, close ups, etc.) in a script. Many scripts available to buy are shooting scripts, which will include these directions. But writers, in their drafts, should not do so. Some directions you may occasionally come across are:

LS	(LONG SHOT)
MS	(MEDIUM SHOT)
CS	(CLOSE SHOT)
C/U	(CLOSE UP e.g. of the face)
Tight C/U	(e.g. on the eyes alone)
Two-shot	MS of two characters
Three-shot	MS of three characters... etc.

But it should *not* be necessary to use any of these terms in your own script; they only clutter. If you really have to use them, be very sparing. If it is absolutely essential to your screenplay, there are ways of getting round them. Instead of 'LS of a mountain chalet' try 'In the distance...' or 'Smoke rises from the chimney of a distant chalet...'

Use of 'We see' or 'We hear' are valid ways of describing what the audience should focus on, for example:

> We see two pairs of hands fumbling for the key in the
> door lock.

> We hear a CRACK of thunder, then a scream.

but they should be used infrequently, as substitutes almost always exist. When in doubt, leave them out.

Remember, your script should focus on the storyline and characters, not the specifics of production. Create the movie in the mind of the reader and leave the job of directing to the director.

Montages

This is where you are creating a series of shots to build up a collective picture or feel (they tend not to include your main characters and there is usually no dialogue in a montage). They can be written in a number of ways. For example:

MONTAGE:

A – The volcano ERUPTS ash and fire into the sky.

B – People run wildly through the streets. PANIC.

C – Looting of stores. People running with armfuls of clothing and food.

D – Military police trying to restore order.

E – Planes flying overhead.

Note the double spacing between the lines. Remember, one script page = one screen minute. If a fight lasts for three minutes on the screen, call the shots so that, on the page, it will run for three pages. Rather than write this:

INT. BAR – DAY

Jake storms into the saloon. He grabs a bottle and breaks it on the bar rail. He advances across the floor. It is a stand-off with Clint.

write it like this:

INT. BAR – DAY

Jake storms into the saloon.

He grabs a bottle and breaks it on the bar rail.

He advances across the floor.

It is a stand-off with Clint.

This way, not only are you using up your minute but you are highlighting the important action. It is also an easier form to read. Lastly, never write something like 'A montage to bring tears to your eyes.' Call up the images, create the picture and atmosphere – think visual.

Paragraphing

Long unbroken paragraphs of business are ugly to look at and difficult to read (a script reader scans the page downwards). So try to break up your paragraphs into units of action or ideas. My advice is never have a paragraph longer than four or five lines. Numerous one, two and three-line paragraphs are acceptable and probably to your advantage. Breaks in sentences within paragraphs are done with dots (...) or two dashes (- -). If breaking from one page to the next always try to end your sentence before going on to the next page.

Entrances and exits

How do you move from one scene to another? The convention is you will CUT TO: (written in the bottom right hand corner at the end of your scene). However, even when it is not written, the Reader knows there is no other way to do it. So don't clutter up the text with CUT TO: each time. You will save space and probably add another three or four pages to your script.

Other terms you will find are:

FADE IN   (always at the start of a script)
FADE OUT   (at the very end)
DISSOLVE TO:
FADE TO BLACK
FREEZE FRAME

Remember, if you FADE OUT or FADE TO BLACK on one scene, you must always FADE IN on the next. But unless you can absolutely justify them, stick to CUT TO: or better still, leave them out.

Character cues

The name of the character speaking that piece of dialogue, in capitals, is situated approximately 1½″ in from the edge of the dialogue; it is never centred (see page 18). Normally all your characters will have names, but characters whose functions in the story are minimal and/or brief may simply be given roles, e.g. FARMHAND, SECRETARY and so on.

Actor direction

This is where you, the writer, issue direct instructions to the actor on how to deliver the dialogue you've written. Best advice is: don't, *unless* the tone of delivery is in direct contrast to the meaning of the words:

JOHN
(sarcastically)
This is gonna be a great party.

They are always in brackets, in a line to themselves and set half-way between the CHARACTER CUE and the Dialogue. Generally, don't intrude on the actor's (and director's) territory.

Actor direction is, however, useful if your character is specifically speaking to someone and there are several people within earshot, for example:

JOHN
(to Sandra)
Where's my shirt?

or like this:

The phone rings.

JAN
Griffin Mill's office... one
moment.
(to Griffin)
Bonnie Sherow.

Griffin nods, he'll take it.

You do *not* put action descriptions here:

(Incorrect)

JOHN
(hitting Sandra)
Where's my shirt?

(Correct)

JOHN
Where's my shirt?

He hits Sandra.

Dialogue

After the business comes the dialogue. It runs immediately below the name of the character speaking, and fits into a column approximately 3″ wide down the centre of the page (see page 18).

All dialogue is single-spaced and there are no large blank spaces in between words unless they are filled with something, either (beat) or (double beat), meaning pause and longer pause. This can be written either of two ways:

(i)
>   THE ANGEL
>   (not even breathing hard)
>   I'll let you fall down for free

He looks down at the stunned quartet.

>   Maverick was mine anyway. . .
>   (beat)
>   . . .' cept now it's personal.

(ii)
>   THE ANGEL
>   (not even breathing hard)
>   I'll let you fall down for free

He looks down at the stunned quartet.

>   Maverick was mine anyway. . .
>   (beat) . . .' cept now it's personal.

Do not use hyphenation to break words from one line to the next (although those that are naturally hyphenated may be broken onto the next line):

(*Incorrect*):

>   JOHN
>   I never said that. No, I dis-
>   tinctly remember.

Likewise, do not use hyphenation to break dialogue from one page to the next. End the dialogue sentence at the bottom of the page and begin the next sentence at the top of the next page.

When a character's dialogue has been interrupted by description (not by another character's dialogue) then it is shown thus:

> JOHN
> I didn't mean to do this.
> I hope you can understand.

He takes a knife and approaches Sandra. She writhes and sweats, the rope pulling tighter at her wrists.

> JOHN (Cont'd)
> You see, I really am so sorry
> about all this mess.

If only one line of description (business) intervenes, do not repeat the character cue unless clarity is threatened.

Sound

Any sounds that are crucial to your script (and are not made or caused directly by the actor) must be included in the Business in capitals, for example:

A police car siren SHRIEKS through the dark streets.

Norma turns as a floorboard CREAKS in the old tower.

Jake HEARS the noise of running water from upstairs.

Sandra's fist CRASHES through the window.

The SOUND OF ethereal music GROWS (or FADES)

A KNOCK splits the silence.

You may also find the term OVER used, which means the same as v.o. (VOICE OVER) but for sounds. So here's how it all comes together:

INT./EXT. WAREHOUSE – DAY

We follow Mr. Blonde as he walks out of the warehouse . . .

. . . to his car. He opens the trunk, pulls out a large can of gasoline.

He walks back inside the warehouse . . .

INT. WAREHOUSE – DAY

. . . carrying the can of gas.

Mr. Blonde POURS the gasoline all over the cop, who's BEGGING him not to do this.

Mr. Blonde just sings along with Stealer's Wheel (OVER)

Mr. Blonde LIGHTS up a match and, while mouthing:

> MR. BLONDE
> "Clowns to the left of me
> Jokers to the right. Here I am,
> Stuck in the middle with you."

He MOVES the match up to the cop

. . . when a bullet EXPLODES in Mr. Blonde's chest.

Note that specifying exact music in scripts is not normal. Tarantino can do it. A danger is that new screenwriters tend to capitalise every little sound so that every other word of their narrative is in capitals. Again: think. Use sparingly; when in doubt, leave it out. Lastly, never write anything in italics.

❢ If a script is not correctly formatted, even with the best will in the world, I'm reading it very negatively from the start because I'm thinking: this person is unprofessional, they haven't even bothered to take the time to find out how it should be laid out. It doesn't have to be glossy, just easily readable. ❷

Paul Marcus, Producer:
Prime Suspect 2

Some useful books on format:

Professional Writer's Teleplay/Screenplay Format Guide, $4.55 + postage, available from the Writers Guild of America (East). For all addresses, see Chapter 22.

Cole & Haag: *The Complete Guide to Standard Script Formats.*
Vol 1 – Film Formats
Vol 2 – Television Formats
(CMC Publishing, US) $16.95 each

3

ORIGINATING YOUR IDEAS

❛ When I started writing full-time all I had to talk to was my word processor. I had to learn how to bounce ideas off myself. ❜

Andrew Davies,
writer and adaptor

———— Pre-writing ————

❛ Why are there so few good scripts around today? It's to do with how much work you put into it before you sit down and write it. It's a very disciplined hard job, but it pays off. ❜

Adrian Dunbar,
co-writer: *Hear My Song*

Any novice writer will naturally put immense efforts into the actual writing, pouring it out in one massive creative burst and then feel it's perfect as it is. But this approach ignores any aspects of craft. In truth, the actual writing (called the *exploratory draft*) is only about 5% of the process. All the preparation leading up to that – developing ideas, creating characters, structure, scenes and sequences – is called the *pre-writing*, and is covered in the next nine chapters.

Generally, the process of screenplay creation breaks down like this:

> Pre-writing = 65%
> Actual writing = 5%
> (exploratory draft)
> Re-writing = 30%

The more you work on the pre-writing, the easier your exploratory draft should become.

Writing a screenplay is a succession of breakdowns: moving from the general to the specific. Now study the flowchart on page 33. It gives an overview of the entire process from idea to delivery. Don't worry if some terms mean little at present. The chart is there to refer back to as you progress through this book.

—— Your goal as a screenwriter ——

❝ Don't try and write a movie you wouldn't want to go and see yourself. ❞

Paula Milne, writer:
The Politician's Wife,
Die Kinder, True Love

Why do you want to write? Most writers will respond: 'I wanted to move people, make them laugh and cry'. How do you do this? In screenwriting teacher Michael Hauge's words:

❈❈❈❈❈❈❈❈❈❈❈❈❈❈❈❈❈❈❈❈❈❈❈❈❈❈
❈   Your Primary Goal As A Screenwriter Is To   ❈
❈   Elicit An Emotional Response In Your Audience   ❈
❈❈❈❈❈❈❈❈❈❈❈❈❈❈❈❈❈❈❈❈❈❈❈❈❈❈

To hook them in and keep them watching that screen or turning to the next page to see what happens next, *seduce the reader*. Every scene described, every line of dialogue, every image created must work towards your aim. Remember this at all times. Engage your audience successfully, tell a great story well, and you will elicit that emotional response. Try to enter the mind of the audience and understand the way emotions affect and work on us.

❝ I once thought drama was when the actors cried. But drama is when the audience cries. ❞

Frank Capra,
writer/director:
It's A Wonderful Life, etc. ... etc.

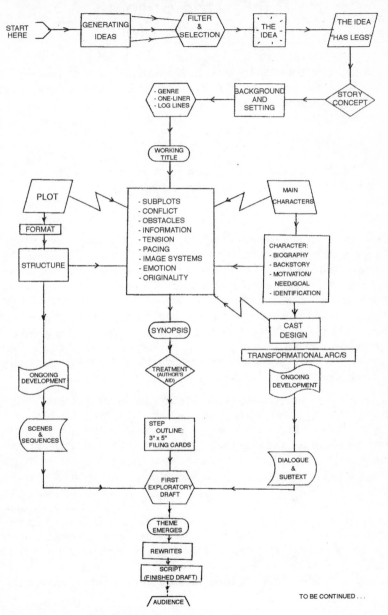

Figure 3.1 Flowchart: The Screenwriting Process

B.P.F. – the Burning Passion Factor

❧ The scripts that really work are those written straight from the heart, passionate pieces with the energy of the writer's voice, even though the structure may not be perfect – that can be fixed later. ❧

Paul de Vos,
screenwriter/
producer

❧ Ultimately, writers need to write what they're passionate about, not what seems to be currently commercial. ❧

David Friendly,
V.P., Imagine Entertainment

Whenever producers or script editors are asked 'what do you look for in a script?' one word crops up every time: *passion*. Passion in the writing, your ideas and their expression. Of course they look for an original core idea, engaging characters and a sense that the writer has a knowledge of structure; it is taken as read that the manuscript will be professionally presented and laid out to the relevant format. But even if plot, characters or structure might be a little shaky, if there is a certain intensity to the writing – the voice that comes across – they may at least be gripped by that (and possibly call you in for a chat).

This is where the writer's voice comes into play. It is the difference between being asked 'what is your script about?' and 'What is your script *really* about?', those deep-down ideas and thoughts you want to put across to an audience (see Chapter 4 – Theme). Do you have them?

❧ What's the point of writing a beautifully structured script, with all the right technical points in it, if the writer has nothing to say? ❧

Lynda La Plante

So, whether you are writing your masterpiece of arthouse cinema or an episode of a soap opera, write about things *important to you*. Dig deep inside yourself, access your own experiences through life, take one aspect or incident that has been important to your own development.

But don't just take this one aspect and write it down exactly as it was for you. Take that specific idea and develop it, fictionalise and add to it, to make some universal truth that will mean something to others – your audience.

❝ If you're not passionate about it, why is anybody else going to be? Besides, you won't enjoy the process anyway. ❞

Paul Marcus

──────── Thinking creatively ────────

Writers think in a number of different ways:

(i)	Inductively	– from the specific to the universal
(ii)	Deductively	– from the universal to the specific
(iii)	Logically	– i.e. causality: how things happen in the world, one thing following another
(iv)	Non-Logically	– i.e. coincidence: by definition meaningless, but life itself contains coincidences
(v)	Creatively	– discovering hidden links or relationships between two unrelated things (ideas/people) no-one has seen before

Thinking creatively leads to you discovering unexpected twists in a plot or character. For example: you have a man and woman violently wrestling on the floor, one has a knife. If one stabs the other, this is predictable; if the nature of the fight changes and they start to make passionate love, suddenly you have spun them off in a new direction and played with audience expectations.

As a writer, always look for the unpredictable, the unexpected twists in everything you write – it will keep the audience on their toes and eager to know what comes next. That same eagerness that makes the viewer glued to their seat until the end is the same emotion that makes your reader turn to the next page. William Goldman said you should have a surprise on every page. Do you agree?

One thing, however, is certain: ideas won't come by just waiting for inspiration:

❝ The art of writing is the art of applying the seat of the pants to the seat of the chair. ❞

Art Arthur,
writer

Now watch *The Usual Suspects*. Note down the moments in the story where you are caught by an unexpected plot twist. Repeat the process with other films, preferably those you have not seen before.

Generating ideas

❝ Today's writers are a weakened generation because they grew up watching movies, so now they're just recycling them. Be original. Real cinema is about the imagination. ❞

Michael Leeson,
screenwriter:
The War Of The Roses

At this stage of pre-writing you will be using two different types of thinking: firstly, *inductive* – a divergent, opening-out, almost stream-of-consciousness thinking strategy. Your aim? To come up with as many and as diverse ideas as possible. It is non-judgmental, because at this stage you are only interested in quantity.

This is followed by *deductive* thinking, where you sift, filter and test your ideas, selecting those you feel are strongest, have the most 'legs' (to use an industry term).

❝ Just sit there putting any thoughts you may have, however stupid they may seem, onto your computer or the page; you want to be as free as possible. Later, your inner critic is your friend – that gut thing that's saying 'this is great', 'this is terrible' or 'this character isn't working'. ❞

Tom Schulman

— How do I generate these ideas? —

- Personal experience: you have lived a life – use it. (But please don't write your life story exactly as it happened.) Take a specific from your experience, extend it into something which might have meaning/ resonances for others.

  ❝ I'd like to thank my parents for making me the way I am, and my analyst for making it marketable. ❞

  Ruby Wax

- Others' personal experience: as above, but pick on something in the lives of your friends, family, people you've met; not the whole person, but elements of that person/their experience. Collect these aspects and make into a new composite.
- Some lines of dialogue/a character: always carry a notebook (and pen) for overheard conversations, characters that catch your eye; note their dress, speech, mannerisms, etc.
- Newspapers: keep a file of clippings/stories that stimulate you (a fertile source area – especially for contemporary TV drama).
- An advertising slogan/song title/newspaper headline: if it stimulates you, create a new story from that source.
- Visual stimuli: look at photographs or a painting. What moves/ intrigues you about it? What story could this scene be telling? Take an interesting newspaper photo: create a new backstory (every- thing that happened up to the moment that shot was taken); what is each character's history? what happened after this photograph was taken?
- Brainstorming: pick a subject, list down a free-association of thoughts and feelings that come to you, unstructured odds and ends. A technique regularly used in advertising.
- Mind mapping: write a key idea or subject in the centre of a page. Write associated ideas in bubbles around, with a line linking each one to your core idea, then draw bubbles of associated ideas coming from those bubbles until you build up a spider's web of words and ideas.
- 'What-If' scenarios: ask yourself 'What would happen if this happened?' For example, if I woke up tomorrow and discovered I was blind/had developed ten-feet arms/turned into a cockroach/if the world were to end in 24 hours/if time stood still? . . . and so on. (a good method for finding surprising twists). Most stories start this way.

- Dreams: keep a notepad beside your bed to record stories/images from your dreams (example: Mary Shelley's *Frankenstein*).
- Visualisation: we all visualise in dreams, daydreams and our imagination. This is conscious creative visualisation you can tap into at will and bring under control, accessing the unconscious via conscious relaxation techniques. Relax *completely* in absolute silence and mentally recall an imagined favourite location or a person in your past: draw on all your remembered senses – visual, auditory, taste, smell, movement, feelings. Use your mind as a film screen to project onto it whatever you are imagining.
- Adaptation: (novels/real-life stories, etc.) Fine as a writing exercise, but if you're serious, obtain the copyright owner's permission first.
- Intertextuality: another word for plagiarism. Steal from others – but don't make it obvious (*Reservoir Dogs* is *The Asphalt Jungle* meets *The Killing* (Kubrick, 1956) meets *City On Fire* (Ringo Lam, 1988 – Hong Kong), *Clueless* a reworking of Jane Austen's *Emma*).

These are just suggestions. You need an eclectic approach to ideas. At this stage, it's not the getting there that is important, but how you do it that's interesting. Keep an ideas file. Whenever one occurs to you, write it down, drop it in the file, forget about it. Writers need to generate a continual stream of scripts and proposals. (Most professionals work on more than one project at a time, all at different stages of development).

❢ I have a shoebox: for ideas, fragments, snatches of conversation I hear. I scrawl it down, throw the scraps in the box. Every time I start a new script I start picking through the pieces. Suddenly you get five pieces together and think: this is almost the first Act of a movie, if I flesh it out a bit. ❢

Shane Black,
screenwriter:
Lethal Weapon

Using any or all of the above devices, generate thirty different ideas or subjects. These may be just one word, but list them. Remember, make no critical judgements on them at this stage – you want quantity. Now put the list aside and read on.

— Filtering and testing your ideas —

By now you may have realised that, for a writer, ideas for stories are everywhere and finding them isn't the problem. Figuring out the story that has the most 'legs' (potential) is more the problem. Even more difficult is trying to discover which story *you* care about, the one that generated in you the strongest gut-emotional response, and which story you feel you can tell well. How can you do this?

Apply the following to each of your story ideas:

(i) Answer all these questions about each idea: Who is it about?/What?/When?/Where?/Why?/How?

(ii) Has it got 'legs'?: Is it going somewhere? Is it dramatic? Can I dramatise it in a series of scenes with a minimum of explanation? Does it have a plot? Can I create one for it?

(iii) What is at stake? It should be something vital and specific – not just for the character/s involved, but for me as a writer.

(iv) Look for the unpredictable, the original, the uniqueness in your ideas and characters. Look for the surprises.

(v) Is it my story to tell, something I really care about? Can I draw upon my own emotions/experiences, then apply them to that idea? Is it something I only partly understand or does it need working out? Is it something I know I *should* care about (war/cancer/famine) but don't truly?

(vi) Is it too personal a story for others to become involved in or be affected by? Can the idea be worked in a caring, original and uncompromising way to make it meaningful to somebody else?

(vii) Now play Devil's Advocate: think of all the objections to that idea: weaknesses, reasons why you should not pursue it further, etc.

Tip: If your idea happens to be a TV script about people working in a TV show, or a movie script about people making a movie, my advice is: *drop it*. Producers passionately hate industry in-jokes. Those that exist (e.g. *The Player*, *Living In Oblivion*, *Get Shorty*) are made by established film makers with track records.

- Now that you have your list of thirty ideas, run each one through the questions above and select those ideas which seem the most promising, have the most 'legs' (use your gut reaction/ emotional response). Put the other ideas aside.

- Take two or three of these unrelated words/ideas from your chosen list and juxtapose them together. Now find or make links between them. Then write one sentence for each group of linked ideas.

- For those ideas you have selected, develop a story for each of them, with a beginning, middle and end. (Use only one or two sentences for each segment.) This may not work for all your ideas, so drop those that don't convince or work for you.

- For the ideas that remain, expand to a fuller outline, including your major scenes (a couple of sentences for each scene) and breaks for each segment: beginning, middle and end.

If, after all this, you still feel strongly enough about your idea, then perhaps it is strong enough to continue. . .

4

DEVELOPING YOUR IDEAS: FROM IDEA TO FRAMEWORK

❝ Movies are about story: is it well told, is it interesting? If it isn't it doesn't matter how talented the rest of it is. ❞

William Goldman

Some definitions

Story This is the series of events which form the screenplay *in chronological order*

Plot The most interesting and dramatically effective way of telling the story

And these are the ways the terms will be used throughout this book.

Getting it clear

Having decided on your story idea, you should now start to move from the general to the specific, asking yourself all sorts of questions about it so you can analyse it and get the best from your story. Questions covered in this chapter are:

- Why do I want to write this screen story?
- Who do I think will want to watch it?
- What is it about?
- Who is it about?

- Why is it mainly about this character rather than any of the others?
- How important is the setting or background? Will the audience need any special information in order to understand the story?
- How do I want the audience to feel while they are watching it and after it's over?

You may find you have a background but need a plot. Often you will have one idea, but it is not enough until you have two ideas – one about character, one about situation – that you can make a story. You also need an end.

Now try to express your story in these terms:

It is a story about (CHARACTER) who wants to (DO SOME-THING) and ends up (SUCCEEDING/FAILING/CHANGED).

This is your *story concept*.

And remember, being a visual medium, these 'somethings' are visible actions and desires that can be seen on the screen – they form the action of your story. Expressing your story concept will help you achieve clarity about your characters and the action of your story.

❝ The success of the independent movie is because people like the story. The story is now the star. ❞

Roger Simon,
screenwriter

— How do I choose my main story? —

Your gut response

What affects you the most emotionally?

Look for the end

How do you know you've got a good story? Many writers reply 'Not until I've got my ending.' Make sure you've got your end. The genre (page 46) of story you're telling might give you clues to what this might be. Remember your story concept.

Is the ending dramatic enough with a big enough final climax? Has it a climax at all? The story with the strongest ending/biggest climax will usually tell you it should be your main story.

Ask yourself: what is original about my story?

And keep asking yourself this throughout the writing and rewriting stages. Originality is not just one element, it is a mix of elements.

Examine the dramatic structure

Not just the overall three-act structure (see Chapter 7), but the smaller three-act dramas going on inside the overarching one (inside Acts/subplots etc); which one is the most dramatic? The strongest one usually leaps out and tells you 'this is my main story'.

Surprises

What are they? Where are they? Always look for the unexpected, the twists in the story that will catch your audience off-guard asking 'what happens next?'

❢ It's so hard to tell good stories. It's very tedious and often mind-bending work to come up with an interesting story with enough twists and turns to sustain a journey. ❥

Chris Carter,
writer/creator:
The X-Files, Millennium

───────── **'Writing backwards'** ─────────

Screenplays are written backwards. That is: the prime focus for both writer and audience is the final climax at the end of Act III. So, having decided on your end climax – where you need to get to – you work backwards to make sure that everything in the plot – other climaxes, set-backs, decisions made, etc. – works 100% towards that scene and moment. However, don't get too disturbed if your end hasn't come to you yet – it will. Remember, they didn't know the end to *Casablanca* even during filming.

Now ask yourself this question: do I believe in this story? If you do, then carry on . . .

– There are only eight basic stories –

How many stories do you think have been told on screen? Thousands? More? In fact, the answer is eight. They are listed below, together with examples. Can you list other examples?

1 ACHILLES

The fatal flaw that leads to the destruction of the previously flawless individual (*Samson and Delilah, Othello, Superman, Fatal Attraction* and *film noir*). This is also the cornerstone of the crime drama – the flaw belonging not to the hero, but the villain (*Columbo, Miss Marple*).

2 CANDIDE

The innocent abroad, naive optimism triumphant; the hero ('good man') who cannot be kept down (*Chariots Of Fire, Forrest Gump, Indiana Jones* and *James Bond* films, *Mr. Bean*).

3 CINDERELLA

The dream come true; unrecognised virtue recognised at last; goodness triumphant after being initially despised; rewards achieved through transformed circumstances (*Pretty Woman, Rocky, Strictly Ballroom, Star Wars, Mighty Morphin' Power Rangers*).

4 CIRCE

The chase; the spider and the fly; the innocent and the victim; mostly the temptress ensnaring the love-struck male (*Godfather I, Othello, Double Indemnity, Body Heat, 9 1/2 Weeks*, film noir).

5 FAUST

Selling your soul to the devil may bring riches, but eventually there is a price to be paid; the long-term debt; the uncovered secret that catches up with us sooner or later and damns us; the inescapability of Fate (*Wall Street, The Seventh Seal, Fatal Attraction, The Red Shoes,* horror and spaghetti western genres).

6 ORPHEUS

The gift taken away, the loss of something personal. Either about the tragedy of the loss itself or the search which follows the loss (*Dr. Zhivago, Rain Man, Jason And The Argonauts*).

7 ROMEO AND JULIET

Boy meets girl, boy loses girls, boy finds/does not find girl – it doesn't matter which (*West Side Story, When Harry Met Sally, The Graduate, Sleepless In Seattle*).

8 TRISTAN

Triangles (eternal or otherwise); man loves woman and unfortunately, one or both are already spoken for (*Fatal Attraction, The Graduate, Jules et Jim, Pennies From Heaven*).

Each of these stories has an original source. Research the original stories and read them. What makes them so special that even today they are still used as templates for screen stories?

These eight basic stories can be presented in many different forms – tragedy, comedy, history, whodunnit, soap opera, etc. and can be mix'n'matched, even inverted, but they still form the basis of all stories and plots.

The most popular story is Romeo and Juliet. Why do you think this is so? List five screen dramas which come under this heading. Now list five where Romeo and Juliet appear as a secondary story element

List as many films as you can which combine the following: Achilles + Cinderella, Faust + Orpheus, Circe + Tristan, Candice + Romeo & Juliet.

You will probably find your own story idea slotting into one (hopefully more) of these categories. This is no bad thing: audiences and commissioning executives want something new and different but also something simultaneously familiar (called the 'comfort zone'). The danger is in sticking exclusively to one archetype (you risk obviousness and banality). Find new ways of telling it: combine, reshuffle, adapt, expand on them.

Now run your story idea past one or more of the above eight outlines. Can you make it better by adding any elements from 1-8? Can you increase the conflict/set-backs/love/character mix, etc? The more elements you add, the more original you may find your story becoming – and the less like other things you've seen.

Remember, you are looking to get the maximum drama and emotional impact out of your script. Once you have decided on what plot appeals to you, your next step is to place it within a genre.

Genre

6 In America, before they make a film, they always ask you: 'What shelf is the video going on?' 9

Anthony Minghella,
writer/director: *The English Patient,*
Truly, Madly, Deeply

Everything we write is in one genre or another, or is a combination of genres. Genre refers to the type of story: the tradition within which your tale is set as it relates to previously made films/dramas. Not simply tragic, comedic or historic, it is more focussed than that. Here are some conventions:

Romance

Two people fall in love, overcoming various obstacles, winning out in the end. (*Romeo And Juliet, War Of The Roses, The Mask.*) In *When Harry Met Sally* the obstacles are themselves; they each believe friends can't be lovers.

Comedy

A funny story where nobody gets willfully hurt (*Airplane, Ruthless People, Throw Mama From The Train, Four Weddings And A Funeral*).

Buddy movie

Two characters who are complete opposites (and thus repel each other) are compelled to stay to work together. The repulsion changes until by the end they are best buddies (*Lethal Weapon, Midnight Run, The Last Boy Scout*).

Crime/Detective Thrillers

The investigation of crime and criminals: crime does not pay (*Philip Marlowe, Dirty Harry, Columbo, Poirot*).

Film Noir

Dark and deadly. A man whose life experience has left him sanguine/bitter meets a woman to whom he's sexually and fatally attracted. Sometimes he comes to cheat, attempt to murder /actually murder a second man. (*The Maltese Falcon, Double Indemnity, Basic Instinct, Body Heat, Devil In A Blue Dress, Seven*).

Other genres are: Western, Sci-fi, Gangster, Melodrama, Action-Adventure, Suspense-Thriller, Mystery, Horror, Biography, Historical Romance, Melodrama, Musical, Road Movie, Martial Arts, Cult, Generation X, Documentary. Can you think of others?

> Now list three films for each genre. Can you list their conventions in three sentences?

It is also possible to mix genres, for example: Sci-Fi/Noir (*Blade Runner*), Horror/Noir (*Angel Heart*), Comedy/Western (*Blazing Saddles*), Romance/Comedy (*Four Weddings And A Funeral, French Kiss, The American President*), Romance/Comedy/Western (*Maverick*), Crime/Noir/Comedy (*Dead Men Don't Wear Plaid*), Action/Suspense/Thriller (*Speed*), Sci-fi/Action/Comedy (*Men In Black*), and so on.

> Can you think of other mixed genres? Name three other films for each type listed here.

However, the only way to really understand this idea of genre is to watch lots of films or TV made in that particular style. Be aware of it next time you watch something.

Look at your own idea in terms of genre: it may help you decide what sort of plot, characters and themes (page 51) you are dealing with. It might give you an indication as to what your story ending might be like. Does it?

Try not to see genres as a limitation. Think creatively, beyond conventional imagination to arrive at original and unique solutions.

❛ When working on a project, I try and think 'what are the great films in that type and their great remembered moments', and try to aim for that. With *Misery* I always had *Psycho* in my head, with *Butch Cassidy* it was great Westerns like *Shane*. ❜

William Goldman

—————— **Whose story is it?** ——————

If an event happens – e.g. a car crash, bank robbery, assassination of President Kennedy – each one of the witnesses and participants will have their own version of that event. Their own point of view (P.O.V) is their story. So, decide on who's telling the story, whose eyes we are seeing these events through, and your main story and sub-stories (subplots – page 55) and their course will begin to clarify.

The three-act linear structure: an introduction

In Chapter 7 we'll be examining the screenplay's three-act structure in detail, but at this stage we should just establish the basics. People refer to this template as the Classic Hollywood Film structure, but its origins lie with Aristotle, and it actually forms the basis of nearly all good dramatic structure.

Act I	The Set-Up	Establishes Main Character(s), Setting, Situation, a Conflict and Goal. Protagonist (or Hero) begins the journey to achieve that goal.
Act II	Development	Develops the main story; establishes and develops obstacles to that goal; develops the Protagonist and other characters; adds depth and meaning to the story concept.
Act III	Pay-Off and Denouement	Contains Climax and Resolution: the main climax occurs; the goal has been achieved /task completed; all the characters' relationships and subplots are resolved, and finally the audience are allowed to wind down, feeling satisfied at the end.

In a film screenplay, these Act lengths generally work out thus:

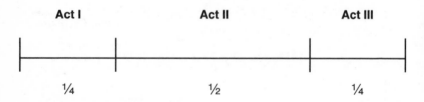

Act I   Act II   Act III

¼   ½   ¼

with each Act ending in a climax and each one being greater than the one before, until we reach the major climax at the end of Act III. Familiarise yourself with it now. Can you begin to create your story in this way?

The one-liner

Now try to express your story in one sentence using no more than 25 words. In this sentence, focus on the core idea of your story. Refer to the story concept, it may help.

This one-liner will not only help you focus on your story, but can be used as a device in your *pitch* (chapter 19) when you are selling the idea to someone. Put simply, this sentence should *make me want to watch this movie* and encapsulate that single solid concept which attracts an audience. For example:

> The story of a hero who goes it alone against a rigid social hierarchy and wins the day – but the hero is a talking pig! (*Babe*)

> A dislikeable man is forced to repeat the same day over and over again and cannot escape; can he find a way out – and love? (*Groundhog Day*)

> A board game comes to life. (*Jumanji*)

> *Romeo & Juliet* – on the Titanic (*Titanic*)

This is similar to what eighties Hollywood called the High Concept – that single core concept which sells the movie and helps the producer imagine the poster, for example:

$$Alien = Jaws \text{ in space}$$
$$Top \ Gun = Rocky \text{ with jets}$$

❝ High Concept means I can hold the film in the palm of my hand, so straightforward, so simple. ❞

Steven Spielberg

When asked: 'What's your story about?' the one-liner is your reply. Now do it.

❝ Making a one-liner out of it is easy. Making a great one-liner is hard. ❞

Julian Krainin,
Head, Krainin Prods.

Log-lines

Now try creating some log-lines for your project. These are the kind of short, pithy slogans you see on film posters that capture, at an emotional level, what it's about, or the kind of short descriptive billings used in weekly TV guides ('a gripping tale of family passion, intrigue and drama'). Their sole purpose is to *attract an audience*. They are about creating the right expectations – in producers, agents, the audience. Although log-lines (also called strap-lines) won't come into play until the final stages, when packaging your script as a selling document, writing them here will help you focus on your project and clarify its 'through-line' (thrust and integrity).

Log-lines consist of *two* key elements:

- The Rule of Three
- Contrasts: start with a factual description, then take the imagination on a journey

Examine how both elements are used in these examples:

'Honour made him a man.
Courage made him a hero.
History made him a legend.' *Rob Roy* (1995)

'Imagine if you had three wishes, three hopes,
three dreams . . . and they all came true.' *Aladdin* (1992)

'Someone said "Get a life" – so they did.' *Thelma And Louise* (1991)

'This is Benjamin . . . He's a little
worried about his future.' *The Graduate* (1967)

'A story of Love, Laughter and the Pursuit of
Matrimony.' *Muriel's Wedding* (1994)

'Don't breathe. Don't look back. The Dark Side
of Nature.' *Twister* (1996)

'Everything is Suspect. Everyone for Sale. And Nothing is what
it seems.' *L.A. Confidential* (1997)

Here are some more for films (with release dates). Can you guess which ones from just the log-lines? (Answers: Chapter 22)

1 "Five Good Reasons to Stay Single" (1994)
2 "The List is Life. The Man was Real. The Story is True" (1994)
3 "Sex is Power" (1994)
4 "In their hands a Deck of Cards was the only thing more dangerous than a gun" (1994)

Now create some log-lines for your project. When thinking them up, ask yourself:
● Does it go to the emotional heart of my story?
● What does it tell me (as an objective observer) about my story?

Note: don't expect the log lines you work out here to be the ones you create later.

Theme

❛ In my younger days I was writing but then I discovered something: I had this great urge to communicate, but I had nothing to say. ❜

Bruce Joel Rubin,
screenwriter: *Ghost, My Life*

Theme is a *vital* ingredient in a screenplay. When discussing your script with an industry professional, two questions always crop up: 'What's it about?' (your one-liner), followed by: 'What's it *really* about?' This is where your theme enters.

Theme is that universal statement about the human condition you, the writer, want to make; those ideas or words you want your audience to take away with them at the end to help them live fuller, happier, better, more rounded lives. Theme applies to your audience, but it also answers the question: '*Why* do I want to write this script?'

Theme gives your screenplay emotional depth. It is not a statement in dialogue. It is more related to and embodied in the development and growth of your main character, it derives from the successful combination of all the elements of a screenplay – and it should take the whole of the screenplay to say it properly. Indeed, theme, like plot, almost always sounds foolish and shallow when simplified into a couple of sentences.

An audience's interpretation of theme is always subjective: *Tootsie* may be about a man who dresses up as a woman in order to get a job. To its director, Sidney Pollack, it was 'an exploration of love that had friendship as its basis, and whether these two could co-exist' (compare *When Harry Met Sally*). For Michael Hauge, the theme is: 'in order for a relationship to succeed, we must be honest – to ourselves, and others' (compare *Groundhog Day*, *The Mask*).

In *Witness*, a film we shall examine in depth in Chapter 7, the theme is the collision of two worlds with opposing values: the city values of the gun and masculine individualism vs. the earthly seasonal non-violent Amish with their high regard for community; is it possible to move from one world to the other without being tainted or affected in some way? Ideally don't we need a balance of both?

Theme is about 'writing from the heart'; you have to trawl into your inner self and emotions to discover what your personal themes are; they are about how you see the world, and what you want to say to your audience about the nature of society and living one's life.

In general, you will not know the theme of your story before you start writing it. Rather, it is something you discover while writing your exploratory draft, or after. Don't worry about it or force it; let theme come to you in its own time. The time to develop and texture it into your screenplay is during the rewriting.

❛ This new generation of screenwriters are completely versed in Hollywood structure, but the depth is missing. They aren't really writing about anything. ❜

> *Dan Pyne,*
> screenwriter:
> *Pacific Heights,*
> *Doc Hollywood*

Watch the following films. What do you think the theme of each one is? (Answers: Chapter 22)

1. *Field Of Dreams*
2. *Jumanji*
3. *Batman Forever*
4. *Jerry Maguire*

Title

Choosing the right title for your script is essential: good ones hook the audience, bad ones put them off. It has to grab their attention, be memorable, impart the essence of your script and tell us something about the setting, core idea and the characters.

What do these titles evoke for you?

Star Wars	*Star Trek*
Strictly Ballroom	*L.A. Law*
Dumb and Dumber	*The X-Files*
Speed	*Brideshead Revisited*
Unforgiven	*Cheers*
sex lies and videotape	*thirtysomething*

Each one conjures up an automatic mental picture and a subconscious emotion about it, and stimulates our curiosity.

Your final title is probably the last thing you decide on after the script has been completed, so at this stage give it a working title, perhaps one word or the subject matter, to give your project an identity.

Background and setting

You need to know completely the world your story is set in to make it believable for your audience (i.e. make them suspend their disbelief). It doesn't have to actually exist, but they must believe that it could.

Ask yourself these questions:

● What type of world is it? How do I want to affect my audience? Will they feel recognition at a world similar to theirs? Can I capture their imagination with a world they've never seen but which will appeal to them?

- Is it a *realistic* world close to the real world the audience live in? Is it one they might live in, in another country or another time in history?
- Is the world *exotic*? Maybe the world exists but the audience would never visit it (e.g. Everest, the moon).
- Is it *fantastic*? Maybe it doesn't exist in reality but it may in some fantasy. (Some things may resemble the world as we know it, but the rules may be different.)
- Is it the world of a particular fictional *genre*? The audience will know this is not reality, that cowboys were probably never like this, but still . . . The rules of conduct will generally be the same as in present-day reality.
- What is the *climate* like? How does it affect the lives of the people? Can they live outdoors or must it be mostly indoors because of the cold? Are there any illnesses/special dangers only found in this world as a consequence?
- *Landscape* – is there beauty in the natural surroundings? Are the inhabitants aware of this? Are there any animals? What are people's attitudes towards them? Are they work beasts or pets?
- *Society* – how do people live in this world? As groups, couples, singly? Are they isolated or does everyone know what everyone else is doing? Are they at war or at peace with each other? Is there enough food? Do they have houses? If not, where do they live?
- *Economy* – how do people make a living? What do they earn? Do they work to live or live to work? Do they work at all? Is there poverty? How do they travel? Is travel fast/slow/organised/chaotic?
- What is the arrangement of *power* in this world? All social situations (including love) have an uneven distribution of power; do people have power over their own lives? Can they decide what to do tomorrow? Are they governed by the need to work or by some over-lord? Are they tied to their job/land or can they study/work independently? Do they have spare time? Do they have wealth and power over others? Do they wish to be free? Remember:knowledge and information are power.
- What are the *rituals* of this world? A family meal, washing your hands, washing the car, catching a bus, all are rituals.
- What are the *ethics* of this world? What are the moral constructs? Where are the boundaries of right/wrong, good/evil, legal/illegal?
- How important is the *spiritual life* in this world? Is there organised religion or cult/s?Does it enrich or limit their lives? Does the religious

establishment have powers over their lives outside of the hours of worship? Is organised religion unimportant but the inner spiritual search paramount?

- Are the *emotions* important in this world? Do people talk/sing about love/hate? write/read poetry? have affairs or feuds? Is it acceptable to express emotions openly or are they suppressed through custom/for some particular reason (institutional or professional discipline etc.)? Is it a world where it is considered important to be controlled and unemotional at all times?

- Are the creative and performing *arts* important (to the society in general, to your character/s in particular)? Or is everyone glued to their home computer game? How do people amuse/entertain themselves/each other? Is there any leisure time?

- Are people in general *content* with this world? Do they wish to change it or long to leave it? If they did, would they miss it?

- If you were an intelligent, perceptive alien landing in this world for the first time, what would strike you most about it? Looking closer, would you find those first impressions misleading?

The setting of your story fixes it in time and space, that is, historically (past? present? future?) and with regard to place (specific locations, streets, rooms).

Although you may feel the setting limits you on what is possible in the story, it focuses you as a writer. A story must not only have a general world canvas as a backdrop, but it must also have a specific setting, a smaller world. That world must be small enough for you to understand all of it, like a creator God. Not knowing fully the world of your story means you will not be able to make real choices in that world. You will then tend to borrow from other recognisably similar situations. This leads to clichés and stereotypes. Be original; the depth of that originality produces better and more believable answers and solutions.

Subplots

Although your script will have a main plot, it won't be enough to sustain your script and give our understanding of the main story and main character/s depth, colour and meaning. You need subplots – additional stories linked to and involving other characters or other incidents which have an influence on the main plot and the way your main character reacts. They are vital. You should have:

- A main plot
- A main subplot
- Other subplots

Short-form television drama will have a main plot and a subplot (possibly even a second subplot); beyond that, it could strain. Films have a main plot, a main subplot and between three and five significant other subplots (seldom more). TV serials, mini-series and soaps will have a dozen or more plot strands.

Audiences are very visually literate today. Even if a subplot is slight, or appears briefly, your audience will still receive it, however subtle.

The important thing about subplots is:

❋ ❋

Whatever Your Main Plot Ends Up Being, All Your
Subplots Should Inform And Feed Into Your Main Plot

❋ ❋

The kind of relationship a subplot has to the main plot must be one of these four:

- **Contradictory:** going against the core idea of your main plot
- **Complementary:** resonating the ideas in your main plot
- Acting as a **Set-Up:** and hooking your audience until you introduce your main plot
- **Complicating:** the life of the main plot (e.g. by introducing a love story into an action-adventure drama such as *Speed*)

Subplots will carry and embody the message/theme of your screenplay; usually they tell us what the story is really about (redemption, community vs. individualistic values, the search for identity, good vs. evil etc.) For example, the main plot in *Field of Dreams* is about building the baseball diamond, but the writer was more interested in exploring the father-son relationship and the role of dreams. In *Witness* the writers were more interested in the John Book–Rachel relationship (as were the audience). They explored this via the subplots, especially the main subplot.

> Now watch *Witness*. Write down what you think is the main plot and the subplots, and what relationship (of the four above) they had to the main plot. Can you chart each one's development?

A fast-moving, complex film such as *Tootsie* has at least five subplots:

1 Michael–Julie (actress in the soap)

2 Michael–Sandy (his insecure friend)

3 Michael–Les (Julie's widowed father)

4 Michael–Brewster (the soap's lecherous doctor)

5 Julie–Ron (the soap's director)

. . . arguably six (Michael–Jeff, his flatmate), each one further complicating the main plot of Michael's attempt to get, maintain and then quit his acting job. Each subplot has something to say about the nature of love and friendship, each has its own internal structure and each grows out of and intersects the main plotline. See pages 58–59.

> Watch *Tootsie*. Did you notice so many stories being carried out simultaneously? Probably not. The joy of a well crafted script is that not only does it manage to carry so many stories simultaneously, it integrates them, along with the theme, with consummate ease – you don't notice it and can't see or feel the joins.

So subplots have a number of dramatic uses:

- *To show parallel action.* Have two distinct stories, linked or not, so you bounce between them to illuminate your main story.
- *To reveal subtext.*
- *To reveal different aspects of your character.*
- *To surprise the audience.*
- *To delay the development of your main story.* This is useful in comedy (where it's easy to divert from the main story for some minutes and create set-pieces) or where your main story is quite thin.
- *To introduce another character.* Each significant character should have their own story (see Chapter 4).

	SET-UP	1st TURNING POINT	DEVELOPMENT
MAIN PLOT →	Michael can't get a job	Michael gets a job – as Dorothy.	Michael becomes very successful.
SUBPLOTS ↓			
1. MICHAEL – JULIE	Michael (as Dorothy) meets Julie on first day at work. He's attracted to her.	Julie asks him to dinner. Their friendship begins.	They become friends. They go to the country. They talk. Dorothy encourages Julie to break up with Ron. Dorothy helps Julie out by babysitting.
2. MICHAEL – SANDY	Establishes the long-term friendship between Michael and Sandy by showing them in various situations (at birthday party, preparing Sandy for her audition)	Michael & Sandy make love, changing the nature of their relationship & putting their friendship in jeopardy.	Sandy's insecurities increase. She invites Michael to dinner and confronts him about his behaviour.
3. MICHAEL - LES	Les meets Dorothy.	Les starts to fall in love with Dorothy.	They sing together when Dorothy visits farm with Julie. Les takes Dorothy dancing.
4. MICHAEL – BREWSTER	Michael is warned that Brewster is a "lech".	Brewster begins to be attracted to Dorothy.	They work together. Dorothy tries to avoid Brewster, who keeps trying to kiss her in their scenes.
5. JULIE – RON	Establishes that Julie and Ron are dating.		Michael notices the condescending way Ron treats Julie.

Figure 4.2 *Tootsie* Subplot Structure

2nd TURNING POINT	CLIMAX	RESOLUTION
Michael tries to get out of his contract – but "she's" so good no one will let him out of it.	"Dorothy" reveals herself to be Michael.	
Dorothy tries to kiss Julie. Development: Julie won't see Dorothy.	Michael says "The hard part is over". They've become friends.	Now they can continue their relationship. They leave together.
Sandy discovers Michael is in love – with another woman – and she discontinues their friendship.	Sandy opens in a new play.	She and Michael are friends again.
Les proposes.	Michael gives the ring back.	Les forgives him.
Brewster sings outside Dorothy's window and makes a pass at her.	Michael unmasks and Brewster realises Dorothy's not a woman.	
	Julie breaks up with Ron as a result of Dorothy's lessons about self-respect.	

- *To reveal backstory* (see Chapter 4).
- *To provide a context or setting for your main story.* For example, *Chinatown* begins as an investigation of someone's wife, develops into a corruption scandal, and ultimately into a story of incest. The subplot can create the context for the final climax and hold the first part of the storyline together, especially when there are a number of characters involved.

In a script, the movement between plot and subplot gives movement to your story. If plot and subplot were unconnected your stories would seem free-floating, unrelated – and irrelevant. It's the skill in how you integrate your subplot into the texture of the whole that gives your script believability as well as complexity. Too many subplots not well integrated will lead to a muddy, unfocused script weighed down by too much going on (cf. Spielberg's *1941*).

—— Some final considerations ——

Cost

Film and TV making is expensive and producers are forever cost-conscious. A first script that is knowingly expensive is a candidate for rejection; it demonstrates lack of understanding of the industry. I am not saying write only small-scale scenarios or limit your imagination, but you should at least be aware of the things that add heavily to a budget, for example:

- special effects
- period drama with many historical settings
- lots of exotic locations
- any scenes with specific weather (for example, an outdoor snow scene in a summertime shoot)
- insisting that a major star be cast as the lead part

❝ The cheaper your budget, the more imaginative and inventive you are forced to be. ❞

Roger Corman
writer/producer/
director

Watch these films: *Reservoir Dogs, She's Gotta Have It, Leon The Pig Farmer, Living In Oblivion.* How do you think they got round the 'no-budget' problem? Did they do it well?

Research

If you are writing about an activity or subject you have little experience of, it is essential for you to do background research, in order to give your setting credibility and believability. But beware the dangers of over-research. You may reach a point where something 'just wouldn't happen in this job'. Tough. You are looking for the dramatic truth, hence it would. So set it up and build it to make it look like it would happen in those circumstances – you're not writing documentary. As they say in journalism: Never let the facts get in the way of a good story.

❦ People are always telling me: 'You should hear about all the funny things that happen at my work.' I say to them: '*You* just tell me about your job. Let *me* make it funny.' ❦

Allan Sutherland,
comedy writer

Medium

When a Reader receives a script or a producer is pitched an idea, they instinctively know the ideal format for that idea. Most novice writers seem to think solely in terms of feature films. But the type and complexity of your story, plots and subplots and the number of characters should indicate to you whether there is enough to fill 90+ minutes of the big screen.

Ask yourself: to do my story justice could it be best told in a full-length feature (between 90–120 minutes)? Would, say, 60 minutes of TV serve it better, or even a mini-series? Is it actually a 30–minute story ambitiously stretched to feature length? Is it really a 4–hour mini-series crammed into 90 minutes?

As a basic rule of thumb, think of it like this:

TV Drama   60 minutes or longer. Up to 6 main and secondary characters; studio based with limited location shooting.

Feature Film	Between 80 and 120 mins. 7 or fewer main and secondary characters; broad visual canvas, location shoots; fits a genre.
TV Mini-Series	Two or more feature-length episodes running on consecutive nights/weeks; very broad canvas with tendency towards family sagas and often set against major historical events. Usually book adaptations.
TV Serial Drama	Anything up to 13 or even more main and secondary characters, with perhaps 50 or more storylines running at different times and of varying length. Usually told in 30 or 60-minute chunks, transmitted regularly (weekly/nightly).

So be objective about your idea and honest with yourself:

- Is it fit for the big screen?
- Is it the right format/length?
- Would it sit more comfortably in a different format, e.g. television or straight-to-video?

Every tale has its own ideal length. This is to do with the decisions you make: where does my story start? where does it end? Picking the right format for your story will give you confidence – in yourself and in the story.

5

CREATING YOUR CHARACTERS

❝ Your characters will lead you through the story maze. You don't know where. Trust your characters and you will trust your story. ❞
Paula Milne

So far we've looked at things in general and abstract terms. Now let's start to flesh things out. The two main building blocks of a script are: *character* and *structure*. They are symbiotic, the yin and yang: both feed, support, illuminate and drive each other.

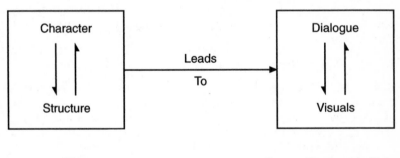

Creating credible and convincing characters is probably the most difficult and elusive thing for any writer. This chapter offers you tools and a starting point to help you come to grips with it.

'Getting' your character is the hardest part of writing a screenplay, and probably the most important. Every story is to a greater or lesser extent character driven, even *The Terminator* or *Speed*. Think of the films you like best. Almost always there is something about the characters that won you over, that engaged you enough to care about them, to feel tense when they were in danger. So how do we do it?

This chapter will examine the two most important factors when creating characters for a script:

- the creation of the characters themselves; their biography and backstory
- the design of your cast

But first, let's give your characters some names.

Choosing a name

The name you give your characters is important, so choose good, strong ones: names evoke certain feelings in an audience. Think of some: Indiana Jones, Priscilla, Bruce Wayne, Forrest Gump, Malcolm X. *Field Of Dreams* has Ray as its main character: an ordinary, nondescript name for an ordinary, nondescript, unmotivated Iowa farmer. *Thelma and Louise*: an unusual name (but sounding like that of a typical Southern American housewife) and a fairly regular name – two degrees of normality for two far-from-ordinary characters. Why do you think the main character in *Witness* is called John Book?

Remember, some names are generation-specific: for example, Rose, May, Blanche, George, Norman, Sharon, Tracey, Kevin, Jason, Kylie, etc.

Also, consider the way names can be used to underscore an emotion: a character who has always been known by their last name might be annoyed by the pointed used of their first name, as would calling them, say, Mike, when they insist on being addressed as Michael; the same applies with nicknames. Watch *Scent Of A Woman* and note its use of Charles, Charlie and Chuckie.

Tips: A good source of names is one of those books that list names for babies.

Try to give each of your characters names that do not share the same initial (unless there is a vital plot reason for it) or that sound the same. Three characters in the same story called Ray, Ricky and Reg, or Jack, Jacques and Jake would only confuse your audience (especially the script reader).

——— Creating 3-D characters ———

❋ ❋
❋   As A Writer, Your Goal Is To   ❋
❋   Create 3-Dimensional Characters.   ❋
❋ ❋

This means characters which are intriguing, which catch the audience's attention, and which are above all believable. The more you know about your characters the more well-rounded they will become in your writing, and the more your audience will enjoy and believe the work. When descriptions are flat, when dialogue doesn't come alive, when characters act in implausible ways, often it is because the writer has not taken the time to really get to know his or her characters fully. When you know your characters inside out, like a best friend, you'll know exactly what they would and would not say and do.

❝ Many of what I thought were my funniest lines were cut, because they were jokes that came from me, from the page, and not from the characters themselves. The audience had to believe a character would come out with a particular line. ❞

Simon Beaufoy,
screenwriter: *The Full Monty*

Even though you will not actually use over 80% of your character information in the script, you need to know it. Not just because it clarifies and focuses things in your mind, but also because at some point, someone – be it script editor, producer, director, or (especially) actor – will point to the script and ask you 'Why does the character say/do this?' You must have a plausible answer, and doing thorough work on your characters will give you that answer.

❝ I approach it in terms of: I'm looking at this character Richard Goodwin, and I'm trying to understand why he makes the choices he makes: why work for this committee rather than make more money in Wall Street? Why does he choose to prosecute Charles Van Doren and champion Herb Stempel and why feel ambivalent about that championing? I try to connect the dots of those actions, understand a personality that would make those choices; understand that character in a way that makes those choices intelligible and believable. ❞

Paul Attanasio
on writing *Quiz Show*

A fundamental principle to understand here is:

**We Learn About A Character
From The Decisions They Make**

This applies most especially to your main character (the protagonist). Their goals (outer motivation) drive the plot: their *decisions* expressed as *actions* dictate the path your story will take.

Consider characters as having three dimensions:

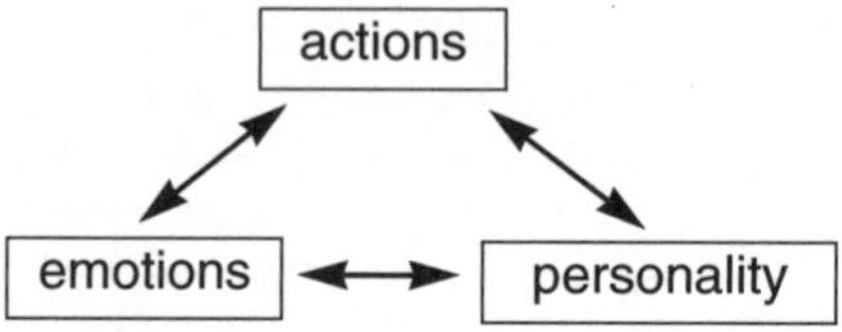

Use just two of these and you will have flat or stereotype characters that don't leap off the page.

Action

- physical (visual) action
- verbal action (dialogue) covering action, emotion and personality
- emotional action (see below)
- psychological action (inside a character's mind, encompassing thoughts, feelings, dreams, states of mind, etc. and manifested externally in *decision-action*, the formulation of a goal, a decision to act or not to act)

Emotions

Screenplays *are* emotion, dramatised through conflict; emotional action derives from a character's *emotional make-up* meeting an obstacle, and in turn generating an *emotional reaction*.

- *Emotional make-up* is your character's capacity or tendency to feel joy/love/frustration/compassion/hate/despair/nothing. It includes their temperament and their capacity to move into an emotional state (anger/despair/etc.) quickly or not.

- *Emotional action* or *reaction* can be a kiss, a special look, a display of grief, etc.

- *Personality* is a combination of integrated interior attributes (attitudes/aspirations/beliefs/life-POV/intentions/etc.)

—— Character functions/categories ——

All characters have a specific function to fulfil in your screenplay. You can divide these into three basic categories:

- **Main character/s** Your protagonist and anyone who advances the story in conjunction with them
- **Secondary characters** Those who interact with your protagonist and have a significant effect on your plot or main character/s (antagonist, mirror and romance – see cast design, later)
- **Minor characters** Those who add colour, atmosphere or comic relief, deliver messages, open doors and generally contribute to the world of the story

—————— The protagonist ——————

This is the character

- you want your audience to focus on
- whose POV they experience the story through
- who will travel the journey in the story of your screenplay
- with whom the audience will most identify
- who, by definition, will be on screen most of the time.

Often called the hero or heroine, the protagonist is the one who should

- drive the plot (their outward motivations and goal/s are the engine of your story)
- initiate the action.

Can you name the hero/protagonist for the following films? *Forrest Gump, Back To The Future, The Mask, Speed, Unforgiven* and *Braveheart?*

Although the protagonist is usually your main character, it is not always the case. In *Rain Man*, Raymond (Dustin Hoffman) is the main character, but Charlie (Tom Cruise) is the protagonist, the one who travels the journey from being a self-seeking avaricious business type to an unselfish rounded person. In *The Third Man*, Harry Lime (Orson Welles) is the main character, but the protagonist is journalist Holly Martins (Joseph Cotton), as with Kane and the journalist in *Citizen Kane*.

Watch *Heat* : which do you think is the main character and which the protagonist – De Niro or Pacino? Now do the same for *Don Juan De Marco* – is it Depp or Brando?

Character biography – analysis/check-list

You should write complete biographies (of between 2 and 10 pages, sometimes more) for each of your principal characters, from birth to the point where they enter your script. Why? Because you will be startled at the end of it to realise just how much you have fleshed out your original character idea. Suddenly you will understand why your character does this action or wears that particular garment. Sometimes you will find your characters changing the direction or thrust of your original story. Don't be afraid of it. Use it to your advantage and re-examine your plot in the light of what you have now discovered about your characters.

This approach can be time-consuming. So here is a handy checklist to speed things up; these are the kind of questions actors ask themselves. Remember, the audience don't need to know all this information – in fact, you probably won't use 80% of what you write down – but you the writer should know and be able to answer every question.

- What is their gender and age?
- What is their weight, height, build, colour of hair, eyes and skin? Are they right or left-handed? Do they have any facial expressions, a squint or any disabilities? Do they have a limp or missing finger? Do they wear spectacles or contact lenses? How do they walk or move? Do they have any mannerisms or habits? Do they smoke? What are their attitudes towards each of these?
- How do they speak? What do they sound like? What pitch and speed is their voice? Any favourite sayings or words? Do they use slang? or swear?
- Do they live alone or with other people? Do they have any children? What is their relationship to them? What kind of children are they?
- Do they have a partner, or one or several lovers? Are they celibate? Married? Do they have dependent relatives, flatmates or pets?
- Where do they live? Do they own their home? How much does it cost? How is it furnished? Are they domesticated, tidy or messy?
- Are they successful in material terms? Do they have a good job with enough money? Are they worried about their finances? Are they financially independent? Do they like their job? If not, what would they rather do? What are the power relationships in their work with co-workers, boss, or employees?
- Are their parents living? Do they like them? Was their family rich, poor, struggling to keep up appearances? What have they inherited from them, both physically and psychologically?
- What kind of education did they have? Was it a military back-ground? What were they expected to do with their life?
- What is their nationality? Do they live in their country of origin? If not, why not? How do they feel about this?
- What is their sexuality and their attitude towards it? How important is it? Do they have any hang-ups? What are their attitudes towards someone else's sexuality?
- When they are at home for an evening alone, are they happy with their own company? Do they read books, magazines, newspapers, the back of cornflakes packets? What music do they play to themselves? What do they eat? Can they relax? Do they knit, sew, write letters, watch television, revise their notes from an evening class? What are their hobbies, if any? Are they quirky? Are they a collector? What do their hobbies, music and books tell us about them?
- Are they a cool or a sexy person? Are their relationships fiery and passionate or calm and carefully controlled? Do they have a nasty

temper? Are they charming? Do they control their emotional life or does it control them? How do they express tension or do they internalise stress? How do they express pleasure?

- Do people like them? Do they do what they want? Do they admire or respect them? What do they most like or dislike about themselves? What aspects of themselves do they praise, deny, or want to change?
- Do they run their own life, or are they usually obeying other people, or doing things in order to please or take care of others?
- What is their favourite colour? What is their star sign and birth stone? Do they believe in astrology? Are they religious or spiritual? If so, what are their beliefs and practices? What are their moral beliefs and code of ethics? Do they have a phobia or phobias?
- What do they want from life? What are their goals in the short, medium and long term? What do they *really* want from life and why? When they die, how do they want to be buried: six foot under, cremated, at sea? Do they want their ashes scattered anywhere specific? Any particular music played at their funeral? Have they thought about death at all? Does death bother them?
- What is their relationship to the other main characters in the story? Who or what is trying to prevent them from achieving their goal(s)?
- Do you like them? Do you respect them? How do you want the audience to feel about them?
- Within the drama/film/story, what is their goal or dramatic need? What are they trying to achieve, gain or change during the course of the piece?
- At the end of the script, what is their development? How have they changed? What have they learned, about things or other people, themselves?

Another handy exercise, and again based on how actors approach their part, is to take your character through a typical day in their life. What time do they wake in the morning? How do they wake up? With vigour, or do they lie there waiting to muster the energy? Maybe with a cigarette? How do they smoke it? What do they do next?. . . and so on.

❛ As I start learning (a part), the character becomes like a photographic plate. The image begins to show itself to me... If I can hear the voice and begin to see how he moves, then all I have to do is become that image or imitate that image and bring it to the screen. ❜

Anthony Hopkins, actor

Remember, the point is not to use all this information but to have it in your mind (and on paper) to draw upon if needed. Who we are effects how we talk, think, what we do, how we feel, what we say, so the more you know who your characters really are, the more you will be able to make their actions and words specific, characteristic and believable. Your characters will sound and act like real people, not cardboard cut-outs created to serve a plot.

Now write a thorough biography for your main character.

Backstory

Besides a character's biography, you should also work out their backstory. This can be defined as the story of your character and the relevant events in their lives that happened to them immediately before they entered the script. Normally, the relevant backstory for your character/s will only be a matter of weeks long, but it can also be hours, months or years – your story will dictate the timeframe. For example, in *Ordinary People,* the drowning of Conrad's brother (seen later in flashback) happened some months before the film opened, yet we know these months were deeply traumatic.

As with your character biography, write a 2–10 page backstory for each of your principle and secondary characters. The key use of backstory is it can provide important information about your character/s and events you can use during the telling of your story. Another advantage of backstory is it helps you decide exactly where to open your script (as the motives your characters possess in Scene 1, Act I clearly derive from events in their immediate backstory).

In practice, writers often write a combined backstory and biography. Remember, these are tools only: you use them, they do not dictate to you. As you develop and write the script, the story will probably evolve away from these original ideas and make you return to both biography and backstory and revise accordingly. Don't worry. Your story is your guide.

Secondary characters

When creating these (particularly with the antagonist/opposition and the romance), follow the same procedure as for your main character. Know them inside out, but beware of letting them get out of hand and becoming too memorable – they must never upstage your main character. Try to make their dialogue as individual as possible, but don't start writing it too soon or they may run away with you.

Minor characters

Beware, it is in the creating of your minor characters that you are in the greatest danger from cliché and stereotype (it usually indicates the writer has not done enough work or thought). Thus it is essential you make as much effort on your minor characters as you do with your principal ones. Nothing is easier than to bring in a couple of stereotypes to chat, hang around for a scene or two and conveniently move the plot on a bit. You may not even notice you are doing it, as you're too focused on your protagonist's tormented soul.

When thinking about minor characters, consider the following:

- Every time you bring in a new character *think what you are doing*. If you have seriously thought through all those 'Getting It Clear' questions in Chapter 4, then you should know what story you are telling and hence the function of your minor character. If you have worked on your main and secondary characters, you should be in the habit of providing depth of characterisation. If you have thought about the world and setting of your story, then you know what background your character has.
- Then consider how complex this character needs to be. There may not be time or space in your script to get too elaborate. So, how are you going to make this character original within the parameters you can afford? Can you give them a distinctive dress style, physical presence or body language? Can you give them a speech idiosyncrasy or dialect, a surprising hobby or area of expertise? Do they have a characteristic emotion – perhaps one unexpected in view of their social role? These all may help as short cuts, but they may not make your character completely original, so don't lean on them too

much. Remember, do all your thinking before you get to dialogue.

- Look around you. People are endlessly fascinating, sometimes odd. Notice, when travelling on public transport, that punk engrossed in a Jane Austen novel or the bus driver whistling an opera tune.
- Learn from other writers. Charles Dickens' bit-part players were often exaggerated but never dull.

As usual, it's down to doing enough work. Stereotype minor characters are usually produced by writers who get as far as their function in the script but no further. Even non-human characters need well thought-through biographies to make them believable (e.g. *Toy Story, Babe, Star Wars, The Lion King*).

As a writer, you invent your characters, or take them from life, and modify them. You don't get them ready-made from some box of stock types. So every time you bring in any new character, think. Don't just look at their function in the script or within that scene. Ask why they are there. Should they be there at all? Could their role or function be performed by an existing character? Ask yourself these questions about each character's relation to your story:

- Is it a main or secondary character, or a bit-part?
- Are they the protagonist, antagonist, or do they switch sides?
- What is their relationship to the plot? Are they essential to the main story, the sub-plot, or simply a conveyor of information?
- What makes them different from every other character in the story? If there are similarities, you should change them.

When creating a character and their dialogue, if it helps you get a clearer mental picture during the writing stage, try imagining the best possible actor in that role. But, be aware that every actor carries with them a 'baggage' of character types they have played in the past, and this baggage may impose limitations on your imagination and creativity. Moreover, when finally submitting your script to someone in the industry *never* give them casting suggestions or include an ideal cast list. This is tantamount to telling them their job and indicates a naivety of the production process.

❝ In *Dead Poets Society* I started with the story and that told me what kind of characters I would need... Start thinking objectively about your characters. ❞

Tom Schulman

─────────────── **Cast design** ───────────────

It is no use having a well-rounded protagonist unless you have other characters to relate to or react against. Your choice of characters may well be the most crucial decision you make in writing your screenplay. Each character fulfils a function in your story and represents or expresses different aspects of your theme. Hence your story, its premise, the problem set-up by the inciting incident (see Chapter 7) and theme will dictate or influence the cast you design and the type of principal characters you create, each one fitting the nature of the problem in some way.

It may seem simplistic, but you have **four main primary character types** to choose from:

1 Hero/ine

This is your Protagonist (page 67). It is this character's job to keep the story moving forward, hence their goal(s) and external motivation drive your plot, their decisions initiate the action. And they must want to pursue these goals to the very limit.

2 Opposition character

The Antagonist (also called the Nemesis) is the character who most stands in the way of your hero/ine achieving their goal and creates obstacles in their path. They are a visible character who visibly confronts the hero – remember, good villains make good drama. Also they must push your protagonist to their utmost credible limits.

Note that occasionally, characters you would normally consider antagonists are in fact protagonists. These characters are called anti-heroes (e.g. Travis Bickle in *Taxi Driver*, Jake La Motta in *Raging Bull*, D-Fens in *Falling Down*). However, even these unlikeable characters are not without some endearing qualities. Why do audiences like these creations? Can you list more?

3 Mirror character

Also called the Reflection or Support, this is the character who is most aligned to the protagonist. They support the protagonist's goals (or are in the same basic situation), add depth to the character of the protagonist via dialogue, making your protagonist more credible, more believable. A protagonist working alone without this Sancho Panza-type figure will cause difficulties for you in letting the audience know exactly what is going on with your protagonist and your plot.

4 Romance character

This is the character who is the object of your protagonist's romantic/ sexual desire, the active romantic pursuit – the prize, if you like, at the end of the journey (it is usually one person; in *Disclosure* it is the concept of wife and family). This character alternately supports and then creates obstacles to the protagonist achieving their goal. The protagonist's emotion grows out of conflict; if there is no conflict in the relationship, things will get boring.

Remember, if you are going to create a romance character, it is important to get your audience to identify or 'fall in love' with your romance as much as your protagonist.

Here are some important principles regarding these primary character types:

- their category is established when that character is introduced
- they should all have been introduced by the end of Act I, certainly by the start of Act II
- each character stays in their designated category throughout the script; changing categories will only diffuse the focus of your script
- you don't need all four, but you must have a protagonist, an opposition and either a mirror or romance; you can have two opposition figures or any two other character types but as a rule-of-thumb, stick to one protagonist or hero/ine
- you don't have to explore all these characters' inner motivation and conflict (although with your protagonist it is vital)

You may find it helpful to construct a cast design chart like the one on page 76.

	Hero /Protagonist	Opposition /Antagonist	Mirror /Support	Romance
Witness	John Book	Paul Schaeffer	Carter (later, The Amish Community)	Rachel
Field of Dreams	Ray Kinsella	Initally it's Mark. Ultimately, it's Ray's image and memories of his father	Annie, his wife (Also, later, Terence Mann)	
Speed	Jack Traven	The Bomber	Harry (then, after Harry dies, Annie)	Annie
Disclosure	Tom Sanders	Meredith Johnson	"A friend" on the e-mail	Tom's wife and family
The Piano	Ada	Stewart, the husband	Flora, the daughter	Baines
Falling Down	D-Fens	Prendergast, the cop		(as D-fens sees it) His wife and daughter
Quiz Show	Dick Goodwin	Charles Van Doren	Herb Stempel	

Now watch each (or some) of the films listed in the chart on page 76. Do you agree with the roles I've assigned to each character? If not, why do you disagree? How would you assign them?

—— The counter-character chart ——

When looking at the relationships between your characters, it might help to draw up a counter-character chart like the one shown below. When creating this chart, ask yourself what your other characters have to be in order to get the most contrast with your protagonist. Make the traits as mixed and as varied as you can to illustrate the different elements of your protagonist you wish to highlight. If it helps, think in terms of opposites and different degrees of dominance. For example, the chart for the sitcom *Roseanne* might look like this. Can you fill in the spaces?

Roseanne	Female	Married *(wife)*	Very dominant	Overly sarcastic
Dan	Male	Married *(husband)*	Easy going	Laid-back
Becky	Female	Single *(daughter)*	Dominant	
Darlene	Female	Single *(daughter)*	Dominant	Cynical/ abrasive
D.J.	Male	Single *(son)*	Easy	
Jackie	Female	Single *(sister)*	Submissive	

And so on …

Character flaws

Try to think of each principal character in your story as being incomplete, as hiding some profound imperfection in their soul. Think of it as a 'hole' going through the middle of their character, like the words in a stick of seaside rock. Perhaps your character needs to be a perfectionist or a control-freak, can't love or trust anybody or must rigidly organise all aspects of their life; maybe they loathe themselves and believe nobody could love them.

When you know or have chosen the flaw, you can begin to see how they have hidden it over the years, probably since childhood. What defence mechanisms have they devised to conceal it? What attitudes and forms of behaviour have grown up to help them survive it? What tentative and probably fearful attempts have they made (or might they make) to heal it?

All characters (just like people) have this hole right through their middle and all of them are desperately trying to hide it and live with it. Grasp this, and you have a powerful tool for developing your character/s even further.

You might trying using this 'flaw' idea, and a character's reconciliation of that flaw, as jumping-off points for creating their developmental arc (p. 81) or your theme (p. 51).

Audience identification

❝ People go to the cinema to see themselves on the screen. As an actor, people must identify with you. You cannot hold up a picture and say 'this is me', you hold up a mirror and say 'this is you'. ❞
Michael Caine, actor

While it is important to establish your protagonist as early as possible in your script (don't clutter it up with other secondary or minor characters first), it is essential you get the audience 'on the protagonist's side', to establish subconscious links so that your audience sees the world and experiences emotion through that character's P.O.V. – and you must do it quickly. The way you do this and maintain it so that the audience completely identify with the protagonist is a key factor in emotionally affecting your audience.

There are a number of ways of achieving this:

- *Sympathy* is the most often used identification device. Make your protagonist the victim of some undeserved mishap or misfortune (*Edward Scissorhands, Cliffhanger, City Of Joy*), preferably in your opening scene(s).
- Put your character in *jeopardy*. We identify with people we worry about, fear for or feel anxiety about, whether the danger is life-threatening or simply loss of face (e.g. the *Indiana Jones* sagas).
- Establish the *likeability* of your character. Perhaps they are nice, highly skilled, hard working, a decent honest person or they may make us laugh. An audience will be more prepared to go along with them; a good example is the joke in the elevator in *Ghost*. But remember, likeability and audience identification are not necessarily synonymous.
- Arouse our *curiosity* in this character: here the character will often be a negative or dislikeable person (e.g. *The Fisher King, Bad Influence*), but we are drawn in by the mystery to follow their actions and choices. It is important with dislikeable characters or anti-heroes to give them at least one redeeming feature such as humour or witty dialogue, or to have a likeable secondary character who likes them. Audiences find it difficult to identify with completely obsessive or mad characters.
- Establish some element of *inequality*. We feel sympathetic to someone who is unjustly downtrodden (e.g. Thelma in *Thelma And Louise*) or vulnerable (*Birdy, It's a Wonderful Life*).

There are also other subtler ways of approaching the task:

- *Empathy* This is the strongest form of identification, but the most difficult to create and sustain. Generally, it is a combination of sympathy, fear for and likeability; we share what the character feels, are involved with them in their life-situation, challenges, failures and dilemmas. The more normal the character (however abnormal their situation) the more chance of empathy there is (e.g. *Field Of Dreams*).
- *Admiration* Courage, determination, luck, intelligence, adherence to their principles in the face of temptation or danger all encourage the audience's admiration. Sometimes this is different from like-ability: we may not like someone we admire (e.g. *Patton*).
- *Familiarity* Familiar and recognisable settings induce a feeling of comfort in an audience. Also, giving a character familiar foibles

might help: forgetting names, getting up late, mis-programming a video recorder, etc.

- *Power* A character possessing complete power is intriguing – we all have a fascination with power (*The Godfather, The Krays*). Power can also be shown through feelings (*Dangerous Liaisons*). You might even make your character a superhero (*Superman, Batman, James Bond*). Here you are building on an already established genre and cultural base with its own pre-fixed values system.
- *Omnipotence* Allow your audience only to see events and characters through one person's (the protagonist's) eyes/P.O.V. (*Maverick*). This is most common in the detective genre (*The Big Sleep, Chinatown*).
- Try to introduce your protagonist into the script as soon as possible (*Maverick, Birdy, The Fisher King, Calamity Jane*). Rather obvious, perhaps, but it needs stating. Later you can strengthen identification by layering on more and more modes.

Watch the openings of *Thelma And Louise, Maverick, Tootsie, Butch Cassidy* . . . and *Field Of Dreams*. From that information, describe each film in one ot two sentences. Does the end result sound especially wonderful? Probably not. Yet we are engaged by each film. In what ways are we drawn into an intense and enjoyable identification with the main characters (Thelma, Louise, Bret, Michael, Butch, Sundance and Ray)?

Watch *Carrington, Falling Down* and *Mrs. Parker And The Vicious Circle*. They are not very likeable characters; were you interested in them? Did you feel involved with them? Or did you feel at the end you were glad you never met them?

Again, don't just stick to one of the above, mix'n'match. Play with the possibilities. The stronger the identification between audience and characters (especially the protagonist) the better.

6 In Europe, producers ask: 'Are the characters intriguing, is the protagonist interesting?' In America they ask: 'will the audience like him?' They call it 'rootability'. 9

Lynda Miles,
Pandora Productions/Pathé Films

6

CHARACTER GROWTH, MOTIVATION AND CONFLICT

Character growth – the transformational arc

Your principal characters, especially your protagonist, must experience growth in order for your story and characters to have any meaning. (If nothing happens to your protagonist, where's the story and the interest for your audience?) And that growth must occur gradually over the arc of your entire screenplay (no less), never instantaneously. This is termed the *transformational arc* or growth line. If your character has grown all they can after just ten pages, all you've got is a ten-page story.

❋❋❋❋❋❋❋❋❋❋❋❋❋❋❋❋❋❋❋❋❋❋❋❋
❋   Growth Occurs As A Result Of   ❋
❋   Confronting Obstacles   ❋
❋❋❋❋❋❋❋❋❋❋❋❋❋❋❋❋❋❋❋❋❋❋❋❋

And remember, we learn about a character from the decisions they make, often under pressure; decisions about obstacles, decisions about conflict, and how to overcome them.

The greater the pressure, the more 'backs to the wall' the situation, the more we find out the real truth of the person. Hence, growth occurs over the arc of your screenplay in a series of emotional 'beats' (moments or leaps of growth/revelation) within each Act and within individual scenes.

Getting started, you have two kinds of characteristics:

- those your character starts the script with
- those that your character will need at different points to overcome the story obstacles, and the final beat of growth leading to the end goal.

Let's look at *Witness*: if John Book, the protagonist, needs to be more sensitive, trusting and less individualistic by the end of the story, then you can already begin to see the characteristics he will need at the start. This means it is possible to start from either end of the story in order to understand who your character is and where he or she is coming from and going to, just like knowing the end of your story to find its opening. Understanding this will make it easier to chart the growth arc of your character. Once you know what characteristics are needed at a specific stage in the story you can then design the scenes and incidents that help create and reveal these characteristics. Often you will create a scene or incident first and then discover what special aspect of the character and/or growth it is revealing. Writing is a mix of both approaches. Let it happen.

For example, in *Rain Man* we first see Charlie (Cruise) cut off, with no emotional connection to other people, even his girlfriend. News arrives about the father's death and the will. Charlie reacts as he would normally do to get whatever he wants: he kidnaps Raymond (Hoffman). Change comes when he purchases the television set, and we now see Charlie moving from the reactive character he has been to one of anticipating Raymond's needs. Charlie teaching Raymond to dance is a turning point: it is the first unselfish thing Charlie has done for Raymond, the two characters actually touch each other, and we can see Charlie moving away from selfishness. Raymond drives the car (i.e. Charlie is now risking his beloved possession). Charlie goes to the doctor and says: 'You should have told me I had a brother'. Finally, we see Charlie willing to give up his money in order to connect with his brother.

In *Witness,* John Book only achieves his final beat of growth by putting down his gun and exposing himself to Shaeffer's gun – risking his life to save Rachel. In doing this he achieves his final beat of transformation which is necessary to solve the 'problem' set-up in Act I (i.e. calling upon the power of the Amish community to witness what is taking place – whereas in our society so much is ignored, allowing some things to happen), and to take away Schaeffer's power despite his shotgun. In this scene Schaeffer realises he cannot fight the whole community, that his power as an individual (the power he's always lived by) is not all-powerful. This is Schaeffer's final beat of character growth, which occurs after he has 'won' – defeated Book according to the rules and values of the game as played in big city cop life. It should also be noted that Book is revealed to be a carpenter before becoming a cop. This is significant to the relative ease with which he is seduced by the values of Amish life.

So, as a writer, first you need to establish the values and emotions in the world of your script, then put your protagonist through various crises where their emotions pitch and waver, their values are challenged, and they have to make decisions, and end with them being changed, with an altered value-system and an altered emotional response.

In any script, your protagonist needs a powerful transformational arc to emotionally grip your audience and hold your story together. Someone sitting at home wanting a glass of water is not powerful – they can go into the kitchen and get one; if that person were stranded in the desert for a week and would, literally, kill for a glass – that's powerful and gripping. A weakness in new scripts is that the story of the life depicted is just a collection of incidents strung together (as in real life); the emotional arc is not there. Bio-pics are especially prone to his, taking that person's life chronologically from birth to death (e.g. *Malcolm X*). You need to depict the most dramatically effective incidents to create that arc. At least Tim Burton's *Ed Wood* concentrated on the most dramatically interesting period of Wood's life, his backstory integrated into the body of the movie, and his 'afterlife' covered via end-credit captions.

❋ ❋
❋   Look For The Emotional   ❋
❋   Development Arc   ❋
❋   In Each Of Your Main Characters   ❋
❋   (Not Just Your Protagonist)   ❋
❋ ❋

Ask yourself:

- Where does the growth begin? Why? What causes it?
- What changes are they going through?
- How do they react to these changes?
- Where do we first see some indication of change?
- How do we see it?
- What do they make of it?

Finally, do not confuse character growth with theme. They are similar and linked, but growth applies to your character/s and is specific to them, whereas theme applies to your audience – that universal statement about the human condition you want them to take away at the end.

Now watch *Witness* complete and try to chart out the beats/moments of growth in the John Book–Rachel relationship (the dramatic emotional beats of the main subplot, starting from when they first meet, moving through significant eye-contact, hand holding, not kissing, kissing etc.) Do the same with another film/TV drama. Continue until you feel conversant with this concept of the arc.

Character motivation

❛ The goal of the character is the most important thing: what the character wants when the story opens, and the character becomes clever by the number of ways they can find in obtaining that goal. How they go about it is down to who they are and the assets they have. When writing I just say 'I know what this guy wants' and a scene is always about what a character wants. ❜

Tom Schulman

If character is the most important element of your screenplay, then it follows that what motivates that character to act is even more important.

Audiences always hunger to know why a character acts as they do. When we read in a newspaper about some horrific but senseless murder, we may be partially interested in the event itself, but our overwhelming interest is not in how he killed his family, but why – the reason. A screenplay character is no different. If you provide this motivational dimension of character, satisfy the audience's natural hunger to know why, then you have already begun to separate yourself from the common herd of would-be screenwriters and those that merely try.

Working on a character's biography and backstory will tell you what generally motivates them in their life. However, you must also know what motivates them in this specific script – their dramatic need/outer motivation/goal in your story. Without this an audience cannot make sense of a character's actions – neither can you.

Motivation in a screenplay is usually defined in terms of 'character-in-action', i.e. we're not interested in characters who tell us what's driving them, we need to see it embodied and enacted.

Hence it is crucial that your protagonist (and your other major characters) have a clear, specific need or goal. They must want to do or accomplish something by the end of your script, and their reasons for doing it must be clear, evident and *visual*. This is your character's motivation. It is the driving force of your screenplay, forms the focus of your story and ties it all together. Motivation is what makes it dramatic: the character in conflict and *why* that character will seek conflict.

A character's motivation exists on two levels:

- Outer motivation: their path to their goal, what the story is about and what ultimately determines your plot. It is *visible*, revealed through action and clearly conveys what visibly represents success for the protagonist.
- Inner motivation: *why* your character is pursuing their path to their goal. This determines your character growth and theme. It is *invisible*, hidden and revealed through dialogue and subtext.

For all screen drama, outer motivation or goal is essential. It is the foundation of your entire script. If there's nothing that needs to be accomplished by the end of the script, where's the story? A character's motivation develops over the course of a screenplay's structure in what is called the *motivational through-line*, examined in Chapter 10. Exploring inner motivation, however, is optional, though no less important; even though you may never reveal it overtly on screen, you must be aware of it. Know your character!

Often new screenwriters will employ inner motivation for their dramatic need but dramatic need is the same thing as outer motivation. Consequently, many scripts appear with characters whose goal in the script is to 'become a better human being', 'find themselves', 'rediscover love' etc. But these motivations are not visible, concrete or strong enough to work successfully as a dramatic need – they are internal needs. Internal needs, therefore, often form the basis of a film's theme.

So ask yourself:

- What does my character want or desire?
- Why? both the reasons they know and the subconscious reasons.
- What are they willing to do to get what they want?
- How does this change over the course of the story?
- What could they lose (what's at stake?) if they fail to achieve their goal, fail in their quest or task? If the answer is 'not much', where's the story and the reason for watching? Failure is the basis of tragedy.

Knowing (a) they have a strong enough need/goal (external motivation) to drive them through your script story and up against powerful, sometimes life-threatening conflict, and (b) that they fear the alternative enough (i.e. not fulfilling their need or achieving their goal) to throw themselves into this conflict and confrontation can only help you reach a deeper understanding of your character. If you can't answer these questions above, go back and rethink your story.

Some important principles apply to character goals within a screenplay:

- The protagonist and antagonist must have the same goal or two aspects of the same goal (e.g. in *Witness*, Paul Schaeffer wants to kill John Book; Book wants to survive). Although ideally your story should avoid having two separate distinct goals, normally this can't be avoided because the main plot goal, which tends to be action based, will not be the same as the main subplot goal, which tends to be relationship based. However, your main plot should stand out and be distinct.

    In *Witness*, the main subplot goal is to get the woman (or man) to form a relationship. This is different to John Book overcoming Paul Schaeffer. To leave these two goals distinct and separate would reduce the impact of the story's end, so ways are found to integrate the two, to unify them into one goal. This is usually done by making one of the goals a necessary stepping stone to achieving the other goal.

Witness unifies them imaginatively, not just in terms of action but also of theme. John Book is fast defeating his three opponents at the end of the film, but then he must give up his gun and risk his own life to save Rachel. He must go through this self-sacrifice stage (his penultimate beat of growth) in order to reach the final stage. This self-sacrifice enables him to call on the power of the community – rather than the power of the individual – to witness Schaeffer's actions and so take away his power, despite the fact that Schaeffer has the gun. Book has discovered the true power in the world we are watching, with both mainplot and main subplot goals unified and fully integrated.

- The goal cannot be shared or divided; there can only be one winner.
- The goal must be strong enough (in the context of the script) to generate the need, and the need must be generated by an equally strong motive; so, audience must believe that your character really needs this particular goal badly enough to willingly endure whatever conflict lies ahead in their path.
- The protagonist's need (for the goal) must be as strong as the antagonist's need (to prevent them from achieving the goal) so that both are eventually and inevitably forced into conflict with each other.
- A character's strength is gauged by the strength or magnitude of the obstacle(s) they confront. (That is, the magnitude, difficulty or counter-intention must equal the strength of the dramatic need, goal or intention at that point in the screenplay.)

Although the above five principles appear fairly logical and straight forward, it is surprising how rarely writers (beginners and professionals) pay attention to them. Ignore them or try to change them and your script will encounter difficulties.

——— Conflict and character ———

So, the most important component of a screenplay is character, and the most important aspect of character is motivation. However, character and motivation cannot be understood in isolation. You need the third part of the equation: to understand the relationship these have with conflict.

A character has to be *motivated* to meet a particular *conflict*. Go to a dictionary: how does it define conflict?

- a sharp disagreement or clash (e.g. between divergent ideas, interests or people)
- (distress caused by) mental struggle resulting from incompatible impulses
- a hostile encounter (e.g. a fight, battle or war)
- to be in opposition (to another or each other); to disagree

They say conflict is the essence of drama; certainly, in real life, it is the one thing we all try to avoid. As a screenwriter, you cannot avoid conflict. For you, conflict must be the thing which you seek out, rush to meet head-on, and when you find it, draw it out, shape it, texture it, deepen it. You cannot run away from it. You cannot write a screenplay without it.

Your character may have a goal or outer motivation and even inner motivation, but if there is no conflict there is no drama. Being confronted by obstacles and problems, and the different ways your character reacts to and tackles them, is how we see the protagonist develop. Hence:

❀ ❀

❀   **Conflict Arises When A**   ❀

❀   **Need/Intention/Goal (Outer Motivation)**   ❀

❀   **Meets An Obstacle**   ❀

❀ ❀

Types of conflict

How many types of conflict do you think there are? Two?

- Outer conflict: whatever stands in the way of a character achieving their outer goal/s
- Inner conflict: whatever prevents the character from achieving inner development and self-worth (or what they *perceive* as such) when pursuing their goal/s and the chosen path to it/them

Wrong. The screenwriter has a choice of three:

- individual against individual (outer): personal conflict with other characters, their different goal/s or counter-intentions
- individual against environment (outer): conflict with the forces of nature (disaster movies: *Twister, Airport, Towering Inferno*); society (*Witness*); the group or system (bureaucracy, the government, the family, etc.) (*An Officer And A Gentleman*); values (*Witness*) or sometimes the supernatural, cosmic or invisible forces (God, the devil, time e.g. *Ghostbusters, The Exorcist, Independence Day, Back To The Future, Groundhog Day*)
- individual against self (inner): conflict within the character from something they have not acknowledged, confronted or overcome; perhaps they are unsure of themselves, their actions or goal/s

Principles of conflict

In screenwriting, a number of very important principles apply:

- Outer conflicts must be personalised as relationships between characters (hence the importance of your cast design)
- Interior conflicts must be externalised in physical manifestations or personal conflicts, or by letting the audience imagine the turmoil (but this relies on clues and information you have carefully set-up earlier in the script)

Michael Hauge noted that the hero's inner conflict is embodied by the antagonist or opposition character, is pointed out by the mirror, and the romance is the reward for overcoming it; hence the protagonist achieves character growth.

As a writer, you will usually begin by working on your outer conflicts. If you have a solid and clearly defined outer conflicts structure to hang things on, then you can move on to your inner conflicts, and they will become all the more believable. Bear in mind, too, that the sooner you introduce conflict into your screenplay, the stronger your story will become.

- Consider scenes in your favourite films/TV dramas.
- Analyse those scenes and actions in terms of these principles of conflict and goals.
- Think also of some of the bad films/TV you have seen and analyse those also.

Obstacles

The obstacles which your protagonist must face can take a number of forms:

- physical: e.g. the *Indiana Jones* and *Batman* canons, and including obstacles of nature (*The Mosquito Coast*, *Earthquake*, *City Slickers*, *Cliffhanger*, *Twister*), environment (*City Of Joy*, *Die Hard*) and distance (*Sleepless In Seattle*)
- other characters: e.g. *Indiana Jones*, *Batman*, *Heat*, *City Slickers*, *Thelma And Louise*, *Seven*, *Dead Ringers*, *Hamlet*, *Die Hard*
- mental: e.g. *Field Of Dreams* (Ray's image of his father), *When Harry Met Sally* (their mutual belief that friends can't or shouldn't become lovers), *Birdy*, *Hamlet*, *Cliffhanger*, *City of Joy*
- cultural: e.g. *City Slickers*, *Ghandi*, *Malcolm X*, *Priest*, *The Crying Game* (Fergus when faced by the culture Dill inhabits), *Rob Roy* and *Braveheart* (the system as embodied in their English adversaries), *Singin' In The Rain* (the introduction of the talkies)
- supernatural: e.g. *Ghost*, *Halloween*, *Dracula*, *The Shining*, *Flatliners*, *Independence Day*
- time (a time-lock or limit within which a certain task must be completed): e.g. *48 Hours*, *Scent Of A Woman*, *Apollo 13*, *Around The World In Eighty Days*, *Seven*, *Nick Of Time*, and of course the nature of time itself (*Groundhog Day*, *Back To The Future*)

Ultimately, of course, the most powerful or effective obstacle is the counter-intention: someone wants to stop you getting what you want. Their intention and your intention inevitably clash and out of this clash comes conflict.

Watch a favourite film and try to fill in the Character Motivation Grid (Fig 6.1) like the one below:

	Goal/Outer Motivation	Outer Conflict	Inner Motivation	Inner Conflict
Hero/ine				
Opposition				
Mirror				
Romance				

Fig. 6.1: Character Motivation Grid

Now draw up a similar grid for your own story's characters.

We will return to Character Motivation in Chapter 10.

—————— Developing conflict ——————

In the overall development of your screenplay, it is important that each conflict met, each obstacle faced, is greater than the one before it. Consequently, the degree of courage it takes to confront and defeat it is stronger each time: there has to be something that frightens the protagonist, be it a physical threat (harm or loss of some possession) or an emotional one (loss of face, embarrassment). Each time the stakes must be raised higher, with more at risk (Chapter 10 – Raising the Stakes). *Toy Story* has many good examples of this, even within the same scene.

This leads us to two important principles:

- each obstacle must be *different* from the previous one (e.g. physical, emotional, psychological, etc.)
- each obstacle or counter-intention must be *stronger or more difficult* than the previous one (hence the set-back or failure will be progressively stronger and the recovery require appropriately more courage)

This kind of conflict development (i.e. minimal) would be predictable and boring for your audience:

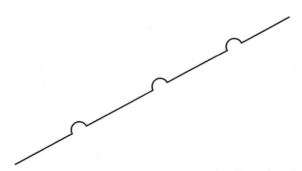

So, in order to extract the maximum dramatic effect from each conflict, you need both conflict (which leads to a climax) and a set-back. In the course of a feature script there will be at least three major setbacks:

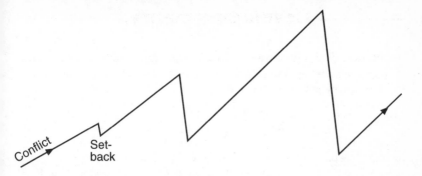

Notice the scale of the setbacks on the chart.

Also a climax does not necessarily mean a physical action climax, it can be an emotional climax (*Field Of Dreams, Sleepless In Seattle* and many European films).

Now try to draw a graph of your conflict, obstacles and setbacks over the development of your screenplay.

Ask yourself these questions:

- What obstacles get in the way of my protagonist? Remember these can be physical obstacles (other characters/environment), internal obstacles or supernatural, cultural and other obstacles.
- Why do they get in the way of the protagonist?
- What are these obstacles willing to do to stop my protagonist achieving their goal(s)?
- Is the obstacle greater than the preceding one? How? Why?

Hence we return to conflict and character motivation – the motivation of those opposing your protagonist.

Final comments

As a screenwriter, your essential task – and most difficult challenge – is to create an emotional reality on the page. The key to this is character and motivation.

How often have you sat watching something wondering what the heck the characters are doing and why? As an audience, we always need to know that there's a good reason for a character's actions, a good enough reason to drive them into conflict. There is always something heroic in a character who 'takes on the odds', always something that touches us... providing we believe.

Emotional realism comes from having strong motivating incidents and personality traits that force the character (reluctantly) into conflict and danger, causing the audience to *identify* with the character *because* they are in danger; a scene with no conflict means there is little or no emotional content or room for identification.

For example, *Tootsie* is emotionally realistic not because it resembles reality but because we are made to believe that Michael would put himself through this ordeal because of his internal emotional needs (inner motivation).

To create emotional realism in a scene and in your screenplay, you must build believable characters that experience conflict, and do so in a way that is economical and dramatically succinct. That means: To show more will dull the edge of the conflict and thus dull the emo-

❋ ❋
❋
    Show What Is Absolutely Necessary – And No More! ❋
❋
                                       ❋
❋ ❋

tional realism you are trying to create. The other essential ingredient here is that the audience most engage totally with the plight and problem/s of the character – hence the importance of identification.

Here is a flowchart you can use, not just in the planning of your screenplay, but whenever you come to write any dramatic scene.

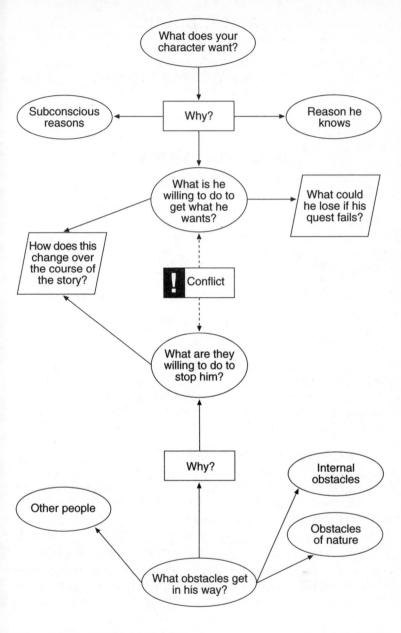

Figure 6.4 Character Motivation Flowchart

Source *Jurgen Wolff*

7
STRUCTURE

The classic three-act linear structure

❝ What's the trick? A good story that catches your attention, good characters that are believable. If those two criteria are correct you're in the top half per cent of screenplays. Then there's good structure. ❞

Tim Bevan,
Working Title Films

❝ When you look at a script, you instinctively know where everything is supposed to fall. With a feature script, if your first Act is under 20 pages you know there's going to be a problem. That's why you keep going back to structure. Because nothing else really works, no matter how avant garde your script is, it still has to be in that structure. And when you're reading a large number of scripts, that's one of the first things you look for. ❞

[A Script Reader]

Having decided on your idea, thought through your story concept and worked on your characters, the next step is to look at the overarching dramatic structure of your story development and script. (Remember, character work and plot structure are symbiotic; they feed and drive, complement and illuminate each other.)

A screenplay – and the course of this book – is a series of breakdowns, moving from the general to the specific. The first breakdown creates Acts I, II and III; the next breakdown gives us the beginning, middle and the end of each Act; we can then break down each of those sections into sequences, then scenes, and finally action and dialogue. But in order to create a screenplay in the first place, it is essential to know how it breaks down. If this feels like writing-by-numbers, it is – to an extent. But it is also the way screenplays are structured. Why do you think this is so?

There are two classic types of poorly written scripts: understructured (writing exactly how it happens in real life; such scripts are boring – rather like real life) and overstructured (all style: over-complex plotting, many special effects, etc. but no story content). You are dealing with events that are dramatic, looking for the dramatic moments that will move your story on, building and structuring an emotional experience for your audience and culminating in a climax.

> ❅ A screenplay is a blueprint for the finished film, it points the way. Most importantly, it lays out a structure, a spine you can hang your visions and dialogue on. A screenwriter's job is to lay out the blueprint. ❅
>
> *Howard Schuman,*
> screenwriter

Screenwriting structural guidelines have been developed and refined since cinema's early days and were first codified by Syd Field. When looking at the most widely used three-act linear template, it seems presumptuous to say most films follow this pattern, but nearly 90% (especially mainstream Hollywood ones) do to a greater extent. As an experiment, pick a film at random showing on television or from the video store and watch it with the chart on page 100. Does it work?

You should not regard structure as rigid rules set in stone that must be followed at all costs. It's an abstract ideal and more about logicality and our eternal need for good, well-structured storytelling: a compelling tale, compellingly told.

Note: Perhaps the most important thing to bear in mind about good structure is: you should eventually be able to get to a point where, when writing, you don't consciously think about it. Structure should be innate in your storytelling and eventually second nature to you when writing.

> ❅ It's a mistake to get hung up on numbers. Writing a script is not a joining-the-dots operation or getting the numbers right. Allow the story to dictate its own requirements. The 'numbers' you get on many courses or in various books should be used to develop your

storytelling instincts, to validate your guesses and intuitions, and then forget them. Learn them, then throw them away. **❯**

> *David Webb Peoples,*
> screenwriter:
> *Unforgiven,*
> *Twelve Monkeys*

Let's recap:

- A television play (of 60 minutes) can be divided by the commercial breaks, usually into three parts/acts.
- Half-hour dramas and sitcoms are divided into two acts (Chapter 8)
- In a feature film, the act divisions are not marked by a break in the action, but they can be seen when the film is analysed. (When a movie is shown on TV, the ad breaks tend to occur at the end of Act I, the half-way point and the end of Act II).

Remember the proportions:

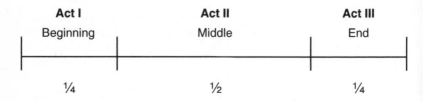

Thus in your two-hour film (120 minutes) the divisions will be: 30 minutes/60 minutes/30 minutes.

Stick to the accepted rule (Chapter 2) with feature script playing time: one page of script equals one minute of screen time. Hence your feature screenplay should be *no longer than 120 pages* (maximum), your Act division being approximately 30 pages/60 pages/30 pages.

There is no law setting in stone this ¼–½–¼ delineation. Indeed, you will find variations such as a 90 minute/90 page feature (dividing into 20/60/10 minutes), but we'll be sticking to the 120-page model.

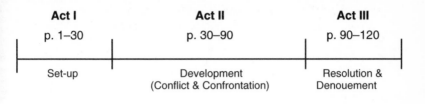

When reading this chapter, refer to the template on page 100. Although following this grid is not a guaranteed formula for success (there *are* no guaranteed formulae for success), it will at least help you organise the telling of your story so that your audience grasp more clearly what you are trying to say.

Now, before you proceed any further, I want you to watch five films: *Witness, The Crying Game, Don Juan De Marco, Field Of Dreams* and *Quiz Show*. Watch each film in one sitting, watch them critically, but without making notes (you can do that later).

—— What goes into each act? ——

To restate: in your screenplay, you are working towards one eventual goal – your final climactic scene in Act III (not necessarily your last scene). Every piece of description, every image, line of dialogue, detail of characterisation, every obstacle met, every set-back, and every conflict resolved, should be pushing towards that final climax to achieve maximum emotional effect.

Note: The 'writing backwards' strategy you apply to your entire screenplay also applies to each Act. Before creating one, you need to know your ending (climax) of that Act; then you can start working backwards, making sure everything works towards that ending.

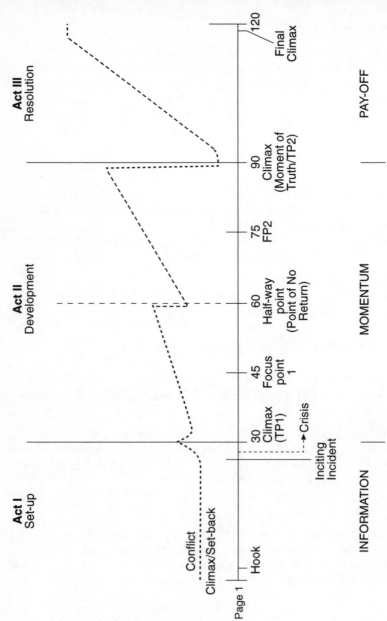

Figure 7.3 The 3-Act Linear Structure

1.1 Act I (Overview)

❢ I read so many screenplays that were boring and poorly written I could tell within the first ten pages whether the script was set up correctly. I gave the writer 30 pages to set up a story: if it wasn't done by then I reached for the next script. ❢

Syd Field

Act I gives your audience all the ingredients from which the story will be made: the main characters, the setting (the social and psychological/environmental 'norms'); tone (gritty-realistic like *Heat*, mythical like *Loch Ness, Field Of Dreams*; lyrical like *Sense And Sensibility, Local Hero*; anecdotal like *Waiting To Exhale*; fairy tale like *Edward Scissorhands*, etc); problems; tension; love interest; the timescale (real or dramatised) and any time-locks (something that needs accomplishing within a set deadline). *No important elements should be introduced later than Act I* (and most definitely by the opening pages of Act II).

In that short space of 30 pages (Act I), a number of things have been established. Let's examine them in blocks of ten pages:

1.2 The first ten pages

❢ The beginning should set up the 'heartbeat' of your script. ❢

Alan Plater, writer

Your first ten pages are critical. All readers tell you if your script hasn't grabbed them in the first ten pages (some now say five), they probably won't continue with the rest of it. If those pages are predictable they'll assume (rightly or wrongly) the last 100+ will be predictable too. People have a habit of jumping to conclusions: after reading just the first 5–10 pages the reader will say to themselves 'this is a good script' or 'this is a bad script'. If they read it with a positive attitude, it is more likely their final Coverage and recommendation will also be positive. So your first ten pages need to demonstrate your skills. They need to be unique, exciting (or, for a comedy, funny) and, above all, grab the reader's interest and make them want to read on to the end.

❢ What's curious about a good screenplay is you can often identify it within the first few pages. One of the key things an opening scene does is present the hero. Having an opening scene that grabs the audience, not necessarily by the throat, it could be a very subtle way; but it has to be something I feel is unusual, something I haven't seen before. But then don't give everything away in the first five minutes. Make me want to turn the page. **❩**

> *Norma Heyman,* producer:
> *Dangerous Liaisons,*
> *Carrington*

In the space of ten pages you have to *set up your scenario*. Establish:

- who your main characters are, and especially who your protagonist is (i.e. the star)
- what your story is going to be about
- the dramatic circumstances surrounding your story
- the genre you are working with

Hence you need to show your protagonist in a setting that is normal and natural for them, i.e. before the changes that are about to happen to them in the story occur. (In TV scripts it is even tighter: the first 2–3 minutes are crucial, hence it is your first *five* pages which are make-or-break.)

1.3 Openings

The first thing a Reader looks for in a script is a *hook* – that something which grabs the audience's attention, draws them into the story and makes them want to watch or read. Ideally, it needs to be in by page three, certainly by page five.

Powerful confrontation between two strongly contrasting characters will always hook your audience. In William Goldman's script for *Maverick*, we first see Bret Maverick on horseback, his hands tied behind his back, and a noose around his neck which is attached to a tree bough. The horse is moving slowly forward; Bret is going to hang . . . very slowly. Then the baddies throw a sack at the horse's feet, from which emerges a snake. The horse, further frightened, moves forward, more agitated. Tension – this time he really is going to hang. But we know he doesn't because Bret is narrating (v.o). His first line is a gag: "It had been a shitty week for me. It had all started when . . . ". We know we are about to follow his (the protagonist's) journey. So how does he escape? We aren't told that until much later in the script, but at least we are intrigued enough to follow and see how he did it. We're hooked!

A hook doesn't have to have a knock-you-over-the-head impact (like the daring daylight heist of *Heat*) to be effective and do its job. It can be subtle, like an arresting visual: *Howards End* – the woman's dress sensually trailing across the grass (man-made natural fabric draping over nature's fabric) drawing us in to follow her – or dialogue-driven, like the 'bugger' hook of *Four Weddings And A Funeral*, or quirky like the modern day film set and clapperboard opening of *The French Lieutenant's Woman*, followed by the arresting image of the lone woman staring out to sea, or as intriguing as the tracking shot of the walking feet in strange two-toned shoes in Hitchcock's *Strangers On A Train* – who is this man? where's he going? – and by the time we see his entire body for the first time we are hooked.

A useful hook device is to have ordinary people doing unordinary things, or unordinary people doing very ordinary things, or pose some question, or have something which holds the promise of more to come.

For the writer, finding the actual opening to your screenplay (the *point of entry*) is often difficult. Most openings are character rather than plot based. Often, a point of entry will see your protagonist at some kind of life-crisis point, a dilemma or decision to face about their life, direction or future. One of the deciding factors on where to open may well be revealed when working on your character biographies and, in particular, their backstories. Whatever you decide, you open the screenplay at the *last possible moment*, usually before the dropping in of some vital piece of information we need to know.

1.4 The key line

Also somewhere between pages three and five you will need to pose the question you the writer are asking in your script, the issue (personal or universal) you are attempting to confront, explore and resolve within yourself – that is to say what the script is really about and the reason you need to write this script. It's to do with your theme. The issue is addressed in the *key line*: it is spoken by a character and gives the audience clues as to what idea will be explored in your script. For example:

"I was part of something. I belonged . . ." (*Goodfellas*)

"Don't climb up there too close to God – he might shake the tree" (*Disclosure*)

"You be careful out there among the English" (*Witness*)

The line from *Witness* evokes the fundamental truth of the film: there are boundary lines between worlds and to step across them is dangerous.

Sometimes the key line is repeated towards the close of the film (sometimes word-for-word), but slightly changed in its meaning (as in *Witness*) – can you explain just how it has changed, and why?

It is not essential to have a key line (but it helps) and it does not have to be set-up on or even near page three but it helps your audience to understand the context of your story or to have something by which to measure the standards of the world of your story.

Watch the openings of *Quiz Show* and *Chinatown*. What do you think are their key lines? (Answers: Chapter 22)

Teasers

Sometimes you will find a prologue (or *teaser* scene) situated pre-credits before your Act I starts. Again this is a hook to grab the audience and/or set the scene (*Pulp Fiction, The Piano, Heavenly Creatures*). It happens a lot in TV drama and sitcoms (*Cheers, The X-Files*). In *Hill Street Blues*, the pre-credit sequence would not only hook and set the scene, it established the different storylines to be followed in that episode. In other TV dramas it may take the form of an 'in last week's episode' montage. Sometimes the teaser is run behind the opening credits (*Golden Girls, The Wonder Years*). The teaser is a useful device to quickly establish the premise your story action will be based on.

Repeated images

Somewhere in the first half of Act I, it helps if you can establish a strong visual image of something that will be repeated (echoed) near the end of your completed script. It doesn't have to be brilliantly memorable, your audience only needs to register it subliminally (in *Witness* it is the image of the Amish community emerging over the brow of a hill). When that image is repeated (usually slightly changed) towards the end, it subconsciously indicates to your audience that we are nearing the end of the story. These two images act like bookends.

> Watch the first 15 minutes of *Witness*. Note its creation of mood, the introduction of the characters (particularly the protagonist), shifts of location (rural to big city), the murder. Ask yourself: how were these various effects created; what does choice of location add to each scene (general information, dramatic value, etc)? Do you think the murder occurs (at 13 minutes) too late, too soon or just right? What about the introduction of John Book (15 minutes) – too late? Should he have entered any earlier?

> Now do the same for *The Crying Game*, *Don Juan De Marco*, *Field Of Dreams*, *Quiz Show*, *Tootsie* and *Four Weddings And A Funeral*. What do they tell you about the nature of the film you are about to see, the characters, settings, genre? Do you agree with some of the decisions the writers made? What were the hook devices used, how were they used and were they effective? Did you notice any key lines? (You should already know the *Quiz Show* key line!)

1.5 Act I: pages 10–30 (overview)

In the remaining 20 pages (20 minutes) of Act I, you need to do a number of other things:

- Environment: fill out the background details to the world your protagonist lives in.
- Beliefs: illustrate by action your protagonist's code of conduct, their value-system.
- Subplots: set them up.

Moreover, usually about half-way through this section (i.e. two thirds into Act I and 20% into the overall screenplay) you should have the first major event of your main plot, the *inciting incident*: a scene, incident or line of dialogue in which something happens or a problem is posed to make your protagonist make a decision and pursue the course of action they will follow for the rest of your script. This causes a crisis which leads to your first climax at the end of Act I. Now let's examine things in more depth.

1.6 Pages 10–20: character-in-action

❦ Between pages 10 and 15 either the arena, theme or direction of the film should be evident, preferably all of them. The audience need some kind of landmark to pull them through the movie, refine their focus on what to look for and where they are headed. If they don't get that they'll get bored or lost. ❧

Steven E. De Souza,
screenwriter: Die Hard I & II,
48 Hours, Beverly Hills Cop III

This section of the script usually focuses on the main characters-in-action (especially your protagonist). This deepens their characterisation by showing their character problem: a mixture of their attitude and personality interacting with a specific situation you have designed for them. For example, in *Witness*, John Book is portrayed as insensitive, ambitious and a user of people. Yet he must work with a woman and child (Rachel and Samuel) whose world and value-system are the complete opposite.

Moreover, this section also acts as a benchmark by which the audience can measure the character growth (how your protagonist and main characters change through Acts II and III, and at the end). In *Witness* the three drive through the streets, being forced to identify possible murderers. Hence in this section you should try to stay focused on your protagonist in all or most of the scenes.

Remember, you illustrate by action, so your protagonist has to be active – this means making decisions. Keep them active and you will keep your audience engaged. And don't forget to start establishing your major subplot, and any others you feel crucial to your story's development (for example, Book and Rachel meet sixteen minutes into the film).

1.7 Pages 20–30

By page 20 your character should have been fairly well established;

you've got most of the essential character information out of the way and established a benchmark. So as we move into the third ten pages we are entering that section of the script that will lead us up to the inciting incident (roughly between pages 23 and 28) and first climax.

In *Witness* Samuel views the identity parades and then identifies the murderer McFee from a photograph, leading automatically to the meeting between Book and his boss Schaeffer, and then to the underground garage shooting attempt by McFee.

Pages 20–30 of a script are often made dramatic by introducing an element of risk to the main character/s. In *Witness* the risk enters when we learn that the murderer is a fellow cop, thus meaning real danger for Book, Rachel and Samuel.

1.8 Pages 23–28: inciting incident and crisis (first turning point/TP1)

As we approach the closing stages of Act I, you will have the *inciting incident*, also called the *catalyst*, *plot point* or *problem*. It creates a *crisis* which leads inevitably to a *climax* (decision made). This is your First Turning Point.

A crisis is a moment in a scene that forces a decision or choice which then causes a change in the character or story. A major crisis (or Act crisis) and climax is a turning point.

At the opening of your script, life is seen pretty much as normal and in balance. The inciting incident comes along (generally between pages 23 and 28, sometimes even at page 17) and upsets that balance; it creates the 'problem' that your protagonist must restore over the course of your screenplay. Your protagonist must be aware of it (although unaware of the effect it will have on him/her), and react to it (even refusing to react is a reaction). The inciting incident gives your protagonist the general need or desire to restore that balance, thereby creating the (general) goal or outer motivation to aim for; these attempts form the spine of your story and the inciting incident sets them in motion.

Your overall story will have two major turning points: at the end of Act I and at the end of Act II (the *moment of truth*). You will also have several smaller turning points in your script, but these turning points, TP1 and TP2, are fixed. Look at it like this: the structure you create for your story is like a bridge spanning a river;

the two turning points are the two main supports that prevent the bridge from collapsing – that's how crucial they are to your screenplay.

A turning point in a screenplay performs a number of functions:

- it *grabs* the story, turns it around and *catapults* it in a new direction by setting up a problem that you protagonist must resolve over the course of the screenplay
- it *pushes* the story forward towards the Act climax (which will then push it into the next Act)
- it *raises the stakes* of the story (increasing risk, danger, level of commitment, etc.)
- it *increases momentum* by raising the stakes, by pushing the story into a new and 'dangerous' direction, by making the achievement of the dramatic need, goal or intention more uncertain. Note: 'dangerous' is relative to *your* screen story.
- it is a crisis point that generates in the audience a 'what are we going to do now?' feeling
- it dramatically *alters* your protagonist's *motivation* (TP1 creates the dramatic need, goal or outer motivation)

Note: if a time-lock has to be set, it will often be established at the inciting incident. Can you think of any examples in the four films you've viewed?

Turning points always happen to your protagonist, are character-related, and caused by their actions (remember: decision is action). Inevitably your protagonist will react to that turning point in some way: they will formulate a goal and an intent to act as a result.

TP1 often occurs at a time when the story seems to be over because of the apparent success of the protagonist. In *Witness*, John Book has successfully found out who the murderer is, has a witness, and has told his boss Schaeffer. Feeling very self-satisfied, he makes his way home. The story is apparently over because Book has 'won'. At this precise moment the crisis (TP1) occurs. Suddenly the story is cata-pulted into a new, different, more dangerous direction.

Lastly, your crisis leads directly into your first climax, at the end of Act I (which creates the momentum to kick your story into the next Act). The climax is the strongest and highest dramatic moment in your first act. (In some instances you will find TP1 coinciding with or even becoming the climax).

In *Disclosure*, the inciting incident scene is where Michael Douglas rejects the sexual advances; in *Misery*, when Annie (Kathy Bates) discovers the fictional Misery has been killed off and shouts 'You murdered her'; when Stanley Ipkiss dons *The Mask* for the first time; the arrival of Buzz Lightyear in *Toy Story*; when Baines agrees to move the piano from the beach in exchange for lessons in *The Piano*; in *Falling Down* it is D-Fens' first encounter with the Hispanic gang members.

When creating your inciting incident, ask yourself:

- What's the worst thing (apart from death) that could happen to my protagonist, which could turn out to be the best thing?
- What's the best possible thing that could happen to my protagonist, which could turn out to be the worst?
- Does it upset the balance of forces in the protagonist's life I have already established?
- Does it indicate or set up the incident and images of my Act III climax scene?

1.9 Pages 28–30: Act I climax (reaction to crisis) and transition into Act II

A climax occurs when a crisis is resolved one way or another. Following the crisis of TP1, we now see your protagonist (and main characters) reacting and responding to it. Because the turning point has transformed your protagonist's original motivation, their original goal has altered or been forced to alter. Consciously or not they will be compelled to formulate a solution, a new (generalised) goal and a line of action they believe will lead them to that goal. Remember, this is their external motivation – what your character must get or win by the end of the story – the thing that drives them through the script. The formulation of this goal and the specific line of action chosen must be strong and visible to the audience (through not necessarily apparent to the protagonist), and demonstrated by visual action. This climax/reaction creates the energy to finally push us into Act II.

In *Witness*, Book bursts into his sister's house, dishevelled and afraid. He is taking Rachel and Samuel with him to escape the threat from McFee and Schaeffer. This climactic action reveals his decision (i.e. his reaction to TP1). The sense of urgency allows the audience to measure the enormity of the danger he feels they are all in. The bleeding wounds engender audience sympathy, allowing us to forgive him if we might have felt his reaction was somewhat exaggerated.

Note: the inciting incident does not necessarily *have* to happen at this point. Sometimes it will even occur earlier in the script. Indeed, a common debate is 'where exactly does TP1 occur?' – at the inciting incident? the crisis? the climax? In practice, you will often find these three moments happening so quickly after each other that they could all be considered a collective turning point. What *is* agreed, however, is that your two major turning points should be at the end of Acts I and II. Whether you want to see it as an inciting incident, crisis or climax is up to you and your story.

❝ By the end of Act I, I want to achieve a feeling of closure, that some stuff is out the way. It's not always the audience understanding everything. A mistake is to try to get all that foundation exposition into the early part of the film, that's why a lot of films start to wind down as you go through them.. ❞

Steven E. De Souza

Now work out the inciting incident in the four films you have watched (*The Crying Game, Don Juan de Marco, Field Of Dreams, Quiz Show.*) Answers in Chapter 22.

2.1 Act II (Overview)

This Development Act tells your main story, shows further your characters in action, and shows the development of those characters through their experiences. All the elements introduced in Act I are now shown working with and against each other: conflict, suspense, tension, action, adventure, passion, romance, murder, mystery, and whatever else you've got.

The nature of this Act, where the problem introduced by the inciting incident is further developed through conflict, is that your characters are operating on borrowed time, underpinned by the existence and nature of the protagonist's solution decided on at the end of Act I. Being a bad or a false solution (even though they don't realise it as such), your protagonist will often find his or herself re-confronting their old problem, though it may take on a new or slightly different shape. They cannot escape the fact that their 'solution' did not solve the problem completely. The audience will of course understand this better than the protagonist. This is the nature of putting the audience in a superior position (we know something you don't) and they know subconsciously that the protagonist will have to deal with this problem at some point later in the film.

In *Witness*, Schaeffer has to deal with the fact he's been betrayed; Book will have to face the fact that running away, for whatever reasons, hasn't solved the problem and has led to Carter's death. This moment of painful realisation usually occurs at the climax at the end of Act II (the second turning point or moment of truth) and this leads to a new and more powerful clarity of purpose.

To get a clearer grasp of Act II, it will help if you see it as two equal halves divided by the half-way point. In the first half of Act II (pages 30–60), up to the half-way point (page 60), your protagonist progresses steadily upwards in their quest and things seem to be going swimmingly. But nothing moves forward except through conflict. If all you have is exposition and explanation, things will get boring and your story will lack momentum. Hence you should be building towards a set-back. Indeed, you will probably have two set-backs in this segment of the script: a minor one as you enter the Act and a more serious one at your script's half-way point. Let's look closer at this first half.

2.2 Act II: Pages 30–45

A *golden rule of screenwriting* is: after a climax, give your audience a breathing space, a pause moment or scene for them to come down, assimilate that climax and all that has happened.

Your protagonist has now fixed their general goal/s and is back on track – or so they think. There is soon a minor set-back but they overcome that and they move steadily upwards. Hence these fifteen pages are usually ones of reaction/response and the setting up by the writer of incidents that will lead to further problems and obstacles later in the story (relationships and complications may begin here).

In *Witness*, we see the potential chemistry between Book and Rachel in the nursing scene (the main subplot's first turning point). This is also a serious complication, because Amish customs state it is not possible for a woman to have an affair or marry an outsider. Through no fault of their own, Book and Rachel belong to two different worlds.

2.3 Page 45: first focus point

At approximately page 45 you will find a *focus point* (also called *focal* or *focusing point*). This is a scene or moment which:

- tightens the storyline action
- reminds the audience of the 'problem'
- pushes the story forward helping to keep it on track (and stopping the audience and the writer from getting lost)
- may indicate the first beginnings of character change or growth in your protagonist

By this stage we have seen some first indications that the protagonist is changing or growing, for example a moment or scene showing a kind of acceptance of the new situation (i.e. your protagonist has adjusted to preceding life-changing events, especially the 'problem' and TP1). It is a marker or 'beat' in the protagonist's character transformation and growth. Up until now they have probably been reacting to events brought on by TP1. The first focus point (or FP1) now sees them making a first significant active move towards achieving their goal.

Forty-six minutes into *Witness*, John Book gives Rachel his gun, even though he knows that somewhere 'out there' McFee and Schaeffer are still after him (a clever integration of main plot and subplot). This is a distinct moment of growth for the Book character in the Book/Rachel main subplot: previously, he would never have done this even if he were in danger. But here he is already responding to the Amish values around him. In terms of main plot (Book has to find the murderer) it reminds us of McFee and Schaeffer and the 'problem' facing all of them.

As with the two turning points, there are two focus points (the other comes at approximately page 75) and they are usually related: what is promised/foreshadowed/mentioned/indicated in FP1 is often delivered in FP2. Hence with the first focus point you the writer need to design a scene that essentially *refocuses* on the storyline.

2.4 Pages 45–60

This section sees your protagonist begin to fulfil the line of action begun at TP1 and tightened at FP1. The line continues onwards and upwards, almost unhindered, because you are building towards your half-way point which will be a *point of no return* for your protagonist. In other words, pages 45–60 sees:

● the obstacles get tougher
● the protagonist get stronger
● the protagonist approach a point after which they cannot quit

In *Witness*, this segment is where Book, formerly a carpenter but now a cop, is seduced by the Amish life (and later, at the half-way point, by Rachel).

Generally speaking, this segment in your main plot restates the external problem. But we also see the protagonist take their first decisive action towards attaining the ultimate goal of the story. More specifically, they will be moving towards the point of no return/total commitment scene at the half–way point (page 60).

In your main subplot, this segment usually illustrates a change taking place in your protagonist. Up till now we have had an indication of that charge, but now we are focusing in on it (e.g. Book helps the Amish build a barn and their communal values are seen in practice; as John falls in love with Rachel, he is also falling in love with the Amish life and values-system).

2.5 Page 60: The half-way point

The half-way point or mid-point of your script (approximately page 60), is your protagonist's *point of no return*, their scene or moment of total commitment. Here, something happens which causes them to reassess and consider giving up their quest or journey. Should they give up or push on? Looking at your script logistically, your character having come sixty pages, it would take them the same time to give up the quest and return to where they started (page 1) as it would if they decided to continue the quest to page 120. In *Falling Down*, 67 minutes into the 104-minute film (i.e. 15 minutes past half-way), D-Fens is on the phone to his ex-wife, and says: 'I'm past the point of no return, Beth. You know what that is? That's the point in a journey where it's longer to go back to the beginning than it is to continue to the end.'

Unlike at other points in your script (i.e. at the end of each act) this half-way point does not necessarily involve any sort of climax or big action scene. But for your protagonist it is a point of no return.

Its main purpose is:

- to force the protagonist to reassess their quest
- to make the protagonist consider giving up
- to make the protagonist then decide to continue on (they must do this)
- to make them formulate a new set of more specific or focused goals
- to make them commit to that new goal totally in a way they cannot back out of

(Remember: we learn about our characters from the decisions they make . . . under pressure.)

The half-way point usually tells us something new, something we didn't know before; it can also represent a major moment of recognition for your protagonist, where they recognise what is really going on, particularly between themselves and the other main character/s. It also evolves and adds to the protagonist's motivation: anyone who reaches the point of no return has, by definition, fewer choices open to them and are compelled to adopt a specific line because they can no longer quit or return home. Also, obtaining a significant part of the solution to the problem adds greatly to a protagonist's motivation to remain on the case; there are fewer options but they are now 'addicted' to finding the solution.

Very often in a film with a love story, the point of no return is when the two people either go to bed together or say 'I love you' for the first time. In *Witness* it is the seduction scene in the barn where Book and Rachel dance, touch and almost kiss. After this Book's actions and options are narrowed: his attraction to Rachel, a woman who could be ostracised by the community, limits the choices he can make. The pair (and audience) realise they are on a path of no return, or what seems like no return; an emotionally dangerous course for both of them.

In *Disclosure* it is when Michael Douglas is forced to tell his wife about the mediation – and the full story; in *The Mask* when the gangsters offer a reward for the stealing of *The Mask*; in *The Piano* when

Barnes and Ada lie together naked for the first time, and the daughter sees them; in *Speed* it is the first time Keanu Reeves comforts Sandra Bullock (on the bus) after the first bomb has exploded.

Returning to *Maverick*, the mid-way point cleverly takes us back to the opening hook of the hanging scene. We discover how Bret escapes and now realise he *must* pursue his quest. We also realise that the first half of the film has been solid backstory in flashback: the audience has been cleverly manipulated – which is the essence of the film. (It also subconsciously prepares us for further manipulation to come; all the more effective when we discover, at the final climactic twist, we have been wrong-guessing all along.) Even in something as vast as Spike Lee's *Malcolm X* (see Chapter 8) the half-way point occurs ninety minutes into the 205-minute story with his conversion to Islam. Up until then Malcolm has been an aimless, self-destructive mass of anger and disruption.

After this mid-point the protagonist will hold to their commitment and be driven along a certain course *because* they have committed to that line in a particular way. From now on your protagonist cannot return to their former life and ways.

Now return to *The Crying Game*, *Don Juan De Marco*, *Field Of Dreams* and *Quiz Show*. What are their points of no return? (Answers: Chapter 22). Notice also how many minutes into the film they occur – are they half-way through? Do they (and your script) fit any of these criteria?

Point Of No Return

Before		*After*
not in control of their life	●	taking more decisive control
a victim	●	hitting back
puzzled by the mystery or 'problem'	●	on track to the solution
uncommitted	●	committed
hunted	●	hunter
living the dream or fairy tale	●	dealing with the reality

2.6 Act II second half: Pages 60–90 (overview)

Your protagonist, having made the decision to continue, and with a new, more focused set of goals in place, progresses onwards. But in this section the stakes are raised, so that now more is at risk, more in danger of being lost (immediately, or in the long term). Raising the stakes also shows us the enormity of what must be committed in order to succeed.

Script readers have noted that if a script is going to show signs of flagging, it always tends to be in the second half of Act II. Sometimes, to combat this, you might find the script exploring one particular subplot or shifting location from the script's main setting. (Both these happen in *Tootsie* during the 11-minute sequence at Les's farm).

In the section between pages 60 and 75, the direction of your protagonist is very clear: they are holding to (or being held to) that commitment made at the half-way point. That point has added some element of compulsion (from within themselves/other people/outside events) where they are compelled to choose more and more specific lines of action to achieve their ultimate goal. The nature of character motivation in film is not allowing your protagonist to do what they want to do, but compelling them to do what absolutely must be done.

2.7 Page 75: second focus point

This second focus point (FP2), at approximately page 75, performs many of the same functions as FP1 (at page 45):

- it moves the story forward
- it keeps it on track
- it pays off FP1 by delivering on some promise or suggestion made at that earlier point
- it may add another significant clue to the solution of the 'problem' or mystery
- it tests your protagonist's new growth

This last function is the most important one.

In *Witness*, it is when Rachel is washing herself, half undressed, and turns to find Book in the other room. Without dialogue and with little physical action happening we see that very powerful decision-action of John *not* to make love to her. At the same time, John's growth (transformational arc) is being tested: if he makes love, it will be because the 'old' John Book is still in charge, the old rules still controlling his actions and choices. His 'success' at passing this test proves that concrete change has taken place in his character; he is a new person. However, it is not only the audience that discovers it; the protagonist himself realises he has changed and moved on. Book now knows who he truly is. This moment of self-realisation is important, and it must be powerful.

Remember the FP1–FP2 linkage: if FP1 plants/indicates the beginnings of change in your protagonist, then FP2 shows proof that they have indeed changed.

The most interesting and engaging type of FP2 is where your protagonist is tested to almost breaking point. The audience must be gripped to genuinely believe that the outcome could go either way (Book might make love to Rachel or he might not).

Sometimes (actually quite often) after this second focal point you will have a long expositionary speech, usually told in the form of a story to someone, which illuminates the real reason for your protagonist's journey, their real inner-motivation. By now your protagonist has probably recognised this inner motivation, although it may be someone else who tells the actual story. Go back to the four films you have watched. Does this happen? Ask why the decision to include or exclude it was made. Was it placed later and if so, why?

2.8 Pages 75–90: complications

The second focal point has tested our protagonist's growth, they've come through it, and we are seeing a new person. The audience now needs to see the true (dramatic) vindication of this test – and this vindication lies in the second turning point (TP2), the moment of truth and the climax to your second Act.

As with pages 20 to 30, this screenplay section is principally concerned with setting up TP2. This is done in two ways:

- TP2 must be strong and well-integrated and the set-up for it clear
- at the same time, your protagonist will usually experience a sense of failure just prior to TP2

This sense of failure is the crisis point for the whole film story and is your protagonist's crisis.

In *Witness*, the set-up for TP2 is begun early in the screenplay: when Book punches out the punks (TP2/Act II mainplot climax), he is wearing Amish clothes – yet for him to get to this crucial point, we must have been able to see John's interest in Rachel and Amish values and their subsequent influence on him. But what is also necessary in this scene is that Book should reach a crisis point which will generate a sense of failure and despair. This occurs when Book learns that his partner, Carter, is dead. Book himself has run away, is living in relative ease on the Amish farm, falling in love, etc. and yet ultimately because of his activities, Carter has been murdered. This sense of failure and despair causes Book to become very angry. The punks choose this moment to annoy the non-violent Amish and Book seizes this as an opportunity to express his anger: he beats them up – but by being dressed in Amish clothes, he draws attention to himself. This information is passed to a police officer who informs Schaeffer and thus we are catapulted into Act III. Note too this is also a crisis point in Book's transformational arc: he has resorted to violence, his old ways – a step backwards. This is part of the story's theme. It also reinforces the idea of the difficulty of crossing into a new world and remaining there, thus foreshadowing the end of the film when Book returns to his own world (albeit changed).

2.9 End of Act II, Pages 85–90: second turning point/TP2 – moment of truth

By the end of Act II your protagonist reaches that second turning point (TP2) somewhere between pages 85 and 90 of the script. It is a major setback and forms the second act climax (or leads directly into it). Here they meet the biggest obstacle in the story, and are defeated by it (although not permanently). This immediate crisis for the protagonist will give them a sense of failure, of having been abandoned or isolated, and of having realised at last (and now being forced to face the fact) that the decision or action taken at the TP1 was false, weak, unprincipled or a terrible mistake. Hence this turning point is called the *moment of truth*.

This creates a new and yet more powerful clarity of purpose for the protagonist, a clearer goal, which accompanies them as they enter Act III. Now, knowing exactly who they are and having faced up to (and possibly accepted) their bad decision or false solution made at the first turning point, they are ready for the final showdown at the end of Act III.

TP2 (the moment of truth) performs the same functions as TP1:

- it involves the protagonist
- it leads logically to and 'causes' the final confrontation scene (and the final climax in general)

In *Witness*, Book beats up the punks and we are thrust straight into Act III. The actions of the active protagonist almost always *cause* the climax. This is the nature of characters in films: they bring about those events which may cause their own downfall and destruction.

Remember that in Act I, just when we though the story might be over, the inciting incident came along, created or posed the 'problem', and caused the TP1, which then spun the story off in a new direction. TP2 often occurs when the story seems to be over for the opposite reason: the protagonist has failed and despair has overtaken them (not all films will follow this format – follow the demands of *your* story). At this precise moment there is a breakthrough, a clue revealed, an inner strength found or (as in Book's case) an action taken precisely *because* of the despair and sense of having failed (his partner Carter's murder); the action causes him to give away his identity and his whereabouts. It also creates the energy and momentum to catapult us into Act III. (Note that the climax to the Book/Rachel main subplot is when they kiss.)

Now return to your four films: can you work out each one's second turning point? (Answers: Chapter 22)

3.1 Act III Pages 90–120: final push and climax

❦ The climax is the principal part of the story and for which ... all the machinery of planning and constructing has been set in motion ... ❧

Syd Field

Your Act III needs to do three important things:

- have a strong **climax** to the story action
- **resolve** the problem or task and the relationships you established in Act I
- provide a satisfying **ending**

In Act III you have to tie up all your loose ends, answer all remaining questions, show how the characters have changed, show what has been achieved or what disaster has struck *and* send the audience away feeling ... however you want them to feel.

So, as we enter Act III, your audience will be experiencing that pause moment or scene after Act II's climax, thus giving your protagonist a chance to regain their stasis, pull themselves together and go for that one last do-or-die attempt. After that, from now on, everything should accelerate towards that final climax.

Your protagonist usually enters Act III with a greater clarity of purpose about who they are (from FP2) and knowing more clearly (usually for the first time) what they really need to do (from TP2) – hence a new and clearer goal is usually formulated and chosen.

After the ending of Act I the protagonist had a general overriding powerful goal: what they believe they need to get in the film. But the character goes through transformation, and is challenged to grow. This has consequences for the character's goal, because if they change and grow, then so will the nature of their goal – the old goal no longer satisfies them. So they are given a new goal at the half-way point and a yet more focused goal at the moment of truth. Each time can mean an alternative goal, or simply the old goal with something added to it. The events of Act II have *almost* led to complete disaster and to a sense of personal failure in the protagonist. Indeed, the low point that follows the Act II climax is usually the protagonist's darkest moment in the script (hence the moment of truth) – a realisation that comes *only just in time*. Act III provides the arena in which to redeem these negative situations.

In *Witness*, John Book's main plot goal is to survive and protect Rachel and Samuel. But as he enters Act III it is no longer just his physical survival, but also the survival of his new Amish values and beliefs. In order to save these he is actually forced to put his physical survival at risk by laying his rifle down and stepping in front of Schaeffer's weapon. So physical survival is no longer the main goal, otherwise why risk it for 'something else'? Surely that something else is now the main goal? Survival now not only involves survival of his new value-system (which includes the importance of the community above that of the individual); the *method* of survival is also crucial: it must be done without the gun, by using the power of the community. In the main subplot, Book's goal is a relationship with Rachel. The second focal point illustrated that this goal was already changing and by the end of the film his goal is to allow each of them to remain in their separate worlds.

Note that in this 'final push' segment you will often find a chase – not necessarily fast cars and screeching tyres – but at least a pursuit of some kind. In *Witness* it is the stalking of Book in the granary silo. In *Tootsie*, after he unmasking on live TV, Michael Hoffman is in the bar with Julie's father. Michael decides to leave the bar, go to the studios and try to talk to Julie. She initially brushes him off and goes along the sidewalk, Michael follows her until they finally talk (the climax) and resolve matters.

Also note that pacing (Chapter 10) is very important in Act III: it is the fastest-paced of all the acts, with more 'crises-per-page' and little let-up. In this segment, incidents will happen fairly quickly and lead inexorably to the final climax. This is also why third acts are often built around a single major sequence. The last acts of both *Field Of Dreams* and *Witness* are single sequences. Sequences will be covered in Chapter 9.

3.2 Pages 115–120: final climax

The climax happens between approximately pages 115 and 119 of the script. It is always a scene (sometimes the final scene) in which the protagonist faces the greatest obstacle of all – the final confrontation with the opposition – and one of them 'wins', the other 'loses' (though note that by winning they may lose, and vice versa). Whatever, this must be seen on-screen. It cannot happen off-screen, or be reported. We want to see it. And this climax must *integrate* three elements:

- resolving the main plot
- showing through action the new transformation in the protagonist
- playing out the theme of the script.

The climax caps off the process begun in Act I: a goal was set but we often discover it was a false or insufficient goal; at the end of Act II a truer goal was set, but at the end of Act III a real or concealed goal is revealed (*Field Of Dreams* powerfully demonstrates this).

It is important to understand that this climax is the *peak emotional moment* of your screenplay (where your theme comes forcefully into play). It may be the screen kiss (as in the ending of *Speed* or as in most romances/romantic comedies – *Four Weddings and a Funeral*, *Sleepless In Seattle, Groundhog Day*) or the much subtler 'wanna play catch?' of *Field Of Dreams*.

John Book entered Act III of *Witness* no longer solely worried about his physical survival, but now more concerned about the survival of his Amish values and less individualistic ethics – all of which are played out in the ending (in the way he now goes about trying to achieve his new goal). Schaeffer, by capturing and threatening Rachel, is also threatening these new values. Book is forced to put down his gun, expose himself to Schaeffer's gun, and then call upon the power of the community to defeat Schaeffer. (This ending powerfully integrates the thematic elements with the main plot action climax.)

Read again the climax quote on page 119 and think carefully about it. This climax is the point towards which you build your screenplay. The value of any incident or character development point in the story is measured in terms of this climax: does it move the story forward to the climactic scene, or not? The question you should ask yourself when creating each and every scene is: how does this screen relate to this climax? As I said earlier, screenplays are written backwards.

Lastly, what comes after a climax? A pause to let the audience come down. Hence . . .

3.3 End of Act III: resolution/denouement

Having got over that final climax – the biggest of your entire screenplay – you must again give your audience a chance to come down from all that emotion. Your protagonist has faced their biggest challenge and either won, or been defeated by it yet still won, or defeated by it and lost (although they've learnt something about themselves and therefore still 'won').

In *Witness*, Book contacts the authorities, the police arrive, take statements and examine the site, and depart. Book then approaches Rachel and they say their silent farewell. In *Field Of Dreams* it is the simple rising crane shot revealing a stream of car headlights ('they will come').

This tapering-off period in your script should also tie up all the loose ends, and any subplots that have not already been resolved in and by your final climax.

This is a moment (or moments) where your protagonist re-evaluates their situation, of how life has changed for them, as if they were setting up a new design for their new life to come (after your screenplay ends). So your story needs to create a sense of an *afterlife*: a feeling that the lives of the characters go on after the story has finished, after your audience has left the cinema. Hence the importance of creating fully three-dimensional characters: if your characters haunt you the writer, and live in your head after the writing is complete, then you're on the right track.

Incidentally, don't forget that resonating visual image (and possibly resonated key-line) near the end of your script, that image or line which is similar to and relates to the one you set up in your opening pages. Here it will be slightly changed or adapted, and does not have to be as obvious a bookend visual as, say, the feather in the wind of *Forrest Gump*. In *Witness* it is much subtler – if you've read this far, you should know what it is.

3.4 Endings

Finally, a fundamental consideration you *must* address: what effect do you want to create on your audience after they have experienced your screenplay?

❦ When we previewed *Four Weddings* . . . in New Jersey, by the end we knew we had a good film, but we were still convinced it would be a small, quiet, almost arthouse, British film. Then one of the US studio heads came up to me and said: 'This movie's gonna make you fifty million dollars.' I said that was ridiculous. Then he said: 'Look at the faces of the people coming out: they're smiling, they've just seen a great movie, they feel good – and that feeling is gonna spread.' ❦

Richard Curtis, writer:
Four Weddings And A Funeral

I'm not necessarily saying give it a happy ending, but give it a *satisfying* ending. The endings of *Leaving Las Vegas*, *The Crying Game*, *Philadelphia*, *Cinema Paradiso*, *Sunset Boulevard*, or even *Witness* aren't exactly happy, but they are at least satisfying. Can you think of others?

Ideally, the audience should feel that there was a reason for your film. They shouldn't be shaking their heads and asking "why the hell did any one make *that*?" Again, this comes down to your ending, your theme and their integration.

❛ I'm very keen to get right the opening five minutes and closing five minutes of a film – they are crucial. ❜

Steven Spielberg

The last 10 to 20 minutes of a film is often what most affects a cinema-going audience. It is also where those vital three elements of Act III (page 122) all come together. The ending is where your theme is integrated into the final action and often makes sense of it – it *unifies* the whole film. What this means in practice is: your choice of ending and how it is played out must be *informed*, *influenced* and *symptomatic* of your theme.

So, get the last twenty minutes of your script right, the ending right ... and write a brilliant screenplay too!

When thinking about structure in relation to your own screenplay or any story you may think of, try approaching it like this:

1 First decide on an end for your story

2 Then design the opening: your first ten pages; then your first Act

3 Ask yourself:
- does it set the story in motion?
- does it establish my protagonist?
- does it indicate what my story is going to be about?
- does it set up the situation?
- does it set up a problem or an obstacle that my character must confront and overcome?
- are my protagonist's needs, goals or motivations clearly stated?

Observations

- Most 'journey' films are geographically plotted. That is, each act takes place in a separate geographical location. In *Rain Man*, Act I takes place in Los Angeles and Cincinnati, Act II in the desert, and Act III in Las Vegas and L.A. More obviously in *Speed*, each act is a separate story: Act I – The elevator (25 mins), Act II – The bus (64 mins); Act III – The Subway (17 mins). In *Maverick*, Act I is set in the town; Act II (first half) on the plains, (second half) on the riverboat; Act III back on dry land. Are there any Act/location correlations in the film you watched? Look again at *Witness, The Crying Game, Don Juan De Marco, Field Of Dreams,* and *Quiz Show.* Ask why these choices were made (or not).

- Looking logistically at the overall three-act structure, one's over-riding feeling is of symmetry and balance (the half-way point being a pivot). Remember too that bridge spanning the river with two central support columns: the two turning points.

- Try to see a film in terms of energy: every scene is a burst of energy; conflict produces energy; new insights or directions produce energy in the audience's mind. The first burst of energy is the hook (it grabs and carries us into Act I); the next is the inciting incident and TP1 which carries you into Act II; the energy that sustains us through Act II comes from the protagonist's realisation that they've had to compromise their values, have chosen badly or wrongly; this realisation (the moment of truth/TP2) is another burst that drives us into and through Act III and towards the climax.

Of course, you will be able to find exceptions and other approaches to this chapter's template (e.g. Christopher Vogler's 'Hero's Journey' construct), but the three-act 'paradigm' is the basic foundation. What you should be asking is how and, especially, why it might differ.

To reiterate: when examining structure in any film or TV drama, it is too easy to interpret any guidelines as rules that *must* be followed (if your inciting incident isn't on page 'X' your script is rubbish, etc.) The things in this chapter are not set in stone; they are there to help you organise and focus your own script.

Remember, you should aim to reach that point where you don't consciously think about structural rules any more.

❢ I do get worried when people get so obsessed about structure in a formulaic way that they forget about character and dialogue and telling a good story – the things that actually do matter most. I would rather a writer came to me with a script that was structurally all over the place but was full of wonderful ideas and characters and sparkling dialogue. Structure you can work on after. What I don't want is something that fits the formulae but actually has no significance, life and energy. ❣

Lynda Myles,
Pandora Productions/Pathé Films

Ultimately, your story dictates the positioning, style and magnitude of your climaxes and turning points.

❋ ❋
❋   ❋
❋   Trust Your Story   ❋
❋   ❋
❋ ❋

❛ Remember the rule – there are no rules. ❜

Jim Sheridan, director:
My Left Foot

❛ There are no rules, but you've got to know them before you can break them! ❜

Adrian Dunbar, screenwriter
Hear My Song

8
STRUCTURAL VARIATIONS

Multi-plotting

What happens if you are writing an ensemble piece – a lot of main characters, each with their own story to tell (e.g. *Independence Day*, *Short Cuts*)? Quite simply, you take it Act by Act. If you have, say, six sub-stories, you have effectively six subplots of equal weight, and you set them up and develop them, one block at a time...

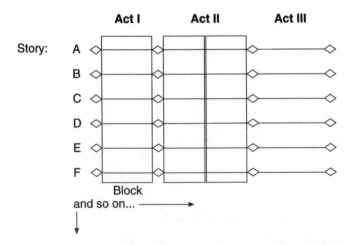

... and you arrange the order of the scenes and plots within each block in the most dramatically effective way possible (you may still find, however, that one sub-story is more prominent – effectively a main-plot). Multi-plots happen more often in television drama series (*NYPD Blue, E.R., Pride And Prejudice*) where there are lots of story strands happening at the same time (but often one particular story will be set-up, developed and resolved in that episode); you may find that the different story strands in an episode are linked in some way, built around a single thematic idea – guilt, rape, trust, etc. Multi-plotting is also enhanced by all the stories taking place in either a single environment, preferably restricted (*Enchanted April, Airplane*), or over a short time-span (*American Graffiti* – one night).

Let's examine *Enchanted April*. The overarching main story is the relationship between Lotty Wilkins and Rose Arbuthnot and their renting of the Italian castle for a month. But the real focus is on the subplots:

- Lotty and her businessman husband Mellersh
- Rose and her husband Frederick
- Lady Caroline Dester's story
- Mrs. Fisher's story
- George Briggs, the castle owner's story
- Lady Caroline and Frederick

And each subplot has its own establishment, climax, turning points, development, final climax and resolution. These climaxes may be the tiniest of events – a decision made, a glance exchanged, an expected reaction not executed – but each is significant within the context of its own subplot. We may have four points of view (told via voice-over, letters and diary jottings), but our main POV is still Lotty.

Now watch *Enchanted April* and try working out each subplot's developmental template. Here are some clues: the inciting incident is the newspaper advertisement; the first act climax is when Mellersh shouts to Lotty: "You are not going to Italy!"; the half-way point occurs with the arrival at the castle of the first man, Mellersh; Act III mostly takes place in the garden after the meal, a kind of lingering extended climax. Also notice the use of voice-over to move the plot along – is this a subtle device or is it overused?

List five more examples of multi-plotted dramas. Watch an episode of each. Do any similar patterns emerge?

Plot variations

There are, of course, other ways of approaching plot structure. For example, when the television detective series *Columbo* started out, it was very innovative. It showed us at the opening who did the murder (using its Act III conclusion as the hook). But the story that drew the audience in was how that murder was actually committed, the back-story that led to it, and how Columbo pieced the puzzle together.

Indeed, the more innovative and imaginative approaches to plotting and structure tend to happen in contemporary television drama. Yet whatever variation you come across it still tends to fall into some three-act logic. It's all to do with the basis craft of storytelling.

A recent development in feature films is *interleafing* (or *interleaving*). Here subplots which juggle with flashbacks and flashforwards intersect and complicate the overarching linear mainplot, and are run as parallel action (*Pulp Fiction, The Usual Suspects, Lone Star, Courage Under Fire*) – but, again, these are by established filmmakers.

The two-act structure

This linear form is found in half-hour (mostly TV) dramas and sit-coms, the act division coming at the ad break. Similar to the three-act linear structure, the conflict starts in Act I and, by a series of climaxes and setbacks, escalates to the highest point of conflict at the end of Act II.

In the two-act structure, the acts are generally of equal length, with three or four main scenes in each act (with perhaps one or two additional transitional or establishing filmed external scenes).

In TV, it is the first two or three minutes which are crucial, hence the hook is in the first three pages and the main plot established early in the first scene. If you have a subplot (you will rarely have more than one – the length cannot sustain overcomplication), it should be introduced, or at least foreshadowed, in your first scene (or second, if your first is short). Prologue 'teasers' (page 104) are an established shorthand for this.

At the end of Act I, instead of an obvious climax, there is some cliffhanger moment of tension (strong enough to hold your audience over the ad break and return for Act II). There is no need to follow it with a pause moment, the break itself will do this. Entering Act II you continue building the action until your moment of truth which in this case is half-way through Act II (i.e. 75% into the drama – like the three-act structure). The remainder of Act II is your resolution.

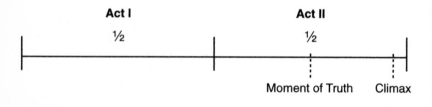

Now watch three randomly chosen sitcoms. Do they fit this template? If not, why?

—— Four and five-act structure ——

You will discover that longer films (e.g. *Goodfellas, Malcolm X, Braveheart, Nixon, Heat, Schindler's List, Casino, Titanic*) may well break down into four, sometimes five acts (each act being generally of equal length). However, the key turning points are still there and similar to the three-act proportions: inciting incident at 20%, point of no return at 50% and moment of truth at 75%.

Portmanteau films

These are the types of film which have a number of separate stories running back-to-back to make a full-length feature and are more director-generated. Most of them, however, do display some kind of overarching link, either the same character/s (*Pulp Fiction, Mishima, Four Rooms, Mystery Train*), the same location (*New York Stories, Grand Hotel, Four Rooms*), the same theme (*Aria*) or author (*Quartet, Trio* and *Encore* from Somerset Maugham), similar storylines (Hal Hartley's *Flirt*), or the same linking prop (*Tales Of Manhattan*). And, of course, each mini-story has its own beginning, middle and end. Mixing your genres within the overall fabric of your feature does not help (*New York Stories, Four Rooms*); that way lies confusion.

9

"DEEP STRUCTURE"

Having looked at the overarching structure, let's now examine what is called *deep structure* (or *sub-structure*) – the elements used to dramatise your story. As you go from the general to the specific, you are moving closer to the heart of your screenplay and nearer to the actual writing of your first (exploratory) draft.

In writing your screenplay you have two devices:

- *Scenes* – the individual incidents
- *Sequences* – the arrangement of those scenes into meaningful clusters of development

Your tools are:

- *Visuals* – the actions your characters enact and your selection of visual images (into an image system)
- *Sound* – principally dialogue, but also the other sounds and effects around them

By now you should have a clearer idea about the overall structure of your intended script and about certain specific moments in your story. But before you can proceed further, you need to know five key things about your story: where you begin; what your inciting incident and TP1 are; your Act II climax/moment of truth (TP2); your final climax and your ending. List them. From there you can go on to fill in the template by dividing it up in terms of sequences as you flesh out your storyline.

The sequence

The sequence is an important concept to understand; it is the organisational framework of your story.

There are two types of sequence:

- *Dramatic* – a series of scenes linked together or connected by a *single idea* that, in themselves, form a self-contained unit of your screenplay (and end in a sequence climax)
- *Bridging* or *Transitionary* – mini-sequences used to link dramatic sequences or to establish character (early in Act I). They do *not* culminate in a dramatic event

The *dramatic sequence* is probably the most important element of a screenplay. If structure is the spine of your screenplay, sequences are the rest of the skeleton, they hold everything together; they are the microcosm, foundation and blueprint of your script. This block of dramatic action held together by one idea can be expressed in one or a few words: escape, chase, arrival, departure, a certain character, a reunion, murder, whatever. For example, towards the end of *The Graduate*, racing to track down Elaine, finally finding her at the church (pursuit); in the wedding sequence that opens *The Godfather;* or the Terence Mann sequence in *Field Of Dreams* where Ray researches, seeks, finds and almost loses Mann.

Sequences are the pegs attached to the washing line of your structure from which you hang your story. Every dramatic sequence has a definite beginning, middle and end – a unit of dramatic action complete within itself – each sequence mirroring the overarching structure of your screenplay. Moreover, each sequence (dramatic or bridging) overlaps slightly with the one next to it, creating continuity and momentum.

A screenplay can have any number of major sequences – however many your script needs – and is related to the pacing of your script. A relaxed, contemplative drama such as *Field Of Dreams* has nine, the brooding *Rebel Without A Cause* seven; *Speed* is exciting, fast-paced, fast-edited, hence more sequences – and shorter ones. Try to work out how many sequences in *Speed*; it's very clearly plotted. Then try delineating the sequences in the films you watched for Chapter 7. Ask why there were so many (or so few).

Let's examine *Thelma and Louise* (total length = 123 minutes) in terms of sequences:

1 *Opening sequence* (escape) runs approximately from 2 minutes to 11 minutes into the film:
- Louise phones Thelma (need sets goal)
- Kitchen: Thelma/Darryl confrontation (problem/obstacles: Darryl's domination, etc.)
- Thelma makes decision (solution: wait till Darryl leaves)
- Thelma packs (action)
- Louise picks up Thelma, they drive away (climax and result)

2 *Bar sequence* (bridging) (at 11m)

3 *Fugitive sequence* (18m):
- (19m) Attempted rape (problem posed by inciting incident: motivates all that follows, gets complicated later)
- (20½m) Shooting (action, crisis)
- Escape (resolution)

4 *Transitional (1st) running away sequence* (21m):
- Driving: no plan (problem)
- Hotel room: make plan (problem resolved)

5 *Losing money sequence:*
- (45m) Pick up Brad Pitt character
- Detour to avoid cops; Jimmy meets Louise in hotel (obstacles in her path)
- (60m) Thelma and Pitt make love; Jimmy and Louise say goodbyes
- Realisation: money left in room (crisis)
- (66m) Discover Pitt has stolen their money (climax, resolution) – major set-back

6 *Thelma takes control sequence:*
- (71m) Thelma robs convenience store – major set-back: point of no return.

7 *Heading for Mexico sequence* (structured around rude trucker):
- (74m) First encounter with trucker
- Pitt in cop station
- Thelma phones Darryl, realises cops are there (problem intensified)
- Driving through night
  (this part of the sequence totals 15m)

- (89m) Second encounter with trucker

- Thelma asks Louise if she was raped in Texas
- Cop chases them for speeding
- Lock cop in trunk
- Thelma and Louise discuss being on the run
- Thelma phones friendly cop again
- Thelma and Louise talk about never going back
  (this part of the sequence totals 16m)

- (105m) Third encounter with trucker
- (108m) They shoot up his truck – climax to this entire sequence

8 *Final chase sequence:*
- (111m): Cops start chasing them
- They are cornered on cliff top
- (120 mins): They drive off cliff

You can see a distinct pattern within each sequence:

Establishment⟶ Problem ⟶ Possible ⟶ Action ⟶
              Posed   Solution

⟶ Crisis ⟶ Climax ⟶ Aftermath

Sequence goals

In each sequence, the central character will have a specific goal, which they believe is a definitive step towards achieving their overall screenplay goal (and fulfilling their dramatic need). This does not mean that there aren't also character development goals which contribute to their transformational arc. Hence:

- the sequence goal is derived from the overall goal
- it is different to all the other sequence goals
- it must help escalate the action (be stronger than the previous sequence goal)

In the sequence, each attempt to get the goal meets an obstacle, which usually fails the first time, then a new attempt is made. Each new attempt will involve your character formulating a new strategy or approach. At the end the attempt either fails, succeeds or is interrupted. Hence the main part of any dramatic sequence is the struggle to reach the sequence goal. Struggle is caused by intention meeting obstacles and conflict.

Sequence setbacks

Sequences generally use setbacks, or reversal, as a burst of energy to move into the next sequence. These setbacks may not alter the story direction but they change the fortunes of the characters, causing them to dramatically alter their strategy for getting their goals. These setbacks will also usually indicate the direction which your next sequence will take. Go back over the *Thelma And Louise* sequences and see how that works.

Revelation

After a setback, a moment or process occurs where the character realises their strategy and/or sequence goal must be abandoned; it may not be conscious but is often embodied in some significant action indicating the abandonment.

Context and content

While there is no rule about how many or few sequences you need for your screenplay, you do need to the know the *linking idea* behind each sequence (the context). You'll then find content will follow.

> Let's create a sequence around the idea of departure. The setting: a young man is flying far away to take up a new job. Beginning: we start with your protagonist getting up in the morning, shaving, dressing and packing their bags and leaving their home. Middle: They load their bags into a car and drive to the airport, perhaps dropping off at a friend's to say goodbye, then arriving at the airport. End: at the airport they check in their baggage, collect their tickets, maybe say their final, tearful farewell to the family and disappear from the departure lounge, onto the plane and fly away . . . but something is wrong. What? You decide.

Suddenly you have created a series of five or more scenes in each of the three sections and fleshed out that sequence. You've created the content – and about six to eight pages of script.

> Now create the next sequence (beginning/middle/end) based on the idea of flying, journey or arrival.

> Now break down your own script story into sequences, using the points outlined in this section.

The scene

❝ If you want to understand the structure of a scene, go get Stanislavaky and read what an actor looks for in a scene. What does each one of these people want? Where are the points of conflict between them? Where does the scene change and go in a different direction? ❞

> *Larry Ferguson,*
> screenwriter:
> *The Hunt For Red October*

The *scene* is the single most important element in a screenplay, the basic building block. It is where something happens, something *specific* happens. It is a distinct unit of action – the place you tell your story and the setting you design for dramatic conflict.

Think of a favourite film; what do you remember? Not the entire film, but great scenes: *Psycho* – the shower scene; *Butch Cassidy and the Sundance Kid* – the pair jumping off the precipice; *Casablanca* – the 'Play it, Sam' scene or the airport departure scene; *Reservoir Dogs* – the ear-severing accompanied by happy pop music; *The Crying Game* – Fergus undressing Dill to reveal her secret; the tango dance in *Scent Of A Woman*. Great scenes make great movies.

By definition, *a new scene occurs whenever there is a change of location or time.*

The purpose of a scene is to *move the story forward*. A screenplay is composed of a large number of scenes – the number isn't important. Your screenplay must have precisely the number of scenes it needs to tell its story dramatically and effectively – no more, no less.

Likewise, a scene is as short or long as it needs to be. It may be one sentence, one line, or just a couple of words. It may also be many pages long. However, Readers frown on scenes longer then three pages (three minutes). Novice screenwriters always include too much dialogue and detail, often failing to find the opening and ending. Your story will determine how long or short your scenes will be, so trust your story.

However, a scene is much more complex than this. It is also part of a whole, a component in a larger structure – the screenplay. Think of a carburettor in a car: its purpose is to assist the functioning of that car; remove it, the car will not operate. In a script, take a scene out and the screenplay will be (should be!) damaged. And just as a carburettor has its own internal mechanism, so does a scene. So look at your scenes in terms of this dual function: as an individual element and as a functioning component of a larger entity.

Scenes come in three types: visual (where something happens visually, with no dialogue – like an action scene or a bridging/transitional scene); dialogue (for example, a conversation between one or more characters); and dramatic scenes (a combination of visuals and dialogue).

Visual scenes are usually very short and undramatic, their single purpose to connect other scenes and act as a bridge or transition between different sections of the action. For example:

EXT. PHILADELPHIA STREETS – DAY
John's car passes by on the way home

. . . or they can act as an establishing shot for the next dramatic scene. For example:

EXT. HONG KONG. MARKETPLACE – DAY
Crowded. Filled with Oriental and British merchants. You can buy anything here. Electronics. Furniture. Food. Anything.

. . . or sometimes they can do both.

Such scenes have little or no internal structure and therefore do not build towards (or open with) a crisis leading to climax. Their purpose is simply to move your story or character(s) from A to B without jolting the audience.

The thing to remember when writing dialogue scenes is: you are working in a visual medium. A solely dialogue-driven scene can only sustain itself for so long. So don't let any of your dialogue scenes last longer than three pages (three minutes); script Readers don't like them and it shows a lack of professionalism about the arena you are entering. Of course you will find exceptions, but most individual scenes tend to last from between a quarter to three pages – remember those assemblages of 'snapshots'.

❝ Conflict is drama, true. But a good dramatic scene could be written over an argument about who does the dishes as much as a train crash. ❞

Mal Young,
Head of Drama Series, BBC

Dramatic scenes are, if you like, the 'ideal' scene, with a beginning, middle and end – though not all of this may be shown on screen; *you* decide. These scenes advance your overall plotline and illustrate character. They escalate the already rising conflict in your story and reach a crisis point followed by a climax.

Each dramatic scene contains:

- text ('the business'): what the characters are doing
- dialogue: what they are saying
- subtext: what is really happening beneath the surface or apparent meanings of the action and speech

Remember, in your script, every image, every piece of description, and especially every line of dialogue must either: (a) advance the action of your plot, (b) illustrate character, or (c) preferably do both. If it doesn't perform any of the above, you should question whether it could be expressed in a better (more visual?) way, or whether it need be there at all. Examine a well-crafted script (like *Four Weddings And A Funeral, Tootsie, Misery, Maverick, The Usual Suspects, Speed* or the films you watched for Chapter 7) and you'll see how every line is there for a reason and justifies its space on the page. It's down to what you choose to show and what *not* to show, both the scenes themselves and within each separate scene.

A scene is made up of two factors:

- the general *context*
- the specific *content*

The context consists of when and where your scene takes place, i.e. *location* and *time*.

- Location: EXT. or INT.
- Time: stick to DAY or NIGHT (Chapter 2)

This gives us

    INT. KITCHEN – DAY

or

    EXT. STREET – NIGHT

A change of either place or time means you have a new scene.

As for content, every scene reveals *at least* one element of necessary story information to your audience. The information it receives is the purpose of that scene. Even if it's just a bridging scene, it denotes we are moving to a different location.

Just like your screenplay and a sequence, each dramatic scene has a beginning, middle and end – but you decide which part of it to show. You are looking for the maximum dramatic impact. Again, there is no rule; your story tells you what to do.

> ❢ I never enter scenes until the last possible moment i.e. before the ending of some specific action in the scene. As soon as it's done, I get the Hell out of there! ❷
>
> *William Goldman*

Tip: When you have written a scene, try editing out the beginning of it and the end of it. Then, condense the remaining information. Your scene may now be only half its original length, but it should be twice as tight. If it isn't, cut front-and-back again, condense the remainder, and go on until you're happy with it. Treat each scene as you would a party: arrive late, depart early.

Creating a scene

As with sequences, first create the context (the purpose, place and time) of your scene, then content will tend to follow. To create context, ask yourself:

- What *happens* in this scene?
- What does each character in this scene want, want to happen, or prevent happening by the end?

- Where does the scene take place?
- At what time does the scene take place?
- What is the *purpose* of this scene?
- Why is it there?
- How does it move the story forward?
- What happens in it to move the story forward?

An actor will approach a scene by finding out what their character is doing there; where they have been and what they have been doing since their last appearance in the script; what they did immediately before this scene happened; where they are going and what they'll be doing after this scene; what their purpose is in this scene and why they are there. As a writer, you have to know all this too.

It is important for you to know what happens *within* scenes (in real time), but also what happens *between* scenes (omitted time) – which you choose not to show. Be aware that the decisions you make regarding which scenes you choose to omit can be as important as those you make about the scenes you decide to show. You leave out what the audience can deduce (Chapter 1). You're in control of this, remember! So ask yourself:

- How did my character get from the end of that scene to the start of this one?
- What were they doing all the time?
- While I've been concentrating on characters X and Y in this scene, what are the other characters doing while this scene is being played out?
- What are the other characters doing between the scenes?

You should know, too, why all your characters are in this scene and how their actions or dialogue move the story forward. If *you* don't know, who does?

The flowchart on page 142 might help when you approach the construction of a scene.

Location

The location you choose should help dramatise the events taking place there; if it doesn't then it's the wrong location. Always look for conflicts: add tension by making something difficult, and then more so.

- Look for the unobvious, the most dramatic setting for your scene. For example, in *Edward Scissorhands*, Edward is frightened not on

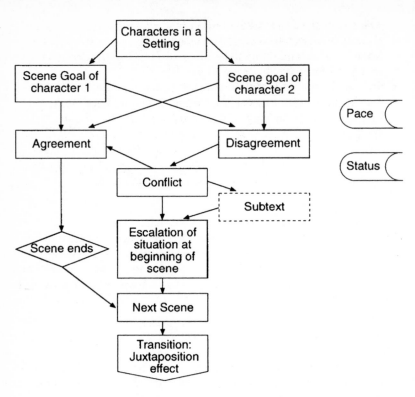

Figure 9.1 Scene Construction Flowchart   Source: *Jurgen Wolff*

a sofa (a neutral choice – with limited action potential), but on a waterbed: a place that is not only visually interesting and humorous but also the place where his hands can create most havoc. So if you wanted to create a love scene, where would it be most dramatically interesting to set? In the bedroom, on a garage forecourt, in a box at a concert hall, at the zoo in front of the lions? Look for the unobvious – the original. Note that a constricted location or controlled environment (submarine, spaceship, airplane, tube train, car, warehouse, etc.) – somewhere the character can't escape from – is highly dramatic (*Speed*, *Crimson Tide*).

- Can you dramatise this scene 'against the grain'? Your couple decide to make love in their concert hall box; they are about to kiss, suddenly another couple enters and occupies the other seats; your first couple have to stop. Do they stay to watch the concert or continue their scene elsewhere? You've added conflict, made something difficult, and then made it more difficult and added tension to their decision: should they stay or leave?

- Can you heighten the emotion by using weather and the elements? Notice how many scenes of high dramatic or emotional content take place in the pouring rain (*Apocalypse Now, The Piano, Witness*, the final scenes in *Breakfast At Tiffany's, Four Weddings And A Funeral*). Rain is very dramatic – as are gales, thunderstorms, hurricanes, sandstorms, restless seas, etc. Can you think of other scenes where weather plays a significant role?

Content

By creating context you determine the dramatic purpose of your scene; you can begin to build that scene line by line or action by action and create the content. So how do we go about that? First find the components or elements within that scene. For each character in your scene, ask the following:

- What aspects of this character's life (professional/personal/private) will be revealed?
- What is their goal in this scene? What do they want to do or achieve? What do they want to happen or prevent from happening?
- Is there agreement? (If so, your scene ends and you move on to your next scene).
- Is there disagreement? If so is there conflict? What is it? What type? What's the subtext? Does the scene escalate the situation at the beginning of the scene? (If so, move on).
- Are the stakes raised by this scene? In what way?
- What has changed at the end of this scene from when we first entered it?

Also ask yourself these questions about your character's attitude:

- What is my character's general attitude within the overall screenplay?
- What is the character's attitude in this specific scene, both at the start and by the end? Has it changed, and if so, how?

Now ask yourself those last two questions in relation to each character's status within that scene.

Lastly, ask yourself if this scene moves your protagonist a step (large or small) nearer to their goal at the end of the screenplay (and the sequence). How does it connect to that Act III climax?

If it doesn't do any of these, drop it, no matter how brilliant it is.

Crisis and climax

As mentioned, a dramatic scene is internally structured. It moves to a crisis then a climax – indeed, there may be a series of smaller internal crises before the major scene crisis arrives. Let's recap the definitions:

● Crisis is a moment in a scene that forces a decision and causes a change in the character or story

After the crisis the forces operating within the scene or act are realigned. A major crisis, therefore, is a turning point.

● Climax is a moment in a scene that resolves a crisis one way or the other

Character revelation

In most scenes your character will discover something, realise something or have something revealed to them. They will gain knowledge. This will affect the storyline or their character development or both. The revelation may be dramatic or merely significant; it depends on your story.

Scene causality

Understand that each scene 'causes' the next one (more or less) and, of course, events within a scene 'cause' the subsequent incidents. Causality is an essential element in constructing your screenplay; it helps you define or even possibly construct your plot, and is a tool in creating powerful momentum (Chapter 10).

Scene ends – writing backwards

Just as it is important to know the end of your script before writing it and to know the end of each Act before entering it, so it is equally important to know the end of your scene. The writing of each scene is, nevertheless, almost always an act of exploration. Once you discover the end of your scene you will probably find yourself going back to rewrite it in the light of your new knowledge.

Finally, consider the effect you create (or want to create) by juxtaposing your scene with the previous or following scene. Are you trying to create a transition, a contrast, conflict, humour, irony, what? (see Pacing, page 164).

Flashbacks

Flashback is a technique of showing past happenings in order to expand an audience's comprehension of the present story, character or situation. It's very tempting to slip into flashbacks in a script, but for the script reader it usually suggests either sloppiness or problems in your script. Execute your story through *action*, not flashbacks; if you do use it, use it sparingly and effectively. The same applies to flashforwards.

The scene is a hi-tech office block. Richard is an accounts executive: 43, industrious, trustworthy, rather shy and weedy. His boss, Steve, is a thrusting high-flyer: 28, ruthless, driven, focused, fit, he hates older people and thinks they're slow. Somebody has made a grave error in accounts: Richard knows it's not him, suspects his boss, but somebody has to take the blame. Steve is in his office 'discussing' the matter with Richard. Write the scene.

Now relocate this scene (preferably within the bulding) and texture it using conflict (direct and indirect – think subtext) to complicate, tighten and enrich the action. Draw out the contrasts between the characters, their relationship, reveal more about each of them to us, anticipate further conflict down the road. What must you show? How can you dramatise it? What scene goals does each have? Can you do it without dialogue? Use the location potential.

If you have already written some scenes for your own script, try this scene relocation exercise on them too.

Dialogue

Dialogue is verbal action which pushes the story forward and which is derived from the character's needs within the scene.

❝ Sometimes you steal dialogue you hear. But normally the way I write dialogue is: I have an idea of how long the dialogue should be – one page, two, three pages, how much the scene will support, and how many points I have to make in that dialogue – either information points or character development points. Then I just start working out conversation . . . using what seems natural to get from one point to another. ❞

Paul Schrader,
writer: *Taxi Driver,*
Raging Bull

Dialogue is the easiest way to impart story and character information. Hence, most new screenwriters will tend to over-emphasise dialogue above the other elements, but the sources of information in a screenplay should be shared by all the script's components.

Screenwriting is about learning how best and most appropriately to use *all* the means of expression: visual action (physical and decision), props, sounds, setting, context, subtext, etc. In general, dialogue should be the last resort of the screenwriter after all the other means of expression have been tried and found wanting.

Did you notice how spare the dialogue was in *Witness*? Did it work against your appreciation and understanding of the story and characters, or did it say more by saying less?

❝ Never let an actor talk unless he has something to say. ❞

John Huston,
director

Film is primarily a visual medium. Images, not words, are your basic currency. Hence the accepted rule is: *show, don't tell*. Despite the popularity of Quentin Tarantino's clever and entertaining 'plotless dialogue' (he's also a director, remember), it is still always preferable to show someone exhibiting a trait rather than telling it in dialogue. Even though TV is more dialogue driven than feature films, the TV writer should still conceive their script visually. Think visual: visualise your character, their behaviour details – body language, gestures, unconscious looks, habits, etc. – as you write your dialogue. And remember, characters interact.

Dialogue performs certain functions:

- providing information
- advancing the story onward and upward
- deepening the characters by revealing emotion, mood, feel, intent (via subtext) and by telling us what would be difficult, time-comsuming or ponderous via character action
- revealing incidents and information (especially motivation) from the past, i.e. from the backstory, so that dialogue can avoid the need for flashbacks
- adding to the rhythm and pace of the script by the ambience it contributes to each scene and contributing to the style of the script (snappy and witty like *Butch Cassidy And The Sundance Kid, Maverick*; sparse like *Witness, Death In Venice*; distinctive like *Blade Runner, Brazil,* etc.)
- connecting scenes and shots by providing continuity
- suggesting the presence of objects, events or persons not seen by using off-screen (o.s.) dialogue

Ideally, all the dialogue your characters speak should be caused by their need to get something in that scene or in a later scene. The true nature of good screen dialogue is that it comes from, is caused by and is driven by the immediate needs of your character at that specific point in the scene and that juncture of the plot, and also by their longer-term needs of the screenplay story.

Screen dialogue is not everyday conversation. What you strive for is *effective* dialogue, to give the *illusion* of real conversation. Effective dialogue sounds natural; it conveys the sense of real speech even through it is more structured than the wanderings of everyday speech. Effective dialogue has more economy and directness than real-life conversation.

Make a recording of people conversing, then listen to it; their dialogue is full of half-completed sentences, 'ers' and 'ums', hesitations and repetitions, rambling, overlapping and rarely focused – the *tone* is conversational, non-literary.

As in conversation, effective screen dialogue is essentially oblique (see subtext), more naturalistic than, say, stage dialogue. Screenwriting uses all the hesitations, half-sentences, etc. of everyday speech, but the dialogue is condensed.

Screenwriting is typically lean and economic. Effective dialogue is sparsely written, with short sentences of simple construction, using simple, informal words. Speeches are brief and crisp. Screen dialogue is written for the ear, to be listened to, not for the eye to read. The basic principle of dialogue (as with all screenplay description) is:

❄ ❄
❄   Say More With Less   ❄
❄   ❄
❄ ❄

Dialogue *can* convey what a character thinks or tell us what is going on in their mind, but it can also be one of the dangers; it encourages novice writers to be lazy.

Screen dialogue words are used more for their implicit rather than explicit meaning. What is important in dialogue is not the literal meaning of the words used, but the meaning being conveyed in the circumstances of that scene. What is not said, or is left unsaid, can be as important as what is spoken (see subtext, page 151).

Dialogue should fit the character, their mood and emotions in the particular situation, with a rhythm and individuality of expression typical of that character. Make your dialogue sound like the character, not the writer. One test is to take the dialogue in your scene and try swapping the speeches around and get those words spoken by your other character. If they can be switched with little evident distinction, then your characters and dialogue have probably not been effectively individualised.

Dialogue works best when it is underwritten and understated. Excessive emotion and spouting platitudes lead to melodrama. And when you *do* get to an emotional dialogue scene, it must be in keeping with the character and their own personal speech patterns. Likewise, avoid clichés and stock phrases, unless they are part of the way that character always speaks.

Most screen dialogue exchanges are short and snappy, speeches bounce off each other like ping-pong, with one piece of dialogue hooking into or causing the next line, building up a momentum. Long single speeches stretching on and on for half a page or more will only alienate your audience. A Reader, upon their initial flick-through fanning of your script, will notice any great slabs of dialogue. It turns them off; to them it indicates that the writer does not understand the accepted rules of writing screen dialogue. If you must have long speeches in your script, you had better have a good reason for them (for example Gordon Gekko's 'greed is good' speech in *Wall Street* is his whole philosophy of existence). So avoid long speeches; cut them out or into groups of smaller speeches. If you must, use very sparingly.

Be aware too of the role of silence: what is not said in a scene can be just as important as what is spoken. Actors and directors learn to use silence as a tool in their box of effects – so should you. Remember, dialogue can be used off-screen (o.s.), or without sound (M.O.S.) – see Chapter 2.

Voice-overs

Try to avoid, or use sparingly and handle with care; it is a literary device and too often is used simply to advance plot. However, voice-over narration *can* be used effectively to set the story and illuminate it:

- If the narrator is a character in your script (often the protagonist) it can supply a personal touch or establish the script's POV, especially at the point of entry (*Field of Dreams, The Great Gatsby, Out Of Africa, Little Big Man, Goodfellas, Sunset Boulevard*)
- If the narrator is not a character in the script (*Tom Jones*) it can supply a certain objectivity
- Some stories need a narrator to supply a unifying structure to the story (*Edward Scissorhands, Trainspotting, 84 Charing Cross Road, Stand By Me, The Wonder Years*)
- It can be used if you need to create a pause moment or give a reflective feel to your narrative (*Badlands*); see Chapter 10 – Pacing

Watch *Truly, Madly, Deeply*, paying particular attention to use of voice-over: did you find it effectively and imaginatively used or was it clumsy and pedestrian?

Any guidelines on dialogue can only be suggestions. Follow any rules too rigidly and you may find your dialogue becoming mechanical or artificial. Ultimately, to learn to write good dialogue, you must *learn to listen*: listen and observe how meaning is expressed, both verbally and non-verbally (in real life and on the screen), listen to the meaning beneath the overt sense of the words – the subtext; listen to the voice, the expressions, even the gestures. Above all, learn to listen to your characters. If you've done thorough work on a character you will know them so well that they will have developed a reality and presence of their own, with their own speech patterns – their own personal grammar. You will find them starting to write their own dialogue, but talking through you.

❝ Dialogue cannot be taught. You either have an ear for it or not. ❞
David Edgar

Some tips:

- Avoid 'passing-the-time-of-day' dialogue: greetings, polite nothings, goodbyes, etc.
- Don't repeat information in dialogue that has already occurred elsewhere in the dialogue; beginners' scripts are full of these repetitions.
- Avoid dialect and writing phonetically: tell the reader when you introduce the character they speak with a Scots/New Jersey/whatever accent. The occasional 'gonna' or 'ain't' is fine but don't overdo it. Script readers don't like reading phonetic dialogue – write it in readable English and let the actors do their jobs.
- If you want to create emphasis try to do it without using exclamation marks; never italicise dialogue; don't use capitals (except rarely); an occasional underlining is okay.
- Not every question asked in dialogue needs to be answered. The use of silence, a reaction, or non-reaction can be as/more powerful than dialogue (e.g. *Witness*). Not every question needs to be answered with the most obvious reply. An oblique open or indirect answer may reveal more about the state of mind of the responding character.

- Select a favourite film which is not purely action driven.
- Work out its Act I division. (If you find an entire act too daunting, try it for a short 30-minute TV drama, or just the first ten minutes of the film).
- View Act I repeatedly, noting down each and every scene and what goes on in that scene, what information is imparted, etc. until you are thoroughly conversant with that act. Better still, work from the script if you can get it.
- Working from your notes (or script), try to rewrite the entire first act as a silent movie, with no dialogue at all. Force yourself to describe and develop character and meaningful action visually.

Why do this exercise? Because I can guarantee that by doing it you will learn valuable insights into portraying characters by showing us who they are and what they're feeling, not by *telling* us. Think visually and you will start to write visually.

Subtext

Script editors and actors will tell you that great drama is all about subtext. Think of the classic eating scene in *Tom Jones*, the unbuttoning of the glove in the carriage in *The Age of Innocence*, the finger caressing the hole in the stocking in *The Piano*; what are they about? Eating? Hosiery? No – the subtext is mutual seduction.

As in real life, the actual meaning lies behind the apparent surface meaning. This is subtext – what is being communicated beneath the text lines or action; the real meaning being conveyed, the real intent (conscious or unconscious) of the character. For the writer, subtext expresses the hidden agenda of a character.

Examine the party scene early in *Tootsie*. Sandy holds up a baby saying how much Michael loves and adores babies. She says this to Michael as he passes; he simply grunts out 'yeah' without even looking at the baby. What subtext is being communicated here – for Michael and for Sandy? How is it used?

Now do the same for *Witness*: examine the scene where Rachel is nursing John's wound and their final departing scene.

You can use subtext in a number of useful ways:

- You can *set an agenda* for your plot and state to the audience what the characters need to do. (Very useful in thrillers, adventure, detective stories and teen romances.) It allows you to believably put together disconnected bits of information.
- You can give the audience more information than the protagonist knows, thus putting them in a *superior position*. It lets the audience know about impending disaster round the corner before we watch the character/s turn the corner and confront it.
- You can *pose a question* that the audience and the characters need the answer to. In *Godfather II*, Michael and Alfredo are discussing their futures. Michael is waiting for his brother to confess his part in the killing of a gangster; he is waiting but Alfredo never gets round to it. We know this is actually a tense death-sentence scene although nobody is killed. Note that this only works because earlier Michael had said 'I could forgive him if he'll confess'.
- You can *establish obstacles,* set up expectations in the audience's mind of the problems your protagonist will encounter. The drama comes from the knowledge that we know these obstacles are waiting to be confronted – this is linked to the 'superior position' (above).
- You can *create an enigma* by denying the audience all the key information until the very last moment. You can drop in tantalising information and unexplained moments that set up the subtext that says implicitly 'if you stay with this long enough, it will all become clear'.

All the above are linked: you are *creating expectations* in the audience's mind – and that's why subtext works (see page 158). Subtext can be used as part of creating a deception: a character says one thing but means another. Another character might not read this subtextual meaning (although they may sense it), but the audience must be aware of the subtext.

As a writer, when writing, you must not only be aware of how a character reads a scene (understands what is going on in that scene, what is said and done), but also how an audience reads a scene. Try to enter the mind of the audience.

Often the subtext constitutes a more enriching emotional experience for the audience than the surface movements of the story, both in main plot and subplots. But what is most revealing are the two levels of meaning integrated together. Screen dramas with appropriate and successful subtext are remembered long after the others have faded in the public mind.

When actors rehearse a scene, they try techniques to reveal subtext. First they speak the line as printed, then follow that by voicing what they feel the subtext is. Do this yourself. Take a scene from a film you like, preferably a scene with some meaty dialogue and some action or movement. Watch it, then write down the dialogue and action in that scene (ideally get the script and work from that). Under each line of dialogue and action, fill in what you imagine the subtext is. After you have done this for a couple of film scenes, try doing it for your own scenes. Another technique is to try reading your scene and subtext into a tape recorder. Play it back and ask yourself: 'Is the subtext clear to an audience in the lines I have written on the page?'

10

ENHANCING EMOTION

Having broken the screenplay down to its micro-elements, let's return to the overarching perspective and consider how certain events on the screen register in the mind of the audience. By understanding the processes you can begin to manipulate these according to your needs as a storyteller, enhancing emotion *in the audience* and *on the page*. It's down to the decisions the screenwriter makes about what to show and what to exclude.

Character motivation and structure

The driving force of your screenplay, and what makes it dramatic, is character in conflict and the reasons *why* that character will seek out conflict.

Generally speaking, main plots are fairly simple and straightforward, though they may contain many twists and turns. The main plot of *Witness* is basically: John Book tries to solve a murder but instead becomes hunted by the murderers who are fellow cops. Doesn't really grab you, does it?

What deepens, complicates and enriches this simple storyline is character. Character influences, alters and deepens the main storyline. It travels through your screenplay affecting every incident and person it comes into contact with, kicking the storyline into new directions, into new and often unexpected territory. Character is the element that engages us most deeply and is an essential component of establish a film's *momentum*, because without character we have no link with the mind of the audience (via their identification with the character).

Rachel's influence on John Book in *Witness* causes him to accept the wearing of Amish clothing which becomes crucial in the second turning point scene where Book beats up the punks, thus drawing attention to himself *because* he is wearing Amish clothing. Hence Schaeffer learns where he is and searches for him in Act III. Rachel's earlier influence also causes Book to hand over his gun, also allowing us to understand that change is taking place in his character. So character deepens and affects the main storyline, making it more interesting and more engaging for an audience. And what makes a character do whatever it is they do? Motivation, which is *character in action*.

Now, armed with your knowledge of structure, we can begin to see how character and growth work within structure. When we first see a character, they have a set of motivations based on their biography and especially backstory. This set of motivations will be assaulted and transformed by you the writer. Indeed, each of the three (or four or five) Acts reflects a distinct phase in the central character's motivation.

Character action follows a distinct path: a character encounters (or creates) a 'problem' which is uncompromisingly threatening; this generates an urgent (dramatic) need or intention to get or do something to cure the problem, which formulates a goal – the external movitation. Having decided what it is, they set out to get it (action) but things don't go smoothly and they reach a crisis. At the point they overcome the crisis (or accept they won't overcome it), their motivations are altered; this is the climax or change point. From this we can draw up a *character action equation*:

$$\text{problem} \xrightarrow{} \underset{\text{(goal)}}{\overset{\text{intention}}{/\text{need}}} \xrightarrow{} \text{action} \xrightarrow{} \text{crisis} \xrightarrow{} \underset{\text{change point}}{\overset{\text{result/}}{\text{climax/}}}$$
$$\text{(motive)}$$

This equation happens not just over your entire screenplay, but within each Act (important), usually within each sequence and often within each major scene.

Using this, and remembering the transformational arc, you can begin to construct the *motivational through-line* for your character and screenplay. For example, Act I of *Witness* runs:

problem	=	the murder
need/goal	=	to catch the killer
action	=	investigating

crisis   =   the killer is a fellow cop
climax   =   the shoot-out scene: betrayal

Can you work out the equation for Acts II and III?

—— **The motivational through-line** ——

This motivation line is another level on which you can structure your screenplay: at the point of entry, the first kind of motivation that compels your character to act often comes from the backstory. The character may find themselves in a life-crisis situation – even if they don't realise it themselves. By showing your character at some crisis point in their life you are putting them in a state of vulnerability. It is then much easier to shift them in new directions. Ideally, they should be ready to move, virtually begging for something new to happen to them.

For Rachel, in *Witness*, her husband has just died. This makes her vulnerable, open to new influences; it also supplies a believable reason for her to travel to Philadelphia (on her way to visit her sister). Given Rachel's background, we need a crisis in her life to shift her, not only physically out of her environment, but also out of her mental environment, so that she could actually consider falling in love with someone like John Book who, on the surface, seems to represent everything that is opposite to her communal Amish life and beliefs. Can you find any life-crisis situations in the four films you watched for Chapter 7?

This life-crisis device can be used at any point in your screenplay, but it is particularly useful in Act I. So: open with a crisis in your protagonist's life, then throw in the inciting incident like a bomb, and the resulting explosion will catapult your characters into the story. The inciting incident creates the 'problem', starts your story, brings all the crucial main characters together, and provides added and more powerful motivation for your character's actions.

At the beginning of *Witness*, the backstory motivation for Book is that he is an ambitious cop (we *see* he wants to catch crooks and advance his career). Rachel's backstory motivation comes from her Amish community values and her loathing of all things and people who represent violence. The two sets of backstory motivation come into almost immediate conflict as soon as the pair meet. They are both affected by the murder (and Samuel's witnessing of it). This heightens Book's motivation, who clearly sees it as a career advancement opportunity. For Rachel, it motivates her to work with Book (and men who live by violence), however reluctantly, in order to get the matter over with as quickly as possible and return to her life. The motivation line of Act I moves up through the inciting incident, first plot crisis to climax. This is a moment the audience knows will intensify the story and the character's motivation (when Samuel points to the photograph of McFee and they/we realise the murderer is a fellow cop). The protagonist's decision to act tightens the story, its direction, and usually adds more risk. The next major event that intensifies the motivation line is the Act I climax, where the protagonist creates their/your script's goal, external motivation or dramatic need (e.g. John Book needs to survive and protect Rachel and Samuel).

The goal of your character (the most powerful motivation in your story) forces the character into conflict with their environment, with other people, or with themselves. It also links the structure of your screenplay from the first turning point to the ultimate climax in Act III. So always ensure that the audience sees, understands or can clearly deduce the motivation of the main character/s.

Over the course of your screenplay, each of these moments adds something to or strongly affects the motivation line:

Backstory ⟶ Point of Entry ⟶ **Inciting Incident** ⟶
                (life-crisis)

⟶ Plot ⟶ **Act I Climax** ⟶ Focus ⟶
   Crisis 1   (Turning Point 1)   Point 1

⟶**Half-Way Point** ⟶ Focus ⟶ Plot ⟶
   (Point of No Return)   Point 2   Crisis 2

        Moment of Truth
   ⟶   Act II Climax ⟶ Act III Climax
        (Turning Point 2)

The four elements in bold are the most crucial; they are the major points on your character's motivation line. The other points shift or intensify the line without necessarily turning it in other directions or creating a point-of-no-return situation.

Remember, external motivation must be very clear and strong in the audience's mind – so it must first be clear in yours. If you are confused, your audience will be too.

> Now write down the events in your screen story which correspond to the points in the above chart and picture how your protagonist's motivation line will be changed by each event or situation.

> Now do this for all your main characters.

—— Momentum: building tension ——

Momentum is the forward movement necessary for any screen story. It is the effect your screenplay has on the mind of the audience, and it's all linked to creating and building tension. Almost every scene in your script should contain tension: it is the energy that propels and sucks the audience through your story. Tension is created when the audience hopes and/or fears that something will happen to the characters.

At its simplest: tension = conflict + contrast. Opposites create tension, (opposite forces, opposite characters and opposite expectations) for your characters and audience; opposite expectations generate hopes and fears in the audience's emotions.

There are a number of devices you can use to create tension:

- anticipation
- suspense
- subtext
- raising the stakes

Tension: building anticipation and suspense

Anticipating that something is going to happen causes the mind of the audience to move forward: they anticipate getting to the goal and the only way of getting there is to mentally move forwards to it, to want it, to hunger for it, etc.

Imagine a small child on her birthday. At 9 o'clock one morning you tell her that today at 4 o'clock there will be a surprise birthday party for her with lots of friends, stacks of food, presents etc. Congratulations, you have just destroyed her day. That time between 9 and 4 no longer exists for her because her mind is now racing forward and reaching for the time the party starts – but you've told her everything and spoilt the surprise. The audience's mind works in the same way: so give them *only* the information they need at the time and don't spoil the surprise.

When considering how your audience reacts to the dramatic incidents you design for them, remember two things:

- There is no one-to-one link between actor emotions and audience emotions. You cannot create specific reactions in your audience simply because you create them in an actor; just because an actor portrays sadness doesn't mean the audience will feel sad. The way you manipulate audience reactions and feelings is via the personality of the character, the situations you put them in, what the risks are, and the degree of audience identification.
- One of the most powerful ways of manipulating audience reactions is via the dimension of future time and its inherent uncertainties – 'What's going to happen next?' 'Will it happen?' 'When will it happen?' It is this future dimension that allows you to affect the audience.

In screen drama there are three dimensions of time: past, present and future. When building anticipation and suspense, the most important of these is the future. This is because the future dimension contains the two elements of *uncertainty* which past and present never can: of not knowing *if* an action will take place or *when* it will take place.

So, how do you create those audience links to the future?

Anticipation

We anticipate something will happen either:

- because it has always happened (it is a normal pattern of life, like the sun rising in the morning)
- because the screenwriter has established it as a norm in the world of your script (for example, in *Logan's Run* everybody accepts death at 31 because of overcrowding), or the norm in that particular character (i.e. it is normal for this character to smoke in bed, beat his wife, rob banks, drink under stress etc.)

Creating *surprise* is one way of manipulating your audience anticipation: this maintains audience interest by telling them that things are unpredictable, that their expectations will not normally be fulfilled. However, an audience cannot be surprised by an event unless they anticipated a different event taking place.

Anticipation, like intention, must be completed: either fulfilled, contradicted or interrupted. You cannot create anticipations and then leave them hanging; loose ends dissatisfy an audience, they feel cheated.

Suspense

Making the outcome of an event uncertain places the audience in suspense. Suspense causes them to hurry towards the end of your story wishing to get through it as quickly as possible, because suspense is a state of discomfort or pain. But is is also a pleasurable kind of pain like entering the horror house at the fun fair – you are alarmed by the scares and screams but as soon as you get out the other side you want to go back in again.

Think of the murder scene in the men's toilet in *Witness*, a very suspenseful scene full of tension; Samuel came very close to being caught and killed. Did you feel a sense of relief after that scene? Probably.

Both these elements are psychological processes and happen *in the mind of the audience*. They cause the mind of the audience to move forward because the audience craves to see the future become the present so that they can reach the anticipated event, or so they can get out the other side of the tense scene and breathe again.

Suspense occurs when an audience becomes uncertain that the goal of your character will be achieved, and it applies to the screenplay as a whole. (You can also, of course, create it at *any* point in your script.) Let's consider the elements in this process:

- To have suspense you must have a character who forms a *need* or *intention* that is vitally important to them
- From that need, the character conceives a *goal*
- If the goal is easy to get then there is no suspense because there is no *uncertainty*
- For the goal to be uncertain there must be difficulties. Not just any difficulties, but difficulties *powerfully challenging* to the goal

Suspense is also created when we do not know the outcome of a particular action. Here your audience must be made to feel two emotions, hope and fear:

- *hope* – that the outcome will occur (but fear that it won't)
- *fear* – that the outcome will occur (but hope that it won't)

Usually, to generate these emotions you must create that linkage between audience and characters which is audience identification (Chapter 5).

Hence suspense equals *doubt*. The choice you have is: *certainty of outcome* vs *uncertainty of outcome.*

A strong, clear goal is therefore vital: as well as helping establish motivation, it gives direction and meaning to your story and to the actions of your characters. If your audience doesn't know the character's goal it cannot measure the strength and quality of the difficulties and cannot know if they are challenging enough to make the getting of the goal uncertain or doubtful. And without uncertainty and doubt there is no suspense. The audience must know the goal *and* the difficulties in getting it.

Suspense starts when you have three ingredients, and not before:

- an intention (setting a clear, strong goal)
- difficulties, especially a counter-intention, that creates . . .
- uncertainty as to the outcome

Normally, as soon as you have conveyed the intention you will convey the difficulties as quickly as possible and this will create the uncertainty. Suspense is best maintained for as much of your screenplay as possible. So you need to establish the intention and the difficulties as early as possible and maintain the suspense for as long as possible. Suspense ends immediately after the final climactic scene because this represents the success or failure of your hero or heroine after which there is absolutely no doubt or uncertainty as to the outcome. This is another reason why you need to end your screenplay as quickly as possible after the final climax, because the suspense is integral to moving the audience through the story, and once it has gone there is no longer any momentum. Any part of the script without these three ingredients will lack suspense.

You should also understand that suspense is something you create on all levels of a screenplay: for the script as a whole, for each Act, for each sequence and for each scene. All these overlap and form part of each other.

Note that suspense need not always be life-threatening. Love stories have their own suspense. In *When Harry Met Sally*, the suspense is: will Harry and Sally, despite their differences (and other obstacles in their paths) get together by the end of the film? What is the suspense in *Sleepless In Seattle?*

Watch *Seven*, an excellent example of generating suspense and anticipation through audience engagement. What elements does it use and how does it use them? Why do we not see the last two murders? Are they all the more effective for our not seeing them?

Subtext

Re-read page 151. Remember, what we *don't* see is often more effective than actually showing something. Watching the reactions of a character standing outside a door listening to the passionate love-making going on inside is more emotionally effective that actually seeing the event. In *Shallow Grave* the murders are all the more effective because we only *hear* them being done, or see the bodies being disposed of in darkness. In *Dumb and Dumber* we don't see Lloyd urinating into a beer bottle, we only hear it and see the end result. The audience deduced it – just as it deduced the ear-severing in *Reservoir Dogs*. Admittedly, a lot is down to the director's decision, but it's also down to what you choose to show and not to show, and the ability and power of subtext to affect an audience's imagination.

Raising the stakes

This means increasing the risk to your characters as they progress through your screenplay, that is, the characters must have something to lose, or something bad would happen to them if they fail (or if they go through with their present action). This risk personalises the 'problem' for them and, through identification, becomes a problem for the audience. Once again your are manipulating the audience through their hopes and fears.

In *Wargames*, the stakes underlying David's actions in the overall film are very clear: the world could be plunged into World War III and millions of people, indeed the entire human race, could be wiped out. In *When Harry Met Sally* the stakes are that both Harry and Sally might never find each other and so be condemned to live their lives of loneliness. What do you think are the stakes in *Witness* – for John, for Rachel, for the community?

Now while a screenplay has major stakes, it should also have minor stakes: risks underlying individual scenes, sequences and Acts.

Rising conflict demands that the stakes are raised higher and higher as the story progresses. This is only logical: if the dangers are at a certain level at the end of Act I, it is inconceivable they will lessen thereafter till the end of the screenplay. The audience's interest would also lessen.

An essential ingredient in raising the stakes is (again) identification. If the audience doesn't care about your character, they will not care about the risk; the more they care about the character the easier it will be to put that character at risk because the audience will experience hopes and fears attendant to that character.

So anticipation, suspense, subtext and raising the stakes are all devices to create *tension* and building tension creates *momentum*.

Insufficient tension is a regular problem with scripts. Are you creating tension in your use of each device? So for every scene you should ask yourself:

- What is the audience *hoping* for here, but simultaneously *afraid* of?
- Are these hopes and fears strong enough to keep the audience engaged and move them on to the next scene?

Watch *The Usual Suspects*: how are the four elements of tension used in the drama? Why at certain points are certain elements used and not others?

Pacing

Pacing means the overall feel of your screenplay, and relates to the flow and rhythm of the climaxes, reliefs and pauses, the highs and lows, the 'crises-per-page', and how they contribute to the 'heartbeat' within that larger structure.

All drama needs variety within its overall structural unity; moments of crisis, confrontation and climax need to be interspersed with moments of quieter reflection – pauses. Audiences need those lulls when characters open up and reveal themselves, when a mood is established, so an audience can catch its breath before being taken to another high. *Falling Down* moves between the tense D-Fens scenes and those of comparative tranquility involving Robert Duvall's cop; even films which from frame one sweep you up and move along in a seemingly relentless romp (*Speed, Ed Wood, Dumb And Dumber, The Mask*) have their comparatively quieter moments. A drama constantly at the same level of intensity (high as in Spielberg's *1941*, or low as in some 'art' films, or with a continuous build like this:

... with no variation, your script will get dull and lose your audience's interest. To give your script movement (and evoke responses in your audience) you need to have a proper balance of high and low points.

And, as with your conflict and setback graph, your highs and lows need to be paced in a saw-tooth construct like this:

To create your script's rhythm you can use the following contrasting *elements of transition* between scenes:

- fast vs. slow tempo scenes
- short vs. long scene lengths
- plot/dramatic scenes vs. theme/character/mood scenes
- scenes presenting information/mood vs. emotion
- day vs. night; light vs. dark
- interior vs. exterior
- dialogue vs. non-dialogue (descriptive vs. action) scenes
- dynamic vs. static activity
- expansive vs. intimate settings
- light (or comic) tone vs. serious tone
- subjective vs. objective POV
- quiet vs. noisy (raging sea/industrial/rock music etc)
- variations in real time and flashback/flashforward

Note that pacing is a function of where you enter and leave a scene. Remember, a scene is a fragment of a larger fragment of a larger segment of continuous action. You enter late and depart early. Hence pacing can also be increased or decreased by the amount of time we spend in a scene.

You will find the pacing of your overall script also determines the pacing of your sequences – the faster the pace or the more accelerating nearer to a climax you get, the shorter your sequences will become. This is especially important in Act III, which should have the fastest pacing of all your acts with incidents happening fairly quickly leading inexorably to your final climax.

Tip: If you want to have a pause moment or give a reflective feel to your script, you might try using voice-over (page 149). For example, *Badlands* is generally a fast-paced action-based story, but there are interludes of voice-over which give it a reflective pace in parts, thus varying the mood, creating light and shade, peaks and valleys. What other films or TV dramas can you think of that employ voice-over in this way?

Scenes do more in the overall context of a screenplay than just satisfy a story function. They interact with each other to contribute to the formal structure (the flow and rhythm, the movement) of your script. The way you interweave these elements – contrasting, complementing, varying, balancing them – contributes to the overall rhythm of scenes. You should consider pacing when you reach the step outline/filing cards stage of your screenplay development (page 174), and the concept is actively used during the rewrite stage.

So, first work out the overall feel of your screenplay: is your script slow-paced and reflective like *Field Of Dreams* or *Sleepless In Seattle*, light-paced as in comedies, romantic comedies and romps, fast-paced and action-driven with fast-cut scenes like *Speed* or *Thelma And Louise*, or does it start slowly and gradually speed up as it unfolds towards its final climax like *Misery*, *The Piano*, most Hitchcock films and the horror genre? Working out this overall feel will help you determine the pacing of your scenes, sequences and final screenplay.

> • Hitchcock's films are skilful manipulations of pace and mood, lulling the audience into a sense of security and then springing on us a sudden shock or surprise – learn from them.

> Watch *Speed* and the original *Friday The 13th*: What elements of transition are used to vary the pacing in these films? Are they skilfully handled? How is it done, and why?

Watch *Reservoir Dogs* : is the pacing gripping for you? Do the lengthy scenes engage or bore you? How does it do this? Why?

Watch Martin Scorsese's *Casino*. Does its use of voice-over work for you, or does it have a distancing effect on the audience? Is it over-used? How does its use differ from that in *Goodfellas*? Was it better employed there? How and why? What elements do both films use to create pacing?

"Upping the ante"

To get the maximum emotion from a scene or moment of high drama, you should:

- before a scene or moment of great joy or relief, precede this with a scene or moment of extreme tension or jeopardy

or

- before a scene or moment of great drama or heavy tragedy, precede this with a scene or moment of extreme release, fun or tranquility

For example, in *Four Weddings And A Funeral*, Gareth's death is immediately preceded by two ante-upping devices: we see him dancing vigorously and joyously and he is given one of the wittiest and most memorable lines in the film (about Oscar Wilde's fax number) which not only makes us laugh but also warms us to him all the more. There is a very brief 'pause' moment, then Gareth collapses – an effective juxtaposition of opposites.

Information in the screenplay

There are many means of expression in a screen drama, and each of these generates *elements of information*. You need to understand both the nature and the effect these elements have on the mind of the audience. Remember, you control the release and arrangement of this information, both in a scene and in the overall screenplay.

Information reaches the audience by:

- what you choose to *conceal* from them
- what you choose to *reveal* to them
- *how* you choose to reveal it

Also, the way in which you *combine* elements of information together in a scene generates extra information but also creates certain effects upon an audience. They make links, automatic assumptions and deductions when presented with individual elements of information.

You must therefore try to *enter the mind of the audience* and decipher what goes on there when viewing your screen drama.

Tip: Wherever you do your writing, try sticking a card on the wall in front of you. On that card draw what you would see if you were sitting in the cinema stalls: the blank screen, the drapes, the backs of people's heads in front of you. Every time you write, try to visualise what that scene would look like when shown on the screen. If you can enter the mind of the audience you can protect yourself from sending out incorrect or unintentional messages. You can also manipulate the process to send out exactly the messages you desire.

- One of the underlying *principles of information* in a scene and screenplay is: once you have established an element of information and given it to the audience, the audience will assume that information remains true for the rest of the screenplay, unless told otherwise (i.e. unless you contradict or update that information).

So whatever they are led to believe, they will go on believing for the remainder of the film. This also means there is no need to repeat information (unless you are deliberately reinforcing or changing it for some reason). Therefore as the story progresses your audience will accumulate a body of information about the world of this story and the people living in it.

The existence of this body of information means that any information which enters later in the script will be affected (informed or corrupted) by all the information the audience already has. For example, in *Witness*, if Samuel had pointed at the photograph in the very first scene, this would have little meaning and he would simply go on his way. But pointing to it *after* the murder sequence gives the photograph scene a whole new and sinister meaning.

- Hence, the second principle of information is: The *order* in which the audience receives information is crucial to the way you want them to understand the information *dramatically*. This is particularly relevant when writing suspense, horror and murder mysteries.

Revealing and concealing information

It is important you know who has information in a scene or in a script and who has not. The basic possibilities are:

- both the characters and the audience have the same elements of information
- the characters have information which the audience does not
- the audience has information which the characters do not
- some characters have information which other characters do not; the audience may be in either position
- misinformation

Each variation creates a different effect in the mind of the audience and on their emotions; curiosity, surprise, stimulation, deep emotional involvement, comic impact, shocked surprise, etc. It is your job to work out and work with these effects, to create them in the audience for the purpose of telling your story dramatically.

Problems you should be aware of are:

- Until a character gets an element of information they cannot act on it.
- If the audience knows something the character doesn't even though it places the audience in a superior position, the character will have to be given the information eventually. From the audience's POV this is a kind of repetition, since it already has the information.
- If a character knows something the audience doesn't, then this information must be given to the audience eventually. (Try bringing on a character who hasn't yet received the information and give it to them.)

Overall, you need to know the effects you are creating within the mind of the audience by the way you release, reveal and conceal information.

Plants and pay-offs

This is also called *foreshadowing*. Remember, everything in your script is there for a reason. Likewise, if you plant something (object, piece of information, characteristic) it must be put there to be paid off later in your script: every action has a consequence, every piece of information has repercussions. If a gun is planted in a scene it has to be used at some later point – within that scene or some later scene. In *Speed*, when Jack (Keanu Reeves) notices the Arizona sweatshirt, he belatedly realises the bomber can see inside the bus. Stanley's dog in *The Mask* jumps up to catch the frisbee, later it jumps up to retrieve the mask in mid-flight at a crucial point in the plot. Even in *Dumb And Dumber*, every plant (from urinating into a bottle to selling the dead parakeet to a blind child) is paid off sooner or later.

Even if the pay-off does not happen until after the final credits (e.g. the inflatable doll-kite in *Priscilla, Queen Of The Desert*, the waiting cab passenger in *Airplane*), the plant *has* to be paid off. If there's no pay-off, what is the point of planting the information in the first place? You're only wasting valuable script space.

Watch *GoldenEye*: why do you think it has Q explaining to Bond all the new gadgets on his BMW car, yet none of these devices are used later in the film? Was it a victim of the final edit or budget cut, a script oversight, or included simply to be in keeping with the Bond genre?

Also, when you plant or set-up the information in your script (the stuff the audience needs to know), it should be dropped in at its most natural or believable moment; more importantly, the pay-off has to be used at the most dramatically effective moment for that piece of information, that is, held back until the last moment possible.

In *Four Weddings And A Funeral,* examine the way the David character (Charles's deaf mute brother) is handled – he has a critical role in the final wedding; we first see him only in passing, standing in the background at the first wedding reception. We next encounter him outside the cinema, and only then do we realise just who he is – and we are already one third into the film. Why was this held back for so long?

Image Systems

An *image system* is a category of images which repeat throughout your script, acting as resonators and reinforcers to the main subject or theme of your story.

Modern audiences are very visually literate, even if they don't realise it; they read something symbolic into every image. And there is a common pool of recognised and accepted symbols, and a more private pool.

- *External imagery*: images which mean the same inside your film as they do outside (the Stars and Stripes, a crucifix, a set of furry dice)
- *Internal imagery*: an object which means one thing outside your film (maybe positive or life-affirming) but which means something else – whatever *you* decide to make it mean – inside your story construct (possibly negative and life-destroying)

Some examples:

Tootsie: images and icons of femininity and masculinity

The Player: blue seas/red seas, film posters of old murder and film noir movies

Forrest Gump: images of innocence and naivety (chocolates, wind-blown feather)

The Piano: images of water, sea, mud all depicting repressed sexual and emotional tension; images of distance and isolation

Chinatown: four image systems woven together – political corruption as social cement, sexual cruelty, water and drought, blindness and sight

❛ In an early draft of *The Fisher King*, the Holy Grail was originally a salmon. I changed it because I realised the Grail was a more universally accessible symbol. ❜

Richard LaGravenese

Your script must operate in both pools, and in a balanced way; operating heavily or exclusively in one will only alienate your audience. The trick is to choose the image(s) carefully and feed them into your screenplay very subliminally: clearly enough for the Reader to pick up, but the audience in front of the screen must never realise they are being fed these images.

- Choose one of the four films covered in Chapter 7
- Work out their image system/s and list them
- Break down those lists into external and internal imagery
- Now do it for your own screenplay

--------- **The rule of three** ---------

There seems to be something magical or mystical in our attachment to threesomes. Watch most dramas and you will see a pattern in the protagonist's quest to defeat an obstacle: tries once – fails; tries again – fails; tries again – succeeds. This applies not only in the overall screenplay but sometimes within a single scene. (The protagonist, antagonist and reflection-or-romance is a threesome). Also, major dramatic speeches tend to be built around log-lines (page 50), which includes the rule of three. A key speech in *Mr. Holland's Opus* runs: 'I will use everything from Beethoven to Billie Holiday to rock'n'roll if I think it will help me to teach a student to love music.'

Now examine Gordon Gekko's 'Greed is Good' oration in *Wall Street*. Are there any threesomes there? Can you think of other examples where action or dialogue is built around the rule of three or contrasts?

What about your script?

11

THE NEXT STEP

The one-page synopsis

Your next step is to write the *synopsis*. This is a one-page (essential) brief factual telling of the entire screenplay story, in prose and in the present tense, typed (singled-spaced) on A4. It shows:

- the twists, turns and final climax of your plot
- the significant characters and their interactions
- an indication of the style of your script

You write this synopsis for your own use, to get a clearer overall picture of your screenplay. It is not essential to write one, but it can be useful as a diagnostic tool to identify any suspected weaknesses in your plot – and certainly which bits can be cut without losing the core essential story. Sometimes the weakness(es) jump off the page at you.

For example, the synopsis for *The Third Man* might run thus:

Holly Martins, an engaging but rather seedy writer of Western stories, arrives in Vienna to work for his friend, Harry Lime. He is told by a cold, disillusioned British police officer that Lime, a notorious racketeer, has been killed in a street accident.

Unbelieving, Martins begins to track down all those who knew his friend: the lonely, frightened actress who forged papers who was in love with him; two acquaintances, the effete Kurtz and the shifty Popescu, who witnessed the accident; his porter and his doctor.

These investigations lead him to the heart of seaminess and corruption in Vienna, to the discovery that Lime (a shameless scoundrel) is still alive, to a struggle with his conscience which ends with the eerie pursuit of his friend, who most aptly retreats to the sewers of the city – and the final showdown.

You might find some neatly delineated film synopses in the reviews of the trade magazines (Chapter 19), and for television in the TV reviews of broadsheet newspapers and listings magazines. Press kits for each production also have neat summaries if you can obtain them (try phoning the press and publicity offices of the relevant production companies).

Do not confuse this one-page synopsis with the one-pager (also called a *synopsis* or *proposal*) which is used as a selling document in your pitch or by a producer to pitch an idea (Chapter 19).

Now write your synopsis – and on *one* page, so be ruthless.

The step outline

By now you should have a pretty firm grip on the jigsaw of your script. The next move is to do a *step outline* (also called a *scene-by-scene breakdown* or *step sheet*).

For this you will need a set of 3″ × 5″ (7.5 × 12.5 cm) index cards. Each card represents one scene of your script (even bridging scenes), so at the top of each card write the scene heading (slug line). Then on each one proceed to describe the action and substance of each scene in, brief, clear notes; include snatches of dialogue if it helps. Pay attention to how you start and end each scene, and how it develops in the middle. Why must the cards be 3″ × 5″? Because industry ethos states if you can't fit it onto one side of the card, your scene is too long.

These cards will help you organise your scenes into sequences and Acts, examine how each scene juxtaposes with the next one, examine your story and character developments and get an idea of your pacing, and where your climaxes occur.

Once you have written out your cards, spread them out in front of you – on the floor or blu-tack them to the wall – and study them. You will start to feel a great sense of control over your entire script. Shuffle the cards around, take out and discard some scenes, insert new ones;

if you feel like colour-coding your characters or plot and subplots with marker pens, do it. Do whatever you have to do to get the best dramatic effect in your screenplay. You may find the following guidelines helpful:

Structure

Mark your most dramatically important scenes. Check how they are spaced out over the entire drama. These are your story's highlights. Ask yourself:

- Does the progression of these major scenes move the story forward at an effective pace?
- Is the overall dramatic suspense of the story maintained?
- Are there enough surprise elements (unexpected twists) to keep the audience interested and involved?
- Do my story crises occur at reasonably spaced intervals over the script or are they bunched up? (Expect some bunching in Act III)
- Am I 'upping the ante' before each crisis or happy incident? Are they sufficient?
- Are the pause or relief scenes used when needed. (i.e. after a climax or heavily dramatic moment)?

Start to get a sense of the rhythm and flow of your scenes and how they interrelate. If you don't, start rearranging the cards around, try different running orders, cut or add, etc. Don't be afraid of doing this or any other new approach that works best for you.

Characters

You should know each character's goals, both overall and within each scene. Look at the function of each scene, its purpose in the script.

- Look at when the different characters appear
- Are they credibly presented throughout in what they say and do?
- Are they consistent throughout?
- Is their development a believable arc?
- Do characters appear appropriately throughout the script or does one (or more) 'get lost' for too long, only to crop up again as an afterthought or for the convenience of plot?

Weak spots

Look for the screenplay's weak spots you can correct:

- Are action high points bunched too closely together? Try inserting a 'break', a dialogue scene illustrating more of your character, or a mood scene, or some delay in the suspense build.
- Not enough exciting high points? Insert some additional crises, build up your suspense more carefully to keep your audience engaged or add some surprising twists.
- Too active or too melodramatic? Add more scenes revealing character or relationships between characters. It gives the audience depth – more time to know your characters instead of continuous scenes of constant high points.

Scene structure

Look at each scene and its internal structure. If the scene doesn't 'work':

- Are you clear about your beginning, middle and end?
- If the scene builds, is the pay-off or high point appropriate?
- Are the characters and the actions in the scene credible?
- Are the characters believable; would they act in that way in the given circumstances of that scene?
- Is the scene basically interesting?
- Is the scene really necessary to the story?

The writer has many tools to use when writing a screenplay, many elements of expression in a scene – organisation, structure, characters, relationships, setting, tone, POV, dialogue, props, clothing, sound. Use them. Think visual: images (not words) are your basic currency. You are not trying to make it real, but *alive*.

Your next move is to write . . .

The treatment

What is it? A prose document (approximately 12–15 pages for one hour TV and up to 25–30 pages for features), typed, single-spaced, on A4 paper (one side), telling your plot as it happens chronologically in your screenplay. Some treatments are available to buy (Chapter 22).

What is a treatment for?

It has two functions:

- Initially, as a device for the writer to organise their own thoughts and develop the texture of script.
- Later, and a treatment's major function, as a selling document used to sell your story to a producer (Chapter 19). So, for your own private use, a treatment can be as long as you need.

What should a treatment do? It should:

- tell the story clearly, identifying both main plot and subplots, but not be solely plot-driven
- concentrate on the main overall dramatic structure
- tell us what we *see*: the characters, their actions
- impart some of the mood, atmosphere and feel of the script
- be written crisply; short paragraphs (try one paragraph per scene), in the present tense, using *active* verbs and *descriptive* nouns to capture the action, verve and pace of your script. Pace is important (try applying the ¼ ½ ¼ dimension to your treatment also)
- include some brief character details (two or three sentences) of your main players. Incorporate these into your text as they enter the script (the first time they enter, their names are in capitals or upper case, thereafter in lower case.) You don't need a separate sheet of characters and their backgrounds; you are selling a story, not a cast list family history
- use dialogue extracts if it helps. But only if it adds colour or helps impart the 'smell' of your script – and do it sparingly
- avoid camera directions or music suggestions

Is a good treatment easy to write? No. Indeed, many writers (and agents) believe it is harder to write than a good script. It may even take half the time that writing a script takes. Writing a treatment is a separate skill in itself.

There is no right way of writing a treatment. These tips are accepted guidelines; each script is special and you must impart that specialness via the treatment.

Is it essential to write one? No, but it's a very important step along the way. Why?

- a treatment exposes any weaknesses in the planned script. It tells you whether it is worth continuing. If everything is fine, you can move quicker to the next stage – the exploratory draft. If your treatment causes you problems, leave it for a week or more, work on another project. Get a distance on it, then return refreshed. Never write your exploratory draft until you are happy with the treatment.

- Eventually you will need a treatment to send to a producer and catch their interest (it's quicker to read than a full script). Not all screenplays made have had a treatment attached. Ultimately your script should sell itself.

❦ Treatments can be a poisoned chalice. They are enormously diffi-cult to write, a nightmare, and they can only give you a sense of the movie. The problem is: you can't write a script before you write a treatment. ❦

Adrian Hodges,
screenwriter

Try to get hold of some well-written treatments (Chapter 22). Compare and contrast their variety. Note how they imparted the energy and feel of the finished film or TV production.

Now write your treatment. Use all and any devices you have to hand: the filing cards, ideas, images, your own storytelling skills, to impart that original and gripping tale.

12

THE ACTUAL WRITING

❝ I approach my exploratory draft like I'm doing a multiple-choice test: if I come to a tough bit I just write something really rough, carry on to the end, then go back to it after. The problem with new writers is they keep rewriting all the time and lose the spontaneity. Just get it down. It's not like this is the only time you can write it. ❞

Tom Schulman

The exploratory draft

You've now finished the pre-writing 65%. Now to tackle the next 5%: writing the *exploratory draft*. You do this in one burst of activity – try spending no longer than ten consecutive days of solid work on it. Using your filing cards as a blueprint to construct narrative and dialogue, just sit down and *do it*!

Set yourself a strategic plan: if your goal is 120 pages, write a minimum of twelve per day. Don't be afraid to overwrite – your task is not to get perfect copy, but to get it all down on paper in screenplay form.

Tip: If writing longhand, try doing it on squared paper and keeping to the appropriate script layouts (Chapter 2). It will give you a better idea of length (1 page = 1 minute), timing, and pacing.

Don't go back over your previous day's work wanting to rewrite it – that comes later.

Try to:

- avoid clichéd images and phrases
- avoid writing 'on the nose' (description or dialogue phrases that stick out as being obvious)
- be clear: avoid lengthy or wordy language, (especially in dialogue)

- keep dialogue short and dramatic
- express action and reaction
- write visual images
- think visual – show, don't tell
- make it vivid, affective, memorable and (hopefully) an *easy read*

Of course, you won't accomplish all these in this draft, but bear them in mind. Now put this book down, take up your cards, go away and *do it*!

— — — — Ten Days Later — — — —

The final full stop: the end or the beginning?

Having emerged from the tunnel of writing this draft, you will feel: 'That's it, I've done it, I can't get it any better'. Wrong! You can – and you will, during the rewrites. But first you need a breather. You've been working closely on your script – too close to get any objectivity on it. You need to *get a distance*.

Put the typed draft on the shelf – for a week (minimum), hopefully a month and forget about it. Work on another project, perhaps from your ideas file (don't feel guilty, most writers work on more than one project at a time). Only return to it when you feel you can read it in an objective, unemotional, critical way. Only then are you ready to enter the rewrite stage (the final 30%), which is where a script *really* comes together.

13

THE CRAFT OF
THE REWRITE

❛ A good writer is not someone who knows how to write – but how to rewrite. ❜

William Goldman

❛ With *Sense And Sensibility*, when it came to having to do a major rewrite, and I've done several, there were tears, actual tears. ❜

Emma Thompson

— — — — X Weeks Later — — — —

Your exploratory draft is the one written with passion and urgency, the reason why you were fired up to explore that idea in the first place. Rewriting is where you apply your knowledge of the technical craft points covered so far to that draft. The trick in making a good script great is to marry the two without losing that sense of energy and drive that originally excited you.

There's no true learning without making mistakes, and writing and rewriting are all processes of making mistakes: confronting dead ends, discovering alternative and better routes, shortcuts – and doing it *your* way.

So, having got a distance on your exploratory draft, now read it afresh in one go at one sitting, without stopping or making alterations or notes (however great the temptation); get a sense of the script as a whole. Then ask yourself the questions in the checklist on pages 182–3, making notes on a separate sheet of paper. (These questions are based on several checklists given to script readers by their production companies.)

HANDY CHECK LIST FOR SCRIPT ASSESSMENT

1) <u>CHARACTERS</u>
   a) Did you believe in them?
   b) Is the speech pattern of each character (i) individual, (ii) true, (iii) consistent?
   c) Do we know enough about everybody important to understand them fully? Are they written at sufficient depth?
   d) Are their motivations clear?
   e) Do they develop or do they end the piece the same actual people as when it began?
   f) Do they have a life of their own or are they puppets manipulated by the writer for his own purposes?

2) <u>CONFLICT</u>
   a) Is there any?
   b) Is the conflict something vague in the background ("Fred v. Life") or is it personalised?
   c) Is the background too much in the foreground?
   d) Is anything of importance to the characters at stake?

3) <u>ACTION</u> (Not to be confused with mere activity)
   a) Do people do things?
   b) Does anything happen?
   c) Does anybody <u>make</u> anything happen?
   or d) Is it all a business of people chattering about things?
   or e) Is it a mere portrait of (i) an individual or (ii) a group?
   f) Does the screenplay mark time while the characters unburden themselves?
   g) Do people actually get to grips with things or is it all shadow boxing?

4) <u>PLOT</u>
   a) Is the story a mere succession of events (e.g. "A day in the life of . . .")?
   b) Is it full of cause and effect?

5) <u>CONSTRUCTION</u>
   a) Is there sufficient variety of pace?
   b) Are the climaxes right?
   c) Does the plot develop at the right speed?
   d) Does the end work?
   e) Are the audience's expectations satisfied?

6) <u>CONTENT</u>
   a) Is the theme implicit or explicit?
   b) Is it clear what the piece is actually about?
   c) Do the characters know?
   d) Should they know?
   e) Is the theme clearly illustrated or brought out by the plot?
   f) Does the writer bring to his theme an individual point of view?
   g) Is it the right length for what he wants to say?

7) <u>PRACTICALITIES</u>
   a) How expensive does it look?
   b) Are all the characters necessary? (Are there enough?)
   c) Are there too many sets? Could we actually fit them into a studio?
   d) If film is suggested, is it necessary?
   e) Do exterior scenes add to the visual and/or emotional content?
   f) If it is (intentionally) an all-film piece, is it containable?

8) <u>THE OBJECT OF THE EXERCISE</u>
   Discounting your own personal prejudices on its theme or subject
   matter and regarding it only as an artefact:–
   a) Did you want to turn the page?
   b) Did you <u>instinctively</u> like or dislike it? Or were you just bored?
   c) Does the writer know his stuff?
   d) Has he got the vital spark?
   e) Would you want to work on it?
   f) Would a wide contemporary audience of ordinary men and
      women (i.e. the same audience that Shakespeare was aiming at)
      be entertained.

THE FOREGOING IS A MERE CHECKLIST. IT DOES NOT
ASPIRE TO LAY DOWN A SET OF UNBREAKABLE RULES,
BECAUSE THERE AREN'T ANY. IF THE SCRIPT FIRES YOU
IN SPITE OF BREAKING EVERY 'RULE' IN THE BOOK,
THEN SAY SO.

Try giving the script and checklist to someone whose opinions you respect (not close friends or relatives) and ask them to make notes.

At the end you will have many notes on many aspects of your script. Separate the notes off into categories: structure, plot and subplots, sequences, characters, dialogue, images, etc . . . however many you need.

A common mistake often made when approaching the rewrite stage is to assume you can fix it all in one massive swoop of a rewrite. *Wrong*. There are many rewrites you can go through – as many as you feel you need – each time looking at different aspects of the script and tackling different questions on each rewrite. All the time you are working towards making your final screenplay stronger. It is a complex task and the final 30% of the writing process, so don't try to tackle it all in one go.

I suggest at least six stages:

> First rewrite: Understandability
> Second rewrite: Structure
> Third rewrite: Characters
> Fourth rewrite: Dialogue
> Fifth rewrite: Style
> Sixth rewrite: Polishing

The idea of the rewrite is to look at common problems that happen in any script and address them in a *focused* way. The point of the rewrite is to decide what stays in your script and (more importantly) what goes. The true craft skill here is cutting: cutting the unnecessary, the redundant, the insipid, without lessening the passion and urgency. These are hard decisions to take but they are necessary. Learn to '*kill your babies*' – cut out your most favourite line of dialogue, description or scene if it doesn't fit, do a job or earn its space on the page.

> ❛ First cut out all the wisdom, then cut out all the adjectives. I've cut some of my favourite stuff. I have no real compassion when it comes to cutting: no pity, no sympathy. Some of my dearest and most beloved bits of writing have gone out with a very quick slash, slash, slash. ❜
>
> *Paddy Chayefsky,*
> screenwriter,
> *Network, Being There*

—— First rewrite: understandability ——

A common problem when you read your exploratory draft is: you don't understand why certain things happen or why a character does something. The reason usually is: the story or character may exist in your mind but you've not put those important elements, reasons or bits of information down on the page.

Ask yourself:

- Is the story I've chosen the most dramatically and emotionally affective one? (page 42 – How do I choose which story?)
- What are the pieces of information my audience needs to know in order to understand the story fully? Have they been dropped in at the most dramatic or effective moment? (page 170 – Plants and payoffs)
- Can I make it better by referring to its genre type? (page 46) For example, if your swashbuckling romance lacks enough romance or danger, perhaps the ending doesn't fit the genre of story you're writing
- Do my characters do uncharacteristic things for no explainable reason? See page 68 – Character Checklist. If you don't have a believable answer, change it for the better
- Is the chosen structure type (three-act, multi-plotted, etc.) best suited to this script? Can it be told better by using a different structural approach?
- Whose story am I telling, whose point of view is the audience experiencing it through? (page 47)

A tendency with many exploratory drafts is understructure (page 97) – it indicates insufficient pre-writing work: for example, of your 120 pages, the first 70 are spend wandering, and the real story action is crammed into the last 50, so you end up discarding the first 70. How do you stop such wandering? Make sure you've got your ending (page 42 – Story Concept)

Now ask:

- What is original, different or distinctive about this story? Keep asking yourself throughout the rewrites. Originality is not just one element, it's a mix.
- What is its dramatic structure? Not just the overall three-act

structure, but the smaller internal ones found within it?
- Flashbacks and flashforwards: are these used dramatically, not just as a device to add another piece of information? Tip: construct each one as a complete dramatic structure in its own right. Now that *you* know why one thing follows another, decide which bits are needed for use in your script.
- What are the surprises? And where? If they are predictable your script won't grip the audience.
- Information: are things held back from the audience until they need to know it? Only give it to them when it makes dramatic sense, when it will be most effective and surprise them most.
- Is it the right length? Does the story fit the chosen length? Is it too cramped or too stretched? (page 61)
- Have you started and ended the script in the right places?
- Theme (page 51): what is the real message of your screenplay? Do you truly know it? (These are questions you *have* to face). Once you know your theme, it will help you sort out just what your plot and subplots (especially main subplot), images, metaphors, cast design, etc. are going to be about, in order to resonate or contradict your theme. Theme is what integrates the act and character development (especially in Act III) and unifies the entire story.
- Why do you want to write this story? Like theme, you often don't discover this until after your treatment or exploratory draft. Decide on the why and you can start deciding on your plot and subplots.

——— Second rewrite: structure ———

❛ I don't necessarily believe in the three-act structure when actually first writing something. However, I do find it a useful diagnostic tool during the rewrite: to go back over your draft to see if and where anything might have gone wrong or become unclear. ❜
Tom Schulman

Every action in your screenplay (physical, emotional, verbal, psychological) must advance the overall storyline and be tightly linked to it. This storyline is, of course, the process of your protagonist trying to reach their ultimate goal within the film – their outer motivation.

Without this relationship an action should be cut. Also, a correct action should be carefully orchestrated as part of the script's rising conflict. Thus, the overall storyline must be advanced and gradually escalate towards the Act III climax.

Consider the elements of each act:

Act I

Purpose: essential story information; introduce main characters; establish conflict, tone, visual style, settings (physical, social-psychological); build theme and mood.

Elements: point of entry; critical life-crisis moment; time frame; character-in-action; dramatic situation; time lock?; inciting incident; crisis; climax/TP1; raising the stakes; character-audience identification

Needs: information; correct dramatic arrangement of story elements

Dangers: lack of clarity and/or direction; insufficient identification with protagonist; unclear who protagonist is; character motivation vague

Act II

Purpose: develop story via conflict and confrontation; build motivation line from dramatic need/goal; move character through point of no return; orchestrate character transformation and growth; advance story via upward progression towards Act climax; maintain momentum

Elements: build from strong TP1 and clear, strong set-up; dramatic need/goal/external motivation; focus points; half-way point; script mechanics (dilemma, obstacles, complications, set-backs – time lock?); sequences; rising action; suspense; scene causality; major crisis; TP2/moment of truth; development of subplots

Needs: momentum; focus; powerful causality

Dangers: a very long section (for audience and writer); often unstructured or understructured; may not have essential incidents/scenes; a too-linear plot line (not enough complications, set-backs, etc); weak or false point of no return; incidents not integrally and logically linked to central 'problem' and characters (i.e. lack of focus, weak causality)

Act III

Purpose: resolve story; heighten tension to climax; integrate theme, unify story; final transformation and growth of protagonist; bring story to satisfying close

Elements: build powerfully from TP2/moment of truth; payoffs; key confrontational scene (protagonist vs. antagonist); increased pacing

Needs: pay off all story elements (including tying-up minor loose ends)

Dangers: momentum lost or weak; payoffs neglected; climax unsatisfactory or disconnected from preceding build-up

Plots and subplots

Examine your subplots, especially the main subplot (the one that will most affect your main plot – and your protagonist).

1 For each subplot, ask: does it perform at least one or more of the eight functions on pages 57 and 60.

2 How do these eight points help me when rewriting?

● Most new writers' subplots don't inform the main story as they haven't worked it out on a thematic level yet
● Crucially, when rewriting, most new writers are not prepared to drop a subplot if it does not inform the main story or perform any of these eight functions. 'Kill your babies' is the core of rewriting
● If the subplots *do* inform and/or perform, do they do it effectively? Are there minor adjustments which would make them more dramatically effective?

3 Know the extremes you can push your protagonist to. Find them, push them further; find their most dramatic elements and place them at your Act III climax.

Climaxes

1 Look at the three end-of-Act climaxes. A climax is a precise moment and a turning point in a story. However, your screenplay is a composite of several stories (subplots). Hence each climax needs to be a turning point within the broader story sweep.

2 Are the subplot climaxes effective, increasing, believable? Look at each climactic sequence and examine it.

3 The end of Act II climactic sequence is often problematic. The protagonist should be as far away as possible from the goal, revelation or realisation of the Act III climax. Logically, they should have

abandoned the quest by now (page 118 – Moment of Truth).
Examine that climactic sequence and its functions. The protagonist:

- denies responsibility for their actions
- abandons the quest (considers it again)
- and faces their moment of truth

If it doesn't do any of these, what's the remedy? You could:

- introduce another character (hence another subplot)
- show confrontation (in present linear time or flashback)
- show evidence of some revelation, e.g. tape, diary notes (and plant earlier the expectation that this evidence exists – another subplot)
- show action to reveal the protagonist's state of mind
- use flashback as parallel action and structure your script to set up the two stories in parallel time, so that the first leads to the second, and hence confrontation (see above)

4 Finally, ask yourself the following:

- Do your climaxes build, from the least significant to the most significant at the end?
- Each climactic sequence should run: plant the possibility of a climax; allow the audience to ruminate on it; present the climax itself.
- Climactic sequence structuring is steered by two factors; your choice of what information is revealed and when you reveal it.
- After a significant dramatic climax you need a pause, and that moment or scene should be in keeping with the rhythm and pacing of the overall script.

Openings and endings

Your choices of where and how you open and end the script are crucial; they tell your audience what *you* think is significant in your screenplay.

Scenes and sequences

Openings:

- are characters, conveyed clearly, effectively, interestingly, well?
- is the visual setting interesting?
- are sound and the pacing of dialogue used effectively?

- is there suspense?
- has the plot been set up?
- is there any conflict?
- does anything happen?
- do you know the protagonist, what they want, their motivation?
- does the writer bring an individual POV, an individual idea?
- is the world coherent? is it different?
- do you want to turn the pages?

Scenes

Work out the aims of each scene

Ask yourself: Why do I need this scene? What is its purpose? What contribution does it make to the overall storyline and final climax? How does it contribute to the action storyline and character motivation storyline? The worst answer is 'because it follows the previous one'. Each scene should have a function in itself.

So ask yourself: What is each character *doing* in this scene (action) both at the start and at the end? Remember: Arrive Late – Depart Early. Cut the intro and departure; you only need the middle of most scenes.

Focusing

Who is the scene about? What is the scene about? What does each character need or want to happen? Why can't the characters achieve this and how best can I express it on the screen? Move away from *your* dramatic needs and towards *theirs*.

What's the character's attitude in this scene? What is their emotional response both to what they have to do and what happens in this scene? Look to subtext in what they say and do: they may mask or contradict each other. Are the audience getting the levels of meaning *you* want?

Remember, a scene consists of: a character's action meeting an obstacle, opposition or disruption, giving rise to tension which is either resolved or heightened; the information is *delivered*, then they *exit*. See the scene construction flowchart fig. 9.1. (page 142)

The scene ending

Is the scene ending surprising enough or is it predictable? Try applying William Goldman's 'a surprise on every page' to every scene. Know the ending and make everything build towards it, but don't take the obvious, predictable route.

Nature of the scene

Does the scene depend on dialogue or on action or a mix of both? Is there dialogue deadlock? (see Fourth rewrite).

Sequences

(See page 133). Remember, the three-act structure is a template; the writer's craft comes in disguising this artifice without the audience realising it's there. So for each sequence you should know:

- What do all the characters *want* in each block? (Not just your protagonist). Why do they want it? What's their state of mind?
- What is actually happening in *each sequence* of the stories and subplots, and how do they underline or reinforce the main plot storyline?
- What's the *emotional engagement* of each sequence? What is it in each one you want your audience to relate to?

Decide on the above, then ask:

- What is the actual dramatic structure of this sequence? How and where do all the subplots fit in?

———— Third rewrite: characters ————

❝ Always try to trip yourself up: look for the places where you've done something which was convenient rather than true. ❞

Clive Barker,
writer/director:

Changing characters

Two key things to address:

- do I *need* all my characters?
- are they distinctive?

Common problems

- there are too many characters
- you've invented a character just to help the story along

Ask yourself if you really need them all, if not, drop them or have their function done by another character. Look at the length and format of your script: are there too many characters for that format to support? (page 61). Too many, and you will lose focus.

Remember, most scripts hinge around three key players (the rule of three again): protagonist, opposition, reflection/mirror, with sometimes a romance character (who may also be one of the above).

❝ The characters have to be clear from what they *do*. Learn to pare down. ❞

Norma Heyman,
producer

Main characters

The first time they enter the script, their presence must be neatly summarised – powerfully, immediately: go for *dominant impressions*. For your protagonist it is worth writing two or three sentences of information (attitudes, background) so the reader has a greater sense of the person in the script. Choose your words carefully. You need to get a *feeling* across.

With main characters, ask yourself if this character possesses a strong through-line: a spine linking their actions to their goals via their motivation (page 156).

The transformational arc

Look for this arc in all your main characters (especially the protagonist). See page 81.

- Which characters have one: the protagonist, other main characters, on-going minor characters? Are they all developed to their fullest extent?

- What changes do they go through? Where do they make those changes?
- Have I established from the very beginning the values and emotions that exist in that world?
- At your screenplay crisis points, do the emotions pitch and waver? Are the characters' values challenged, especially the protagonist's?
- How have the characters changed by the end? What value systems and emotional responses have been altered?

Distinctive attributes you can use to make a character unique include:

- Attitude (crucial): distinctive and unique ones make for interesting unpredictability. Also, how does that attitude work in terms of the other characters in the script?
- Characteristics: the way they look, talk and move on the screen
- Surprise: look for the unpredictable action (not one that comes from attitude). At a key moment in the script, get them to do something completely unpredictable
- Motivational uncertainty: can you generate any enigma around why this character is doing what they're doing in the script? Establish and maintain that uncertainty for the path of the story. (If another character doesn't understand why the protagonist did a certain action, it signals to your audience that we *will* understand it by the end)
- Originality: add it by making your character: the opposite of audience expectations or of their character type; give them a distinctive attitude or characteristic or occasional unpredictable actions; you might also like to make them a 'fish-out-of-water'; give them motivational uncertainty
- Minor characters: although on screen for only a short while, the audience must know everything they need to know about them to work believably. Create your cameos believably (without disrupting the script's overall tone) through dress style (usually related to their job), through physical presence and body language and also through the way they talk
- Stereotypes: how do you avoid cliché in a character? Try to ensure their story contains unexpected outcomes. (Comedies rest on stereotypes and their contradictions.) There is no problem if your character starts out a stereotype (quick audience identification is

an advantage); but *stay* there and boredom soon sets in. Do something unpredictable with your stereotype – enough to make the audience stay with it.

───── Fourth rewrite: dialogue ─────

❢ Dialogue comes because I know what I want my characters to say. I envision the scene – and the dialogue comes out of that. Then I rewrite it. Then I cut it. Then I refine it until I get the scene as precise as I can get it. ❢

Paddy Chayefsky

This is always a difficult rewrite. Writers don't like cutting their dialogue once it's written. However, the best dialogue is rewritten dialogue which is *cut, compressed* and *focused*.

"Dialogue deadlock"

Classic problems you may encounter include:

- Blocking: the exchanges block each other and don't allow anything to develop. For example: 'Are you ill?' 'No.' This is wrong, as it blocks any further development. Try it like this 'Are you ill?' 'Mmm, feeling queasy'. Now you can continue the exchange.
- The dialogue may ramble, lack direction, get nowhere or be too 'talky' (especially in scenes lasting five or six pages) or refer to something happening outside the scene. Get them to say the things that need to be said, but keep it relevant to what's going on inside the scene and in that location.
- The scene may be too flat; the words may do their job, but the result may be unemotional; with no spark, as if the scene died in the writing. Try swapping styles: conceive the scene in a radically different style. Heavy drama? Rewrite as comedy. A purely dialogue scene? Try it as visual slapstick. Try it anyway. Find ways to bring a scene back to life. Do whatever tricks you must, whatever works best for you, to bring the scene back to life.
- Most major speeches in screenplays are built around the two concepts of log-lines: the rule of three and contrasts (page 50). Do yours echo these ideas?

- In dialogue and scene rewriting there are a number of classic strategies you can use to try to make the scene come to life. One is to change the focus and/or attitudes of one or two of the characters. Another is to ask yourself: can I do this *visually*?

Don't think of a scene as 'people talking', think: 'how can I put this onto the screen or page *without* talking?' Think visual and use the medium to its absolute limits.

Subtext

Examine your scenes, their dialogue and action, in the light of your new rewrite knowledge. Is there any subtext there at all? Does it fulfil any of the functions outlined on page 152? If not, change it – either the dialogue, action or subtext.

Fifth rewrite: style

Pacing

(See page 164) Pacing: overall; your sequences (length); scenes; within scenes. First decide on the overall feel of your screenplay – this decision determines the pacing of your sequences.

Next, determine the dramatic pace within the scene itself. Always look for the most dramatic way of using what you've got. If you're in danger of losing your audience, throw in something to keep them interested or set up something for the next or a later scene. How do you determine the dramatic pace?

Use of tone

Look at the use of tone expressed in:

- the scale of dramatic action: are you employing the right lengths for the moments (love scene, chase sequence, climax, etc)?
- lengths of scenes and sequences: do the longer scenes all occur at one point in your script, slowing the pace?
- characterisation: do all your characters belong in the same screenplay?

- *mise-en scène*: look at the settings, locations, weather, costumes, choice of day or night – do they make a whole and add to the dramatic tension of the moment?
- dialogue: review it; does it fit consistently with the storyline and the genre?
- images (page 171): work out the visual references, what they symbolise and what they tell the audience; look at the symbolic meanings of location and landscape (for example in Merchant Ivory films)
- soundtrack (including the use of v.o.) – does it contribute to the mood? Don't specify the exact music track you want, but say, for example 'ethereal pop song that creates a mood of . . .'; describe the atmosphere without dictating the musical language

Transitions

Every scene must end and lead into the next one. Apply those tools of similarity or contrast to each scene juxtaposition. (See page 165.)

Decide what the last line of your scene is: visual description or dialogue? Moving or static? Is the transition one of continuity, jump-cutting or overlapping? If it's dialogue, can you change it to a reaction shot?

The next scene's opening: visuals are always noticed first in any new scene – your choice is crucial. How does that first visual relate to the last visual of the previous scene? What does it establish about this new scene? Normal 'rules' are: if you end on a moving image then you start on a moving image; if you end on a static shot then start on a static shot.

If you have a big transitional jump (in time and/or space) try:

- inserting an extra bridging scene that establishes the next scene
- using DISSOLVE TO: for the next scene instead of CUT TO:
- using FADE TO BLACK then FADE UP: into the next scene

If you've got a dialogue-driven scene or sequence and need to make a big jump, try overlapping your dialogue from one scene into the other, denoted as:

JOHN (v.o.)   or   JOHN (over)

It is important that the audience should not be aware of the jarring nature of these transitions.

Reliefs and pauses

Don't forget those pause scenes or moments following highly climactic or emotional incidents – let your audience breathe and assimilate.

For reliefs *within* scenes, the general rule is: high drama scenes can only stand one moment of light relief (unless the scene or screenplay's purpose is light relief).

When considering reliefs and pauses in pacing, look for the opposites and use them.

Emotion On The Page

Emotion is at the core of a story's believability, and expressing emotion on the page is difficult to discuss: one can only watch, read scripts and experience it to see how emotions work on the screen and are expressed on the page.

What is important in this rewrite is: *you must know the emotion you are aiming for* – within each scene, each sequence, and the overall emotional tone of the screenplay. The wrong level in a scene or climax can throw a script off-focus (if you *do* spring surprises, set them up first). Again, look to the post-emotional climaxes. Pause moments, allowing your audience to absorb the emotion, are crucial to emotional writing.

Even though each of your characters may speak in their own voice, the scene's emotional level *should* be the same for all, with one character (the protagonist) who goes beyond the emotional range to focus that emotion on. To discover the real emotional pitch of this character, ask yourself: how do they engage with the world, the way they express their own emotions? Also, keep the language consistent with the emotional pitch so that you milk the most emotional power from that moment.

In your script, if strong relationships have been set up, the strong emotional climax should be capable of being shown with looks and reactions rather than forceful emotional dialogue (especially by the end). Credible characters + credible desires + credible situations + credible relationships create credible emotion.

The important thing in this rewrite stage is to look for the pitch of the emotion, focus it, and then tighten it.

Engaging your audience's emotion

The basic underlying principle is that the words you use on the page must reflect the type of emotions you want to reflect on the screen and push the right emotional button/s in your audience. A comedy script? Describe the action in a funny way. A tensely dramatic scene? Describe things spartanly. And so on...

Remember: don't put anything on the page that is not on the screen.

Sixth rewrite: polishing

By this stage, you know your script works. With this rewrite you go through every single line with a fine-toothed comb, nit-picking over specific words of dialogue, description or action, asking all the time: 'is this the best word or gesture I can use here?

There are no firm rules about how many rewrites you need to do; you should do as many as you feel is needed to make your script work (in America, nine or more is normal before sending it out). The important thing is: with each rewrite you address specifics, and each successive rewrite should make your script easier, more fluid and more enjoyable and engaging to read. Get used to doing rewrites; they are the mainstay of the production process.

> ❛ The older I got, the more scripts I sold, the more I came to realise there's always something in criticism. You're always going to improve a script. ❜
>
> *Ian La Frenais,*
> comedy writer/producer

Now you've got this far, you should be pretty confident about your script. You can literally hold it like a crystal in the palm of your hand, examine each facet and say 'it works'. You'll also probably feel a temporary 'post-natal' depression (writing a script really is like giving birth!) Don't dwell on it, because you haven't finished yet . . .

14

THE "FINISHED" ITEM

Getting feedback

Now you need to get feedback. Ask a wide variety of people to read your screenplay. Not your mother or favourite relative (they will be biased) but someone whose writing advice you respect; a member of a writers' group (if you belong to one) or someone who might not even like you very much. If that person likes your script, it probably really does work – and it might just work on the screen. Ask them to make notes of constructive criticism. When finished, read their notes, listen to their comments and if you find them perceptive and helpful, rewrite again incorporating some of their suggestions.

Try making a recording with actors (access your local amateur dramatic society): sit them around a table with your tape recorder. Give them the script and record a straight sight-reading (no rehearsals) – and don't direct them. At the end, ask them questions: not just 'did you like it?' but things from the checklist (page 182–3). If they were unclear about certain things, ask them if they'd be prepared to improvise that scene or situation. If so, record it. Make notes.

Now get a distance: next day (or week), play back the original reading. Is what is coming across aurally what you wanted to transmit visually? Are you creating the drama in the mind of the audience, the movie in the mind of the reader? Does the dialogue sound like newly minted thought, as if that character were speaking it for the first time? Does it sound like words spoken or words read off a page? Does it flow? Does it sound natural? Go through your notes; rewrite again if necessary.

Eventually you'll reach a point where you know any further rewrites will only take you further away from the original intentions of your script. Stop there. Decide on your final title.

Titles

❝ Think of a great title: something that stands out, something the audience can hold on to. ❞

Julian Krainin,
Krainin Productions

Re-read page 53. If you are happy with your working title, that it imparts the essence of what's in your script, keep it. If not, brainstorm other possibilities with more impact or hook. Tip: when handing out your script for critiquing, try doing so without a title; ask them to suggest one after it has been read. If the vision you had in your mind has translated onto the page and transmitted to the audience, they may come up with a good, hopefully better, one.

Now start printing it off: you can now officially call this your first draft.

Presentation

This is the total 'look' of your screenplay as it lands on the desk of the reader or producer. Your job is to make it look professional: properly typed, no spelling mistakes, properly covered and bound. Assume the recipient has received your script on a bad day and that they'll look for the slightest reason to reject it. Script readers already have to read over 50 scripts a week, so whittling down the unsuitable is ruthless. Don't give them a reason. Presentation is important, and here rigid rules apply.

Covers and binding

The covers (front and back) should be plain thin card, no gaudy colours (be conservative), no pictures, photos or graphics. The binding is by two (or three) metal paper-fasteners (or 'brads') – see left – through punched holes in the left-hand margin of the script. Some screenplays use comb or spiral-binding and clear PVC covers (acceptable in the UK but *never* in the US).

The title page

Now type your front page. Look at page 202. What strikes you about it? It is plain, simple, clean and bare, with no unnecessary information. No year of copyright, graphics, cast lists, set lists – it's not your job. The title page should contain the title, author's name, and a contact name and telephone number (your own or your agent's, if you have one) in the bottom right or left-hand corner. Nothing more. There's no need to add 'an original screenplay by' under the title. If it's based on a life-story or an adapted script, you state it thus:

<u>Black Beauty</u>
by Caroline Thompson

Adapted from Anna Sewell's novel of the same name

Never use log-lines on the title page. If you need to use them, they go on a separate sheet immediately after the title page, before page one where the screenplay starts. A good title, by-line (author) and contact point is all you should need.

Script length

Remember, you are a first-time writer; your script must be the right length. For feature films, especially for Hollywood, this means a maximum of 120 pages. Some say they now prefer a maximum between 105 and 115 pages. Comedy and horror genres tend not to go beyond 95 pages.

In television, it is even more important: know the page length (how long one page plays on the screen) for the type of series you are writing for (commercial or non-commercial TV). Don't forget the ad breaks if it's for commercial TV – never send a script with breaks to a non-commercial company (e.g. the BBC). Remember, commercial TV scripts run shorter (to accommodate the ads), hence a 60-minute drama would be about 54 minutes.

The covering letter

Everything you write – especially your letter of enquiry, covering letter and title page – will be judged as part of your ability as a screenwriter. Be professional, brief and to the point – no 'I wrote this

THE USUAL SUSPECTS

by

Christopher McQuarrie

Fig. 14.2 The Title Page

especially for . . .' 'This is a sure-fire blockbuster' or 'The reason I wrote this was . . .'; say more by saying less. Your script should sell itself. Mention the title and a brief one or two-sentence description of the script (page 49). If you want to include a *brief* short paragraph on your aims and career ambitions as a writer, that's acceptable. Ideally, the only time your presence need be noticed is when the reader or producer says: 'Hey, it's great. Who wrote this?'

When you mail the package off, enclose a stamped self-addressed envelope, and move on to your next project.

❝ The key is to get your script into as many hands as possible and not take rejection. Be dogged about submitting your material, until someone who senses your ability likes it. ❞

Lew Hunter,
Professor of the Screenwriting
School, UCLA

15

ASSEMBLING YOUR PORTFOLIO

> ❛ When you finish writing a script you cease to be a screenwriter and become a business-person; you then embark on a series of strategies to market and sell your work – and yourself. ❜
>
> *Emma Darrell,*
> agent

Before you read further, look at the flow-chart on page 205; it refers to the information covered in the next 6 chapters.

So, having completed your first script, it's only natural to want to start sending it to people, especially agents and producers. By all means do so if you wish, but my advice is, don't start sending any scripts out to the industry until you have at least two completed ones you are happy with, and a third nearing completion. These should show the breadth, depth and variety of your writing styles, subjects and themes. Take a tip from Shakespeare: try writing one tragedy, one comedy and one history.

> ❛ It's a mistake to think that what you write and send to people will be accepted as it is. Production companies and broadcasters tend to view first-time scripts as writers' calling cards. ❜
>
> *Charles Elton,*
> producer

When you are ready to begin sending out your script(s) you will need four things:

- Your 'calling card' script: the one to hook them and make them ask 'have you got any more?'
- Another script (or two) to follow through: good agents and good producers look for the potential to develop a possible long-term

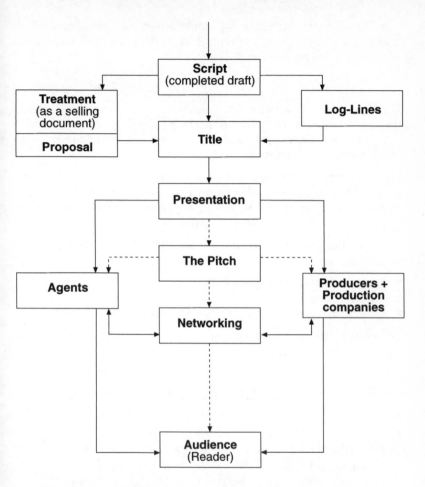

Fig. 15.1 Flowchart: The Selling Process (continued from the flowchart in Chapter 3)

career relationship (Chapter 19), so prove your calling card is not a one-off.
- A very thick skin; you will be rejected – a lot. Get used to it. *Reject Rejection*. Remember, they are rejecting bits of paper, not you.
- Persistence – bags of it.
  (Persistence and rejection will be covered more in Chapter 20.)

❻ There are two struggles: the struggle to write something good and the struggle to get it read. You have to attack both with single-minded persistence. ❾

> *Christopher McQuarrie,*
> writer: *The Usual Suspects*

Tip: If you receive back one of your scripts in the morning post, make sure that script goes out to someone else by the afternoon collection – but make sure it's in good condition: no dog-ears, coffee cup rings or pencilled margin annotations.

Prior to sending it out, make that all-important phone call to agents to ask if they welcome unsolicited manuscripts (page 216), and to producers to ask them if they're looking for projects and if so what type (you should have an idea already – page 226).

When sending your script (and *never* send the original, *always* a photocopy), also enclose:

- a short covering letter (page 201)
- a short, *relevant* CV
- a stamped, self-addressed envelope big enough to return your script

And don't worry about feeling insecure; all writers feel like that – it comes with the territory.

Log-lines

Now try creating a new log-line for your project based on what you now know about the script. Re-read page 50. If the slogan is good, you should use it in your pitch or script presentation, either as a cross-heading on the proposal, or as a tag-line on a separate sheet after the title page. When pitching, they may well ask you 'What's the log-line?' – have it prepared.

Remember, a log-line has one main function: to make people watch. At a very basic level, it's about managing (manipulating) your audience's responses.

The one-page proposal

All media people's time is limited. They are continually bombarded with ideas every waking moment – producers by writers or agents, commissioning heads by producers. Hence the increasing practice of asking to be sent a *proposal*.

This is a *one-page* prose *selling document* intended to hook your audience with the originality of your project idea, and make them want to see the treatment or (preferably) your first draft script. It has to contain enough of the story to draw them in. A proposal should not be confused with the writer's one page synopsis.

The important things about a proposal are:

- it should fit onto a single side of A4 paper
- the fewer words and the more white space the better

A proposal has one goal only: to create interest in the story – but to do this it doesn't have to tell the whole story.

A one-page proposal has to:

- let the reader imagine the project; where you start from, what the journey is, the setting, location, mood and period, an idea of genre; if *absolutely* necessary indicate the *kind* of actor who might play the lead
- tell them who will watch, who the target audience will be
- tell them (for television) where it will fit into the schedules
- contain 'the question'; do Thelma and Louise get away with their crime? will Fergus and Dill stay together? does Griffin Mill get away with it?
- tell the reader if any 'elements' (actor, director, executive producer, etc.) are 'attached', i.e. interested in the project

A good example of a proposal is the one used to attract backers for *Strictly Ballroom* (page 208). Note its energetic use of short descriptive phrases, visual language, active verbs, vividly imparting a sense of energy and excitement about the project. Note too that it encapsulates the project on one sheet with plenty of white space.

Now write your proposal.

SYNOPSIS

Borrowing from the classic Hollywood dance films of the nineteen-forties, STRICTLY BALLROOM is a romantic comedy in the style of PRETTY WOMAN and DIRTY DANCING.

Set in the glamorous world of ballroom dancing, it is the story of a young man's struggle against the system.

When twenty-one year old ballroom champion, Scott Hastings, commits the cardinal sin of dancing his own steps and not those laid down by the all powerful Federation, retribution is swift. He is dumped by his partner Liz, his hopes of winning the coverted Pan-Pacific Grand Prix are dashed.

All seems lost when out of the shadows emerges Fran; a beginner and the ugly duckling of the studio. Through sheer persistence she convinces Scott to give her a chance, and an unlikely partnership is born.

Scott and Fran's first public appearance sends shock waves of excitement through the dance world. The Federation must stop them at all costs.

Scott's Achilles' Heel is his father, Doug. The night before the Pan-Pacifics, corrupt Federation President, Barry Fife, reveals to Scott the terrible secret of Doug's past. Scot is trapped. In order to save his father, he must turn his back on Fran.

On the day of the Pan-Pacifics, minutes before Scott and his ex-partner are to take the floor, the truth is revealed – Barry Fife has lied; Scott is free to follow his heart...

Scott and Fran burst onto the floor; the response from the crowd is "unearthly", but, Barry Fife will not allow it – the music is stopped.

Defiantly, twelve thousand spectators clash their hands together. Scott and Fran dance to their rhythm; the Federation are destroyed; and the floor is flooded in a sea of celebration.

Fig 15.2 The Proposal document for *Strictly Ballroom* Source: © M&A Film Corporation Pty. Ltd.

The treatment as a selling document

❝ A treatment may not get a project made, but if it's good and interesting it will at least get you an interview with the powers that be. ❞

Allon Reich,
Channel 4 TV/Films

We've already looked at the treatment as a vehicle for focusing your story ideas (page 176). Re-read that section; everything discussed there still holds true.

Now let's examine the treatment as it is mostly used: as a selling document sent by writers to producers (or by producers to commissioning heads) so they may decide if they want to commission the project, with you writing the screenplay (or see the already written script – increasingly executives expect to see completed first draft scripts first before they commission).

As with the earlier piece on treatments, the rules remain: single-spaced typed on one side of A4 paper, present tense, short paragraphs, crispness and pace, visual appeal, event-driven, outlining the main characters and imparting the essence of your project. The only differences are that as a selling document it is unwise to let this treatment go over twelve to fifteen pages for feature length or eight to ten pages for an hour-long drama. Creating impact in your first two paragraphs is also very important, as is your presentation (neatly printed and pleasing to the eye, no spelling mistakes, sometimes with photographs and interesting graphics, although these should not overwhelm the text – again, there are no rules). Lastly, if you want to put a list of characters and locations, do so, but put these on a separate sheet at the end as a caveat; at the front they have no meaning.

So make it look:

- professional (Style)
- interesting and different (Substance)

> Now write your treatment.

16

COPYRIGHT

A brief and painless guide to knowing your rights

Prior to sending your script to the industry, you may want to register its copyright i.e. to officially register your claim as being the rightful author of that said original work. Probably the question I am most frequently asked is: 'I've got this idea for a film/TV series/treatment – how can I copyright it and protect it from being stolen?' The facts are: you cannot copyright an *idea*. An idea is just that: an idea. You *can* copyright work (a synopsis, proposal, treatment or script), which is defined as the material form in which an idea is expressed. Technically, according to law, the very fact that the idea is now expressed on paper in black and white means that it is copyrighted. However, effectively it is meaningless and only a small part of the scenario. Also, a work marked © by the owner's name and a date does not guarantee protection, but it does provide evidence both of the date of the work's creation and the claimed ownership of copyright.

Copyright is precisely what its name suggests. It does not offer protection against another individual coming up with the same idea separately and independently. (There are only eight basic stories, there is nothing new under the sun, and remember, talk is cheap – so don't chatter about your ideas until you've put them down on paper and done something about it.)

The more you become involved in the media industry, the more gossip you will hear concerning ideas, formats, even whole scripts allegedly stolen and later screened with someone else claiming authorship. But in truth copyright theft forms a very tiny part of the industry. In practice, it is easy to steal something like a treatment simply by abandoning the original copyright holder's existing text, grammar or language, and rewriting it in your own style.

A common industry practice today, when a company acknowledges receipt of your script, or subsequently when they send you a rejection, is to include the following rider (or similar) in their covering letter:

'(This company) receives a very large number of proposals, many of which are similar to or the same as each other. For this reason, I am sure you will appreciate that even if, in the future, we produce or commission a (film/programme/project) which you believe is the same or similar to your suggestion, but which has come, coincidentally, from another source, we cannot compensate you.

I am returning your (submission/proposal) with this letter. I have not circulated it to anyone else.'

This action might just be to cover the company over things like moral rights and intellectual property claims, but to the untrained observer it looks like an attempt to have one's cake and eat it. In truth there is little you as an individual can do.

Release forms

Another common industry development is the release form, whereby the receiving party gets the submitting writer to sign a form or indemnity waiver before the receiver even begins to read the submission. This short document (between one to three pages) will contain clauses like the following:

'Although we have not read the work we recognise the possibility that it may be similar to and/or competitive with material which we (or one of our subsidiaries or affiliates) is contemplating, developing and/or considering for production. Accordingly, in order to avoid any potential problems:

1. You recognise that the work may contain similar concepts and material which we have or are developing.

2. You agree that in consideration for our reviewing and discussing the work with you, you may not at any time assert or attempt to assert any claim against us (or any of our agents or employees) with respect to our use of similar material in any pro-

ject or series, which we may develop, produce, distribute, license or sell to a third party.'

And if you don't sign the release form your manuscript will be returned to you unread and your masterpiece undiscovered. Catch 22. The final decision on signing obviously rests with you and how important it is for you to get your work read and circulated. If you do sign, just go in with your eyes open, because you could still end up with your ideas being taken, only now you've got no leg to stand on. However, your first task is to get someone – anyone – to read your submission at all.

❛ Release forms are generally not to the writer's advantage. But writers, especially new ones, are paranoid about having their ideas stolen. Put your paranoia aside. Life is risk! ❜

Jeff Polstein
Head of Story Department,
ICM (US)

Some American writers are now submitting their original manuscripts on red paper. Why? Because red paper cannot be photocopied!

Useful publications

Copyright legislation is a quagmire, particularly now since most modern Acts also cover moral rights and intellectual property rights. But a good place to start to understand the fundamentals are the excellent articles by Amanda L. Michaels and Gavin MacFarlane (on UK and US scenarios) in the latest edition of The Writers' And Artists' Yearbook (Chapter 22).

One useful booklet is *Protecting Ideas and Copyright*, available from BECTU for £1 (plus SAE) and free to members. It gives practical advice on how creative ideas may be protected and covers the most widely used practice: mailing your script back to yourself in a sealed (do not use sealing tape) *registered* envelope and keeping it stored away unopened. The key points of this practice are: the envelope is clearly date-stamped over the seal, and the envelope remains sealed and stored away (at a lawyer's, bank or at home) – the theory being that if matters ever came to court, you could produce the envelope and have it opened by and inspected in front of legal representatives. If mailing a computer disk, wrap it in silver foil and then in some cardboard for added protection.

Another handy publication is *Copyright*, one of the many guides printed by the Society of Authors, and available from the publication department for £1 (post free). Lastly, Helen Shay's book *Copyright And Law For Writers* (How To Books, 1996) may prove useful.

Copyright registration schemes

Birmingham's Central England Screen Commission have a copyright registration scheme run in conjunction with a local reputable solicitor. You can send them your script, treatment, synopsis, proposal or format, and they will register its receipt. The document will be securely stored at a solicitors and you will be issued with a numbered, dated certificate of registration. At the time of writing it is a free service, although they may be forced to charge a nominal fee imminently. The industry organisation PACT also runs a free registration scheme for its members – although it is more for programme proposals. A similar scheme for scripts is currently under consideration with the UK Writers' Guild. Registration schemes in the US are run by the Writers' Guild of America (West) and the US Copyright Office in Washington. WGA(w) offer a five-year (renewable) registration: $10 for members, $20 for non-members. However, they have strict submission rules, so check first.

While registration does not guarantee that your ideas won't get stolen, it does at least mean your work is dated and registered with an independent legal entity. It may give you a sense of security, and make you both feel more able to openly discuss that work with others.

Similar registration schemes are multiplying, possibly a symptom of a growing fear (or incidence?) of industry plagiarism. All furnish you with a signed and dated registration document, but they do charge. The decision is yours.

One thing you could do on your submissions is to type on the front page (and on every page if you feel it really necessary) the words: 'Commercial In Confidence', together with the legend ©, following by your name and the month and year it was written. Again, it may not guarantee against plagiarism, but at least it dates your manuscript and formally notifies claimed ownership. It gives clear signals to the receiver, both that you are aware of your legal position and that you are completely paranoid about ideas theft. But it might give you some peace of mind.

All screenwriting is a risky business; be aware that similar ideas are often in circulation at the same time. But you have to distribute your project widely to find the right person to get it on screen, and nothing is gained by leaving a script on the shelf gathering dust. The choice is yours.

Addresses:

Central England Screen Commission, Waterside House, 46 Gas Street, Birmingham, B1 2JT, UK (Tel: 0121-643 9309 / Fax: 0121-643 9064). 'Nominal fee' (tba) gives registration for life.

National Copyright Archive Ltd., PO Box 88, Burwell, Cambridge, CB5 0BU, UK (Tel: 01638 741223) Charges approximately £10 per document.

Stationers' Hall Registry Ltd., Stationers' Hall, Ave Maria Lane, London EC4M 7DD (Tel: 0171-248 2934) Charges upwards of £47 for 7-year registration

US Copyright Office, Washington D.C. (Tel: 800-688 9889)

(See Chapter 22 for other relevant addresses)

17

AGENTS

What they do, how to get – and keep – one

❛ Having a good agent is very important, an agent who under-stands what your goals are, and looks at career in terms of 30 or 40 years. It 's important to have someone there to remind you, when you forget, what your career goals are and what the big picture is. You will be ill-served by an agent only interested in the immediate 'what's hot' one-off quick-hit. ❜

Paul Attanasio

What is an agent?

Essentially an agent is a writer's eyes and ears and business manag-er. He or she (many agents are women) handles everything for you, supposedly leaving you free to write. For a percentage (usually 10% and upwards) an agent will negotiate contracts, wine, dine and schmooze contacts, keep an ear to the ground for future work, (theo-retically) generate new work, even suggest changes in your script to make it more marketable. You the writer are the commodity, and the agent is there to get the best deal without losing the contract. It has been suggested that a writer must earn at least £10,000 per annum before the agent will cover their overheads and start to see a return on their investment.

Do I need an agent?

If you don't have one, you are operating with a handicap. In the marketplace of screenwriting, having an agent is the equivalent of having a merit badge saying: 'This writer can deliver the goods'. It is a sign that some other independent, respected person believes you have talent. If the agent says you can turn in scripts, and to a deadline, it helps a producer trust their own judgement (and blame someone if the project fails). Putting it bluntly: many people with the power in this industry have a reluctance to commit themselves to new untried talent – it's the inherent insecurity of the business. So, if a producer receives a script from an agent it means that at least *they* think you can write. Consequently, that script will be read by the producer rather than the reader, or at least given some precedence. Basically, having an agent is a rubber stamp of confidence – a reinforcer. Hollywood generally only accepts scripts submitted via agents.

Of course, you could always handle your own contract negotiations, but do it with a good (preferably media specialist) lawyer at your side.

How do I get an agent?

As much a Catch 22 as an actor trying for an Equity card. Even assuming an agent likes your script, if there is no guarantee of work (i.e. a percentage) it is not that likely you will get taken on. Then again, actually getting work is ten times more difficult without an agent.

Conversely, if a production company or director is interested in your script and talking money, just watch the agents flock around and invite you in for a chat.

> ❦ One responds instinctively to good writing, you get that feeling in your stomach and know you're in the presence of something quite special. ❧
>
> *Mel Kenyon*, agent

Where do I start?

The Writer's Handbook (Chapter 22) has a section listing agents, contact names, numbers, their catalogues, percentages and attitudes to unsolicited manuscripts. This is your bible.

Make a list of agents you feel might be interested in your type of work and who accept unsolicited manuscripts. Then send a preliminary letter (it's quicker to read) briefly (in two or three sentences) outlining your script and career ambitions. Better still, pick up the phone (*never* be afraid to do this), get to the person by name (important) or their secretary, and ask whether they would mind your submitting something. They can only say no. If they do, go to the next name on your list. They may tell you they are not taking on new names at present, so ask them when they might be trawling again (some agents have an annual or bi-annual clear out which is where your opening may come). But know your agencies first – their international contacts (Europe? US?), specialised fields – and target your script. You may find the larger agencies with new young blood (i.e. an ex-tea boy who wants to be a budding agent and is looking to build up a roster) more approachable. Also some agents charge a small (£5–10) reading fee. Be professional: at all times be business-like, to the point and, above all, courteous. And don't forget that SAE.

Responses

Remember, everything in this business is based on a purely subjective response, and that goes doubly for agents: your script may be slaughtered by one, criticising character A's outdated and stereotyped attitudes, whereas another might praise character A's wonderfully old-fashioned views. So don't give up. Rejection is part of this industry and your learning curve, and if you can't take rejection or criticism, you are not the kind of writer media people are looking for.

Follow through

If you manage to send your 'calling card' script to an agent and (heavens!) they don't dislike it (they rarely say they totally love something), they may ask you if you have anything else. Remember: *you must have that back-up*. You send in your second script (the one more likely to convince them), together with about five or six further script ideas in synopsis. So having that portfolio of scripts is essential (page 204).

It is inadvisable approaching an agent until you have your portfolio together. There's little point in an agent taking on a writer with just one script or one idea – where's the potential for developing that writer's work and career? Agents want writers who are marketable, not just a script that *may* be sellable.

And don't fret if, after sending in your calling card script, you hear nothing. Agents are seemingly perpetually busy, so expect to wait up to three months for a response. Perhaps give them a reminder call after four to six weeks.

If they call you in for a meeting they will want to discuss your career goals. Do *you* know what they are?

Final points

If taken on by an agent, there is usually no signing of contracts; it's a loose arrangement, made either verbally or by an exchange of letters, after an initial meeting. However, once you've got an agent, it is not a meal ticket. Don't expect them to get work for you. They may be able to point you in certain directions, but you must go out into the industry and network, hear where the breaks are and who's looking for what.

Remember, getting an agent is not an end in itself, it is a beginning – the beginning of your career as a writer, and keeping one depends on how that professional relationship progresses. They can drop you from their books just as quickly if you are unsellable (you're only as good as your last script), or if you prove 'difficult to work with'.

I would advise against the 'my agent, my best friend' attitude. The bottom line is business, and ultimately you must feel able and happy to trust your agent's business and literary judgement.

Try to remember that the agent works for the writer, not vice versa. Look at the split of the percentages: who gets the 90%? In a very real sense you 'employ' the agent – but just who needs whom more is debatable.

❝ You don't have to have an agent in order to write. ❞

David Thompson,
executive producer, BBC

Contacts:

The Association of Author's Agents:
c/o 37 Goldhawke Road, London W12 8QQ
(Tel: 0181-749 0315) Secretary: Carol Heaton

List of Writers Guild of America approved US agencies:
$1 + mail + SAE available from WGA(w) – Chapter 22

18

ADAPTATIONS, SHORTS, SOAPS, SERIES, SITCOMS AND COLLABORATION

——— Adapting for the screen ———

Adaptation is the process of changing or transforming material from one medium (novel, stage play, short story, real-life story, etc.) into another medium (i.e. film or TV). Although over 60% of all produced screenplays are adaptations (mostly from novels), the vast majority of first-produced screenplays are original. Why? Because most adapted screenplays are done on commission by already established writers; and before a writer can begin any serious adaptation, the commissioner (usually a producer) must first obtain the screen adaption Rights to the source material, and that costs money – often lots.

Writing screen adaptations is not really the territory of this introductory book. It is a specialist skill for which you will find many specialist publications on the existing market. Understand that each medium has its own underlying principles of action and conflict, its own unique limitations and liberties. In adapting for film you are searching for those basic strong elements that can be dramatised and will play on the screen. If considering adapting something as an exercise, ask yourself:

- Can I reduce the material to a simple strong storyline and a two-hour slot? (A novel has many pages to tell a story; you have only 120).
- Does it have an *intention* which seeks a *goal* which can be made dramatic, and expressed visually on the screen? Are the needs strong and clear enough and do they drive to a final climax?

So: *find the spine*, that central storyline that fulfils all the key screen requirements and can be described in one sentence, your story concept (page 42). Then ruthlessly decide what fits with the spine and what doesn't. Next, creatively decide what to keep and what to dump (select, compress, cut, rearrange, transform; clarity is essential). Then reduce that work to its basic essential story elements. Next, find the beginning, middle and end of your potential script story. Finally, distil out the *spirit* of the story.

This spirit is your jumping-off point, and what demands loyalty. Screen adaptation is creating a new type of reality, so obey the underlying principles for that form. It doesn't mean throwing the book away entirely. Clarity is essential: know what you seek and what the screenplay's ultimate shape will be.

❝ Being faithful to the book isn't the same as repeating every word. ❞

> *Andrew Davies,*
> Adaptor: *Price & Prejudice,*
> *The Old Devils*

Remember, to the media industry, a book is a property to be purchased – and with the Rights comes the licence to do anything necessary to make it work on screen.

One final tip: adapting your own novel rarely works – you are too close to your precious source material!

They say "Good books make bad movies, bad books make good movies" (e.g.: *Bonfire Of The Vanities* and *The Bridges Of Madison County*). Do you agree? List three of each type. Can you think of exceptions? List them.

Writing short films

Short films (generally anything between 5 and 30 minutes) are often a good way for new writers to enter the industry. Many are made by film schools, but increasingly independent low-budget/no-budget/

'guerilla' enterprises are emerging. Some TV channels are increasingly supportive of the short (for TV transmission, the maximum length is 11 minutes).

Writing a short is a different skill from writing longer form drama – possibly the most challenging and difficult of all screenwriting forms to do well. Here are some considerations:–

- One thing all successful shorts share is: the idea and its expression 'fits its space'. It's not a longer story forcibly squashed to fit the allotted time or a sketch idea artificially stretched; nor is it a promo for some future envisaged feature – a good tactic if you can pull it off.
- The tenets of screenwriting (every line justifying its existence) are even more important in a short: you only have approximately 15 pages. Economy of form and expression are everything. So try dropping straight into the life or world of your protagonist immediately; take a particular incident in that character's life which, when dramatised, illuminates their wider existence and history.
- Think twice about 'twist in the tail' stories. Readers are cynical enough to predict endings and generally get them right.
- Humour seems to work well in the short, as long as you are not using it as a sketch substitute.

Despite their denials, industry executives still see shorts as a director's medium, a calling card demonstrating their ability to go on to make their first feature. So link up with new directors and producers; view the project as *your* calling card.

—— Soaps, series and sitcoms ——

Lose your prejudices about writing for TV soap operas and series being downmarket 'hack' work. They are a regular and proven entry point for many new writers and a very good training ground in the writing discipline. Be professional: be adaptable.

❝ Soap at its best is dramatised gossip in a kind of never-ending middle act. ❞

Adrian Mourby,
writer-producer/former
editor of *The Archers*

Part of any TV script editor's job remit is looking for new writing talent, for which they are ever hungry. Each series will have its own 'Bible' – a hefty document containing full details of the series characters, story backgrounds, its ethos and approach, and other production information. However, obtaining one is difficult and you may not see one until offered a chance to write for the show. More established series (*EastEnders*, *Brookside*, *The Bill*) will have writer's intern schemes where novice writers shadow established ones through the production process.

How do you get on these schemes? Target the programme, watch as many episodes as possible and get the rhythm of the show inside you. Speak to the script editor and/or send them a speculative script you've written. What they *don't* want is a spec. (speculative) episode of that series using the same characters. They want something in the same genre or background as that series. Mostly, they want evidence that you can write, potential they can nurture.

If they are impressed, you'll be invited in for a chat (see Chapter 19). Always have five or six one-page story outlines ready. Upon meeting you, they want to feel you know the series well, its structure, and can (or can be trained to) deliver to deadlines. *Never* criticise the show destructively (you are criticising these people's reasons to exist!). Be enthusiastic and receptive; listen and learn.

Be prepared to have your initial outlines rejected – don't take it personally. Be persistent: with every batch rejected send them another, better batch; eventually one will hit a target.

A typical soap/series commissioning cycle might run:–

February:	writers meeting – agree storylines
Late February:	story draft delivered
April:	story modified by producers
May:	first draft commissioned
Mid-July:	second draft with the production designers
Late July:	final draft
Early September:	episode recorded
Mid-October:	episode transmitted

Many soaps and series have annual or bi-annual open trawls for new writers – find out when the next one is, and have a good script ready.

Sitcoms

Sitcoms are, again, a specialist area with their own separate books. As with 30-minute soaps, two-act Structure applies (see Ch. 8). Remember, sitcoms have *two* components: situation and comedy. It's the characters responding to a situation that makes it funny. Audiences respond to memorable characters – so create them! Comedy dialogue is the difference between saying funny things and saying things funny. People want the latter. Producers say they like to see at least three 'laughs' per page, but natural ones. Also note the cyclical nature of sitcoms: at the end of the episode the characters may have travelled a journey but their basic predicament is exactly the same as it was at the start (e.g. *Steptoe and Son, Hancock, Friends, Frasier*). And *don't* write something you think someone else will find funny; write what makes *you* laugh.

When submitting something, producers want to see:

- a completed first episode (pilot) script
- half-page story outlines for each of the next six to seven episodes (at least)
- a one or two page series format digest, including six to eight lines on each of the main characters

Finally, a note on writers collaborating: before you start, set out some firm ground rules, i.e. who does what in this relationship (know your mutual writing strengths and weaknesses), the writer credits order (usually done alphabetically) and the payments split. It will save many arguments later.

19

THE INDUSTRY: HOW IT WORKS AND YOUR PLACE IN IT

❝ If you don't conduct your relationship with the industry, it will conduct you. ❞

Paula Milne

Breaking In

They say it's not what you know but who you know. That certainly goes for the media industry – over half of it is down to knowing the right people, which means networking and contacts: selling yourself as well as your scripts. Luck also plays a significant part – having the right script in the right hands at the right time. So, how do you get that first break?

- Use your initiative. Is there a conference or seminar being organised where the speaker is an established writer or industry executive? Attend it.
- Attend an extensive weekend or week-long writing course (Chapter 20). Fellow attendees are aspiring and established writers and key industry professionals. Many writers get their first break (particularly into TV soaps or series) through meeting someone at a course.
- Some TV networks (BBC, Carlton) and film schools run occasional courses or schemes, mostly free. Entry is by script submission. Find out when the next one is.
- Regular competitions and scholarships are publicised via the monthly writers' magazines.

- Join a Writers' Group (local libraries have lists). Attend, network, suggest a seminar with an industry player. Volunteer to organise or help in its organisation; don't be scared, it's not as daunting as it seems. Many executives (especially writers) are prepared to do it for expenses or a bottle of wine – diaries permitting.
- Join one of the industry bodies (LSW, NPA, PACT, etc. see Chapter 22), meet fellow emerging talent, especially producers and directors. You stand a better chance of breaking through if part of a package (with other elements: producers, director or 'name' actor). It also boosts your confidence.
- If your local theatre has a writers' group, join it. I know you want to write for the screen, but there are more openings here. Also, when executives look for new writers, often their first thoughts turn to the theatre (even though it is a totally separate skill!) If you get something (however insubstantial) performed, it establishes an all-important track record – as does a radio play.
- Some production companies (Alomo, Hat Trick) and TV series (*EastEnders*, *The Bill*) run intern schemes (Chapter 18).

When interfacing with the industry, at whatever level, at all times be pleasant, courteous, confident, professional; not pushy, overpowering, over-confident or loud-mouthed. Learn to listen and take advice. Networking is another skill in your box of tricks. However, remember: you can have as many contacts as you like, but if you don't deliver a good script, it will embarrass people.

—— **The industry: your place in it** ——

❻ There are more stars on the Hollywood Walk of Fame for dogs, cats and horses than there are for writers. ❾
Brian Helgeland, screenwriter

❻ Power? Writers have got fuck-all power, unless they're rich or famous. ❾

American TV executive
(who requested anonymity)

In the industry hierarchy, writers have traditionally been near the bottom and the worst paid. The maxim runs: if a film's a success, the director gets the praise; if it flops, they all blame the writer. However, the importance of a good script is becoming increasingly acknowledged; those who can deliver are getting highly paid, heavily feted and respected (so long as they continue to deliver).

───────── Targeting the market ─────────

You need to know as much about the industry and how it works as you do about screenwriting itself. You need to acquaint yourself with the names (especially of producers and production companies): who's doing what, who's looking for what, commissioning trends, writing initiatives, budgets and box office.

Immerse yourself in the 'trades' (the weekly trade papers) for films – *Variety*, *Screen International* or *The Hollywood Reporter*; for UK television – *Broadcast*. Read them thoroughly, and regularly – ideally subscribe to a couple. Similarly, take as much interest in the end credits of a film or TV programme as you do in the production itself.

In all cases note the names, create a filing card system for yourself: one each for producers, agents, comedy, etc. The key people to look for are: in film – script development executives, heads of development (HoDs), producers and directors; in TV – script editors, producers, directors and commissioning editors. Build up a database, cross-referencing names with productions, projects, their track records, tastes and preferences, their attitudes towards new writers, of industry people you may meet (note where and when met, what was discussed, opinions exchanged, general impressions, etc.) As the database grows these names will become second nature.

When sending your scripts out to the industry you shoot with a sniper not a blunderbuss: target your market – and this database is your market. Information is power.

─ Producers and how to survive them ─

❛ A key factor in *Four Weddings And A Funeral* ending up a strong film was: I had a producer and director who shared my vision regarding how this film should be, and we all remained loyal to that shared vision. ❜

Richard Curtis

The key figure in any production – the one with the ultimate responsibility for a project – is the producer. Good producers get things made; bad ones waste your energy, talent and time. Good producers generate the 'heat' (enthusiasm and commitment) necessary to get a lot of different people with different talents to come together into making a movie or TV production, and then sell it. Crucially, producers also find the money – the single most important fact of life for them. Their aim is to get the best production made for the lowest cost. Get used to the idea that film and TV making is the art of the possible: what the budget and time allow. Sometimes producers take a more hands-on creative role in the project.

Today the producers with talent, energy and vision predominantly work in the independent production sector. Target the people and companies whose work you admire. Know their past track record: are their productions similar in feel to your script? Phone and ask the switchboard if they accept unsolicited material. If yes, they'll probably suggest a specific name (HoD or script editor) to send it to. Mail off your package, but don't expect an instant reply. It may take up to three months for a response. After six to eight weeks try phoning the recipient or their secretary and politely enquire about your submission. (At least you've made another contact.)

Some companies may require you to sign a release form before submitting your script (see Chapter 16). The decision is yours. New writers are always paranoid. If you want your script read you have no choice; if you don't sign, nobody will discover your masterpiece.

Acknowledge the mutual differences and priorities: the screenwriter's primary concern is getting the script right, the producer wants to find the money and get the thing made.

Taking a meeting

So a producer likes your script and you're invited in for a meeting or a 'chat'. This first meeting is usually a casual affair with both sides trying to sum up the other. You should be deciding if you want to work with this person, for they are certainly trying to decide if they can work with you. Just remember that fundamental principle: screen production is a collaborative medium.

❝ Producers look for 'personal chemistry' when working with colleagues. ❞

Adrian Hodges

If there's an obvious personality clash, or if they feel you're a writer who is totally inflexible or too precious about changing your words on the page (i.e. you aren't open to rewrites), they'll probably say 'thanks, but no thanks'. They are seeking to be reassured in this meeting: they want to have confidence in you as a writer who is not only good, but also reliable, can deliver the goods and to deadlines. Never be rude or sycophantic about their work. Be punctual, dress well (smart-casual at least), and be open, constructive and confident.

They won't usually discuss money at this meeting. They may want to discuss your submission in depth, they may want to talk about other ideas you have (have the synopses ready: see page 173), or they may well have a project or idea of their own they'd like you to flesh out and write the screenplay for. If there is agreement it is usually just verbal. Follow up this meeting with a short, appreciative letter; if anything was agreed in the meeting, state them here.

The producer may offer you an option agreement. Taking an option means for an agreed amount (from £1 to £500, but nearer the former), they own the full Rights on that script or synopsis to exploit for a set period (usually one year, renewable annually). This also obliges you to do rewrites from their 'notes'. Get used to it. If you don't do it, someone else will.

If you are offered a decent amount of money, consult the appropriate Writers Guild for the relevant rates (see Chapter 22). If offered, say, one pound, ask yourself: can this person get the project made? Remember, you need that first screened credit. Besides, you'll get your first major payment when the project starts shooting. Subsequent script sales fees are based on how much your last script sold for (or your agent). A growing practice is the Buy-Out, where you sign away *all* rights in perpetuity for an up-front payment of 2-3 times the normal Guild rates. The decision is yours.

Good producers (with their hopefully shared vision) will help you realise the full potential in your project, and if the relationship proves fruitful, enjoyable, challenging or fun, it may develop into a mutually beneficial long-term partnership. Many producers like to build up trusting long-term working relationships with a stable of favourite writers they've discovered, can nurture and rely on.

❝ If you've been paid to write something, the ultimate sin is not late delivery, but non-delivery. ❞

Colin Clements,
screenwriter/
script executive

The Pitch and pitching

Many articles have been written about, and entire courses been built around, acquiring the skills of pitching. For the novice it can be quite a daunting prospect, but some basic thoughts are given here.

A pitch is a verbal presentation of your script or idea to anyone with the power to say 'Yes'. Although more often done by producers to commissioning HoDs, writers are increasingly pitching to producers. Traditionally, you have no longer than three minutes – nearer two – to get it all across. (In *The Player*, Griffin Mill tells a writer, 'tell it to me in 25 words – no more'). This is where your work on the story concept, one-liner and log-lines pay off.

Formal pitching is not as common, or as frenetic, in the UK (where it's sometimes called a *presentation*) as in the US, but it's on the increase. There is a lot of informal pitching: every time anyone – agent, producer, script editor, or director – asks you over a meal or drink, 'what's the project about?', your response is the pitch.

A pitch contains: the main characters, the journey they take, the ending, and who will want to watch it (i.e. the same people who went to see such-and-such a film).

❝ A good idea, badly presented, sounds like a bad idea. ❞

Stephen Cannell,
US producer

So, how can you make your pitch effective? Have a strategy before you go in to pitch:

- **Know your objectives:** to make a good impression on the pitchee (be professional: be punctual, dressed smart-casual, cheery; speak clearly, confidently, with regular eye contact); to show your passion and commitment to the idea; express that idea so clearly the pitchee understands it completely, and do it so enthusiastically, so dramatically *they* get fired up by it too – enough to convince them this is the project they *must* make; to depart with a clear idea of that person's intentions for your project; to leave the door open for you to return with more ideas, even if they rejected this project. Remember: passion is great but please don't be manic.

- **Know who you're pitching to:** be aware of their production track record. Do they have the power to make a decision? If not, how close are they to someone who can?
- **Prepare:** you have only three minutes so be able to express your story concept in three or four sentences; the first sentence should contain the title, the type of story it is and an overview that hooks them; then focus on the story, main character/s, major story moments. A great log-line is useful. Be prepared to give a longer explanation if interest is shown (you'll then have 10–15 minutes).
- **Practise:** on your friends, family, tape recorder, mirror. You're not trying to memorise it; just be clear on the basics of what you're trying to say.
- **Anticipate** questions and possible objections ('it's too similar to . . . *x*', 'too different', 'how do the audience identify with the Protagonist?', etc.) and have *constructive* answers – even build them into your pitch. Be able to explain your creative choices succinctly.
- **Have ready** the appropriate back-up material (one-page proposal, preferably a full treatment) for the pitchee to sell to their boss.
- **Sell** one thing at a time (and have the appropriate synopses ready, if needed).
- Overall, make it feel like a wonderful experience for the listener (keep the cinema poster in your head).

The bottom line is: the commissioner wants to feel the confidence needed to invest in the person they are commissioning. Ultimately, it is the script that will do the selling – or not.

In development

Once your script is in development, you will be working with or to either a script editor (in TV) or a development executive/HoD (film). They work with you to get the fullest potential from the piece. But, of course, they also work for the producer and, as such, act as a conduit between you and 'upstairs', and for the producer's 'notes'. Again, it's down to the mutual working relationship between you and your editor. Generally, they are there to assist you, especially as you probably won't see the producer again after your initial meeting. Also, beware of 'development hell', where your script goes into permanent development and never gets made.

❝ You'll get rewritten even after you're dead. ❞

(Sunset Boulevard)

20

YOUR CAREER AS A WRITER

— Know yourself – market yourself —

❝ Most writers don't have the sort of nature that lends itself to self-promotion. Today's writers and agents are teaching writers how to be better self-promoters; and that's making a major decision in why some scripts sell. ❞

Stephen Rebello,
screenwriter

Generally speaking, most successful writers treat what they do as a business: a job, with regular work patterns, goals and deadlines, and a professional attitude. Of course, this does not negate your other reasons for writing, but you must know yourself and know *why* you are writing.

Remember screenwriting is a collaborative medium; you shouldn't get too precious over a particular line or scene or even entire script premise. Some see writing as a route to some ultimate career goal like directing (especially) or producing. So why not go straight there and direct a short film by some other (possibly better) writer? Most writer-directors are directors first.

Marketing yourself is down to knowing your strengths and weaknesses, as a writer and as a person. It is also about networking: opening up lines of communication that will hopefully prove fruitful later.

Few writers subscribe to or even read the trade magazines, believing they deal in information not of concern to them. They do. Remember: your database = information = power = advantage over other wannabees.

❦ The writer naturally concentrates on the creative work, spends hundreds of hours writing a script, but almost none on marketing themselves. But when you're out in the marketplace, you're not just selling a piece of work, you're selling yourself too. The way you come across and are perceived is often more likely to bring you work than what you write, assuming you write reasonably well in the first place. ❦

Julian Friedmann,
literary agent

Moreover, learn adaptability. Don't get obsessive about only wanting to write features; be prepared to tackle soaps, series, whatever comes your way. You want to work regularly, don't you? But you need that first break, to build a track record and a good reputation.

———————— Reputation ————————

❦ In this industry, your reputation is everything. The media village is very small, everyone knows everyone else and so much is based on word of mouth; your name crops up in conversation, somebody else says 'I've heard he's a bit difficult to work with'; effectively it will kill you. ❦

Malcolm Gerrie, MD:
Initial Film & Television

Think about how others see you. Get a reputation as being a new, talented writer who's good to work with, the word will spread. Producers, agents and others will be eager to meet you. Get a 'difficult' reputation and your career is already dead.

Some writers can be incredibly temperamental if they don't like what's being done to their work and sometimes behave immaturely. I am not saying roll over and take it, far from it. You have to react in a calm, considered logical way and negotiate. If a producer suggests changes you find unacceptable, don't have it out there and then in some unproductive shouting match. Say 'I'll have to consider that' and return a few days later with some good reasons why you think it won't work and offer constructive alternatives. Try seeing things from their point of view, create a positive debate and argue from a position of knowledge and confidence. There is always a middle ground without compromising totally. And never assume that a writer-producer partnership is entirely controlled by the producer.

Lastly, beware also of getting a reputation for managing to sell lots of scripts or treatments but none of them ever being made or reaching the screen.

❥ It is very important to protect your reputation. Your reputation is more than just the sum of what you write, it is how you inter-relate with other people in the industry – especially the key players: producers, directors, your agent – and how good a team player you are. ❥

Julian Friedmann,
literary agent

— Rejection – and how to deal with it —

❥ I can identify with screenwriters' frustration. I wrote over a dozen scripts before finally getting one made. ❥

Michael Tolkin, screenwriter:
The Player

You are trying to enter one of the toughest and most cynical industries around. Hence you will face rejection – a lot. Get used to it. Bounce back. Grow asbestos skin. In Art Arthur's words: reject rejection. Just remember they are rejecting the bits of paper, not you.

❥ When rejecting material, it's not necessarily due to the quality of the writing. There are so many other factors at play; even well written pieces are rejected because either we're not presently in the market for them, or there's no room in the production schedules or the budget's too high, a number of reasons. ❥

Jan Leventhal,
Carlton-Central TV

You can send the same manuscript out to a dozen people and get twelve different responses. The only time to start worrying and taking another look at your screenplay is if they all reject it citing the same reasons. Perhaps they're trying to tell you something: about your script or about yourself.

Most rejection letters will be short, curt and vague: 'not what we're looking for at the moment'. Try phoning them and asking exactly what they *are* looking for. Better still, try writing to them, politely, asking if they might expand on precisely why the script was rejected – weaknesses and strengths. You probably won't get to see a copy of the reader's coverage, but you could always try asking! At least you've opened up a constructive dialogue with the producer or company.

Ultimately, it's down to commitment: how committed are you – to your script, your writing, your career? And, to quote Michael Hauge, commitment is scarey – just ask anyone who's due to get married tomorrow! This attitude may also help you tackle writer's block. Should it happen, ask yourself: how committed am I to this script, scene or whatever? How much fear am I prepared to face in order to see me through this script or scene?

> ❢ It's very hard to continue to believe in yourself when, with all the work you've done, you have so much trouble getting it read or a response. But a good screenwriter will always rise to the top given time, if you stick with it. What works over time is just persistence. ❢
> *Tom Schulman*

—— Writing courses and seminars ——

An emerging fringe industry: intensive weekend or week-long screen-writing seminars are often led by an American screenwriting 'guru' (page 249). Whether attending will be of use to you, only you can judge. Each has something to offer. Some observations on the plus side:

- they are useful as a kind of painless revision to remind you of things you may have forgotten or don't fully understand
- you may pick up some practical tips or opinions that illuminate or revise your own views on screenwriting
- they can be *very* good for networking (page 232)
- they *are* very intensive: you will leave exhausted but also energised and fired-up to write – harness that enthusiasm and write.

On the minus side:

- they can be expensive: most novice writers are poor; your money might be better spent on buying original scripts, some 'how-to' books, renting videos, or on a computer; if you are desperate to attend, speak to the organisers, offer to help them in exchange for a reduced fee (or freebie?) – they can only say 'no', but an entrepreneurial attitude in this business can only be positive

- they tend to concentrate exclusively on the Hollywood three-act linear structure; think for yourself, draw up your own conclusions and interpretative templates
- be aware of the dangers of attending courses as a substitute for actually writing (serial course goers exist). My advice? Write a script, take a course, then write another script, take another course, and so on.

So approach them with the right attitude:

- don't go expecting to be given the keys to screenwriting heaven or some quick-fix answer (beware those who claim to offer such); each tutor has their own unique 'take' and approach to things
- take from each course what you feel is useful to you, put the rest into storage for future possible relevance; make up your own mind and don't feel 'this is how it *must* be done' or you'll end up with indentikit scripts; *you* are the writer, with your own voice, so use these courses as tools to help expand your talents
- ask yourself if you will actually get any writing done on this course; at this introductory stage you might find it more beneficial to attend those (mostly residential) ones where you will at least exit with a full or part-completed script
- as a newcomer you may fear feeling out of your depth; don't – there will be others attending more novice than you – honest!
- after the course, follow up the contacts met and keep in touch; you never know when they will bear fruit
- whatever approach works best for you, do it

A final word about correspondence courses: I am not an enthusiast.

❝ Carry on having a talent for your talent. Create an area for it. You know you possess it. ❞

Alan Plater

21
FINAL COMMENTS

What do readers and producers look for in a script?

❝ The honest answer is: I don't know, but when a good script comes across my desk, boy, you certainly know it. It literally sits up and bites you in the nose. It's something to do with my 'gut' response. ❞

Duncan Kenworthy, producer:
Four Weddings And a Funeral

❝ What's lacking in most screenplays today is resonance: they don't stick to you. You not only forget them after you've read them, you forget them while you're reading them. They feel like they're written to order, with one eye on the box office or a star name. ❞

Stephen Rebello

They want what everybody else wants: A good story. And that's down to the basic art of storytelling – making people wonder what's going to happen next. Master that and you're nearly there.

Because they read many scripts each week, Readers look for reasons not to continue reading the submission: bad layout, poor presentation, no concept of structure or characterisation, wasteful dialogue, etc. So unless you hook them early they will toss your script onto the 'to be returned' pile.

A Reader has in their head a kind of template which they lay against your screenplay. This allows them to automatically sense if your story fulfils the requirements of that form: character credibility, character consistency, character distinctiveness, action credibility, plot consistency, dialogue credibility, structure, thematic integration and passion.

What they *don't* want is:

- last week's or year's movie or production but slightly changed; they all want something new, exciting, innovative, moving – give it to them
- something you think is commercial; they want what moves and excites you, makes you rant or dash straight to your typewriter
- something that has been written to meet a clearly perceived trend. They come in waves: revived classics (*Sense and Sensibility, Little Women, Pride and Prejudice, Richard III*); baseball movies; cop shows, legal and hospital dramas; women in jeopardy; disease of the week; gothic horror revivals; romantic comedies; Tarantino-types etc. Films especially take at least 18 months to reach the screen. A trend popular now will be way out of date by the time your script is read. Screenwriters start trends, not follow them
- stories which fail to excite them, hook them, make them passionate; they don't want stories that fail to engage them (on some level) within the first ten pages
- they *hate* bad spelling, bad punctuation, bad grammar, awkward over-written prose, incorrect/inconsistent margin placement; mostly, they hate language which advances the story by *telling* them everything and *showing* them nothing – it's a visual medium, so tell it visually
- they hate anything not the right length (that's rigid).

Remember: *seduce the Reader*.

❝ The way to learn is to read stories, watch movies and trust your instincts. The more movies you watch the more the rhythm of film gets inside you. ❞

Caroline Thompson

So screenwriting, to be successful, must connect with the mind and emotions of the audience. To do this, the writer must know how what you create on the screen and on the page affects the viewing and reading audience; you must understand and create audience identification with the characters, and you must seek to draw out the common elements of our universal experience as human beings, truths that people can recognise and grasp; give new life to old stories and mythic structures; by finding the conflict, then personalising it, then increasing the stakes by putting your characters at risk, and go on raising the stakes; by drawing out, shaping and *integrating* your theme, *unifying* the whole story in a way that is internally valid and profoundly satisfying for an audience. The artifice is there *but the audience doesn't notice it.*

❝ Write a screenplay that is personal and integrated. By personal I mean simply that whatever genre it is, it must address its author's most personal concerns and considerations. And by integrated I mean that each and every aspect of it – all that we see and hear – accomplishes simultaneously the tasks of advancing the story and expanding character and theme. ❞

Richard Walter,
screenwriting tutor, UCLA

Employ any device you can to affect and entertain your Reader: imaginative and emotive terms of description, funny or quirky lines of dialogue or in 'the business', whatever – as long as it has a reason for being there and does a job. Just don't go over the top.

Look on your script as a dialogue between writer and audience, and from the page *create the movie in the mind of the reader*. What excites, grips, stimulates or moves you, may well have that effect on the Reader.

But knowing your market is also essential. Immerse yourself in the industry: there's no point in sending off a story that someone else already has in development. Being derivative – writing scripts which have thematically already been done to death – will also be of little value to you.

Ten things you must do if you want to be a screenwriter

1 See lots of movies and television (i.e. the arena you want to write in). See what the marketplace is generating. See the good films at least twice: once in the cinema, once on video. (Ideally, see them several times in the cinema: first as an enthusiast, then with your craft templates, then watch the audience reactions.) Look for the *why* and *how* they were so great or awful. Try writing your own reports and reviews about them.

2 Read screenplays – as many as possible (see Chapter 22).

3 Join a writers' group (recommended) for information, networking, moral support and positive feedback.

4 Become knowledgeable about the industry: subscribe to and read the Trade magazines. Get information about the industry: for the UK, for the US, for Europe, worldwide. Be an industry watcher – then a participant.

5 Don't listen to statistics: you want a statistic? Try this: 100% of all screenwriters working today at one time weren't working.

6 Apply the seat of the pants to the seat of the chair *daily*, and *regularly*, even if it's for only an hour. Do a minimum of 30 minutes or set yourself a minimum daily word target. Make an appointment with yourself and write – or get written off.

7 Don't get it right, get it written and finish what you write. Don't lose time. Enjoy it! Worry about perfection during the rewrites.

8 Have persistence and commitment: if you don't have it, learn it. Reject rejection.

9 Believe in yourself and your talents: *you* are the commodity, not your script. If you don't believe in yourself, how do you expect anyone else to? You weren't born with an agent, and getting one isn't an instant ticket to fame and fortune.

10 Every six months or so, ask yourself: 'Am I enjoying this process?' If it becomes painful, find another game to play.

❢ It's a collaborative process, sometimes you get pushed around. But it's a game and you don't have to play it . ❧

William Goldman

To say any script is truly finished is a fallacy; things will change or be changed by others. Try to regard every script as work in progress until it finally gets shown on the screen.

Ten guaranteed ways to fail as a scriptwriter

1 Don't write anything
2 Write badly
3 Show ignorance of the market
4 Be rude
5 Promise what you can't deliver

6 Don't take criticism
7 Show ignorance of the production process
8 Fail to adapt
9 Be a nuisance during the shoot
10 Think it's easy

And finally...

As a writer, you are what the industry calls a 'creative'. The writer is learning all the time: from each successive script written, from meeting other people (especially fellow writers and industry professionals), from everything you do; learning – about life, about yourself. Every day is a day in the classroom.

Experienced screenwriters expect to spend up to six months of full-time work completing a feature script. So anyone with the stamina and dedication to finish a script (especially a feature), whatever the quality, deserves admiration. It takes a lot of effort and hard work. But the more you do it the swifter it becomes.

> ❛ There are certain assumptions about the nature of cinema which should guide most screenwriters: one, cinema is visual; two, cinema is largely a storytelling medium; three, once you have committed to telling a story, you have to tell it vigorously, economically and directly. After those assumptions are taken for granted, everything is up for grabs. ❜
>
> *Larry Gross*, screenwriter:
> *48 Hours, Geronimo,*
> *Streets of Fire*

> ❛ Every great writer was a new writer once – even Shakespeare. ❜
> *Alan Bleasdale*

. . . and finally, William Goldman's famous words about the industry:

> ❛ No-one knows anything! ❜

Now stop reading, stop talking about it – Go Write!

22

APPENDICES

Answers

Chapter 1:

You only need steps 1 and 10 – the rest can be deduced by the audience.

Chapter 4:

(Log-lines) 1 *Four Weddings And A Funeral*
2 *Schindler's List*
3 *Disclosure*
4 *Maverick*

(Theme)
1 *Field of Dreams*: It is important for us to have dreams – even if those dreams are not ultimately fulfilled, it is important for us to have them.
2 *Jumanji*: In life you should always 'face what you fear. Stand up for yourself. Finish what you start', even if that means facing up to the unpalatable (owning up to a wrong-doing) or saying the hard-to-say: from 'I'm sorry' to 'I love you'.
3 *Batman Forever*: We all have two sides to ourselves and our identity (two faces, two personas): the one we show to the world and the one inside we try to hide. For us to function as human beings the 'good' side must control or at least balance the 'bad' side (our inner true self must control and balance the outer personality).
4 *Jerry Maguire*: Self fulfilment comes from selflessness.

Chapter 7:

(Key-Lines)

Quiz Show: "All is not well in America" (spoken on the radio)
Chinatown: "You gotta be rich to kill somebody, anybody, and get away with it"

(Inciting Incident)

1 *The Crying Game*: When Fergus pulls out the photograph of Dill from the soldier's wallet.
2 *Don Juan De Marco*: When the Don Juan/analyst therapy sessions start, and a time-lock of ten days is set.
3 *Field of Dreams*: When Ray, having built the baseball diamond and the story apparently over, hears the voice 'Go the distance'.
4 *Quiz Show*: Where Richard Goodwin is watching the video play-backs and realises something is up.

(Half-way point/point of no return)

1 *The Crying Game*: When Fergus uncovers Dill's physical secret.
2 *Don Juan de Marco*: The death of Don's father and the subsequent threat of medication, plus the notification of only five days left to finish the sessions.
3 *Field of Dreams*: At the baseball game with Terence Mann, when Ray sees the sign about Archibald 'Doc' Graham and again hears the voice saying 'Go the distance'.
4 *Quiz Show*: Dick Goodwin's meeting with the producers, when the Stempel tape is played and Goodwin's case seemingly falls apart.

(Moment of Truth/TP 2)

1 *The Crying Game*: The scene where Fergus finally says 'I love you, Dill'.
2 *Don Juan de Marco*: The final session; the conversation where Don throws the plant pot, and Brando finally admits 'My world . . . is not perfect'.
3 *Field Of Dreams*: Ray's expositionary speech while driving the van home, having just picked up the young Archie Graham.
4 *Quiz Show*: The scene at Van Doren's home where Dick Goodwin confronts Charles with the registered letter evidence; Dick makes a decision and tells Charles to disappear.

Useful addresses

NOTE: whenever writing to anyone, enclose a stamped self-addressed envelope or sufficient international reply coupons (if abroad). It is common courtesy – and professional.

Script suppliers

Many screenplays are now published as books. Beware, they are generally products prepared after the event, i.e. someone transcribing what happens on the screen in the released film. What you want are original drafts or shooting scripts. Film and TV scripts printed in their original formats, early drafts, treatments, film analyses and storyboards are available to buy (approximately $15–20 per script/ $10–15 per treatment) from:

USA:

Book City of Burbank, 308 N. San Fernando Boulevard, Burbank, Ca. 91502 (Tel: 818-848 4417)

Hollywood Book and Poster, PO Box 539, Los Angeles, Calif. 90078 (Tel: 213-465 8764/Fax: 213-465 0413) Catalogue: $3 + $7 postage

Hollywood Scripts, 11288 Ventura Blvd., No. 431B, Studio City, Calif. 91604 (Tel: 818-980 3545)

Larry Edmunds Cinema and Theatre Bookshop, 6644 Hollywood Boulevard, Hollywood, Ca. 90028 (Tel: 213-463 3273/Fax: 213-463 4245). No catalogues

Script City, 8033 Sunset Blvd., Suite 1500, Hollywood, Calif. 90046 (Tel: 213-871 0707) Cat: $2, deducted from first order.

UK:

The Screenwriter's Store, PO Box 11008, London SE10 9ZH (Tel: 0181-293 1144)

Script City, Dept "A", Suite 5134, 19 Cheval Place, London SW7 3EW (Tel: 0171-413 9985/Fax: 0171-581 4445) Note: this has no connection with the above US outlet

[See also Internet Web Sites section]

Specialist bookshops

Cinema Bookshop, 13–14 Great Russell Street, London W1, UK (Tel: 0171-637 0206)

Elliot M. Katt Bookstore, 8568 Melrose Ave., Los Angeles, Ca. 90069 (Tel: 310-652 5178/Fax: 310-653 2778) Specialist in rare/out of print/signed books and published screenplays. Regular lists.

MOMI (Museum of the Moving Image) and NFT (National Film Theatre) Bookshops, South Bank, London SE1 8XT (Tel: 0171-928 3535)

Samuel French Theatre and Film Bookshop, 7623 Sunset Blvd., Hollywood, Ca. 90046 (Tel: 213-876 0570). Many specialist mailshot catalogues, including 'Books on Screenwriting'.

[The above US script suppliers also sell books]

Books – general reference

B.F.I. (British Film Institute) Film and Television Handbook. Published every November. Available from the BFI (see below)

The Hollywood Creative Directory (Hollywood Creative Directory Pub.*)

Low Budget Funding Guide (free annual booklet). c/o BFI Regional Development Unit (see below).

PACT Directory (Published annually; information on all Indie Production Company members. Available from PACT, see below). Very useful.

The Scriptwriting Pack, Ross Smith (British Academy, 1994)

The Writers' and Artists' Yearbook (A & C Black, UK. Published every November).

The Writer's Handbook (Ed: Barry Turner. Macmillan/PEN). Published every November. An essential UK reference book.

The Writer's Market (Ed: Garvey. Writers' Digest Books*). Annual US equivalent to The Writer's Handbook.

* = US or Canadian imprints.

Screenwriting books

Books on screenwriting are many. The consistently recommended ones are by Edward Dmytryk, Syd Field, Michael Hauge, Lew Hunter, Viki King, William Miller, Linda Seger, Dwight & Joy Swain, Christopher Vogler, Jurgen Wolff & Kerry Cox.

Marketing screenplays

Elane Feldman – The Writer's Guide To Self-Promotion and Publicity (Writer's Digest Books*).

Syd Field – Selling A Screenplay: The Screenwriter's Guide To Hollywood (Dell*).

Carl Sautter – How To Sell Your Screenplay (New Chapter Press*).

Cynthia Whitcomb – Selling Your Screenplay (Crown*).

Background books

John Boorman – Money Into Light (Faber and Faber) Diary account of making *The Emerald Forest*

John Boorstin – The Hollywood Eye: what makes movies work (HarperCollins). Good on affecting your audience.

Joseph Campbell – The Hero With A Thousand Faces (Abacus*) The classic study of myth in storytelling. Any of his books are heavy going but worth reading.

Jake Eberts & Terry Ilott – My Indecision Is Final: The Rise and Fall of Goldcrest Films (Faber & Faber). Sharp industry insights.

Lajos Egri – The Art Of Dramatic Writing (Citadel*) deals mainly with plays; essential reading but rather insistently polemical.

Jan Fleischer – An Approach to Screenwriting for the Feature Film (free from SOURCES – Tel: 31-20-672 08 01 or from the UK MEDIA desk c/o BFI).

Julian Friedmann – How To Make Money Scriptwriting (Boxtree). Insider tips on the industry, written by an agent.

William Froug – The Screenwriter Looks At The Screenwriter (Silman James*)
" The New Screenwriter Looks At The New Screenwriter (Silman James*)
[Interviews with Hollywood screenwriters]

William Goldman – Adventures In The Screen Trade (Warner Bks) Life in the Hollywood jungle: acute and funny – a good place to start.

Lindheim and Blum – Inside Television Producing (Focal Press).

Roger von Oech – A Whack On The Side Of The Head (Thorsons/ Harper Collins)
" A Kick In The Seat Of The Pants (Thorsons/Harper Collins) Both good on freeing-up creativity.

Ross Smith – The Scriptwriting Pack (British Academy, 1994)

Ronald Tobias – Twenty Master Plots And How To Build Them (Piatkus)

[Most US Books are available in the UK]

Magazines

Brainstorm, 85 Ridgmount Gardens, London WC1E 7AY/ PO Box 2271, Bellingham, Wa. 98227, USA. Bi-monthly creativity/ productivity newsletter from Jurgen Wolff.

Broadcast (see EMAP subscriptions) Weekly UK Television Trade paper.

[EMAP Subscriptions, Readerlink, Lansdowne Mews, 196 High Street, Tonbridge, Kent TN9 1EF]

Empire, 1st Floor Mappin House, 4 Winsley Street, London W1N 7AR (Monthly UK Film magazine) Tel: 0171-436 1515. Contact:

Tower Subscriptions, Tower House, Lathkill Street, Sovereign Park, Market Harborough, Leicester LE16 9EF (Tel: 01858 468888)

Hollywood Reporter*, PO Box 480800, L.A., Ca. 90048 (Fax: 213 525 2387. Weekly US Film Trade paper)

Hollywood Scriptwriter*, PO Box 10277, Burbank, Ca. 91510 (Tel: 818-845 5525). Monthly, subscription only newsletter.

Moving Pictures International (for films) and MPTV (for television) 151–3 Wardour Street, London W1V 3TB (Tel: 0171-287 0070/Fax: 0171-734 6153/US: 5225 Wilshire Blvd., Suite 900, L.A., Ca. 90036 (Tel: 213-965 7110/Fax: 213-965 8645) Both monthly.

Premiere, (Monthly Film magazine) see under Empire.

Screen International (Weekly UK Film Trade paper) Tel: 0171-837 1685. See EMAP subscriptions.

SCR(ipt) Magazine*, 5638 Sweet Air Road, Baldwin, Maryland 21013 (Tel: 410-592 3466)

Sight and Sound, Freepost WD 3159, Leicester LE87 4AG. (UK Film Monthly).

Variety*, Cahners Publishing (Netherlands), International Circulation Center, Postbus 9000, 2130 DB Hoofdorp, The Netherlands (Weekly US Film Trade Paper).

Writers' Forum, 9–10 Roberts Close, Moxley, Wednesbury, W. Midlands, WS10 8SS (Tel: 01902 497514) Annual subscription.

Writers News: monthly, subscription only from PO Box 4, Nairn, Scotland IV12 4HU Tel: 01667 454441/Fax: 01667 454401.

Writers' Monthly, Market Link Publishing plc., The Mill, Bearwalden Business Park, Wendens Ambo, Saffron Walden, Essex CB11 4JX (Tel: 01799 544200) Annual subscription: £33 New incarnation; no link with former publishers.

Writing Magazine (Printed bi-monthly, also available in larger bookstores. Address as per Writers News).

Industry organisations

B.E.C.T.U., 111 Wardour Street, London W1V 4AY, UK.

British Film Institute, 21 Stephen Street, London W1P 1PL (Tel: 0171-255 1444/Fax: 0171-436 7950). Annual memberships (various grades), discounts, excellent library reference and research facilities.

First Film Foundation, 9 Bourlet Close, London W1P 7PJ (Tel: 0171-580 2111). Excellent support organisation for first time writers and film-makers. Free.

Independent Film Workshop, 81 Berwick Street, London W1V 3PF (Tel: 0171-437 3991 & 0171-287 1870/Fax: 0171-439 2243. Contact: Elliot Grove). Regular seminars, newsletter, annual Raindance Film Festival). IFW is also home of the European Film Institute.

London Screenwriters' Workshop, c/o The Holborn Centre for the Performing Arts, Three Cups Yard, Sandland Street, London WC1R 4PZ. (Tel: 0171-242 2134) 600+ members nationwide; £25 annual membership). Regular courses, industry seminars, workshops and newsletter.

New Playwrights Trust, InterChange Studios, Dalby Street, London NW5 3NQ (Tel: 0171-284 2818/Fax: 0181-482 5292; they also accommodate screenwriting).

New Producers' Alliance, 9 Bourlet Close, London W1P 7PJ (Tel: 0171-580 2480/Fax: 0171-580 2484) Annual membership starts at £45. Energetic new, young producers' body (mostly film). Monthly newsletter and seminars, good for networking.

P.A.C.T. (Producers Alliance for Cinema and Television), 45 Mortimer Street, London W1N 7TD (Tel: 0171-331 6000/Fax: 0171-331 6700). Main industry body for UK Independent Producers (mostly TV).

Player Playwrights, 9 Hillfield Park, London N10 3QT (Tel: 0181-883 0371) Bi-weekly meetings in London: seminars, rehearsed readings of members' new writing. £5 annual membership.

The Script Factory, c/o BFI Production, 29 Rathbone Street, London W1P 1AG (Tel. 0171-636 5587/Information line: 0171-580 1052). BFI-supported regular performance script readings.

Scriptpool, 10 West Savile Road, Edinburgh EH16 5NG (Tel: 0131-668 4377) Packaging organisation for UK writers with scripts to source US producers, directors, studio execs. Send 1-page Synopsis first.

The Society of Authors, 84 Drayton Gardens, London SW10 9SB (Tel: 0171-373 6642).

T.A.P.S., (Television Arts Performance Showcase), Teddington Studios, Broom Road, Teddington TW11 9NT, UK. (Tel: 0181-977 3252). Industry supported body; regular showcase readings of new screenplays.

Writers Digest Books, 1507 Dana Avenue, Cincinnati, Ohio 45207, USA. (Tel: 513-531 2222). An extensive and comprehensive catalogue.

Writers Guild of America (east), 555 W. 57th Street, New York, NY 10019.
Writers Guild of America (west), 8955 Beverly Blvd., West Hollywood,
Ca. 90048-2456 (Tel: 310-550 1000/Fax: 310-550 8185).
Writers Guild of Great Britain, 430 Edgware Road, London W2 1EH.
(Tel: 0171-723 8074).

Script reading services

A small selection. Each, for a fee, will read your script and give you
either a detailed written assessment or one-to-one personal seminar.
Write first regarding rates.

Raymond G. Frensham, PO Box 53, Ilford, Essex IG1 2AL
Independent Film Workshop (above)
London Screenwriters' Workshop (above)
New Playwrights Trust (above)
Player-Playwrights (above)
Writers Digest Criticism Service (above)

Course and seminar organisers

The Arvon Foundation, Totleigh Barton, Sheepwash, Beaworthy,
Devon EX21 5NS, UK (Tel: 01409 23338). Also centres at:
Hebden Bridge, West Yorkshire and Beauly, Inverness-shire
Long established, highly regarded organisation.
Fen Farm Writing Courses, 10 Angel Hill, Bury St. Edmunds, Suffolk
IP33 1UZ, UK. (Tel: 012834 753110 or 01379 898741).
Excellent week-long residential workshops.
Independent Film Workshop (above)
Kent Enterprises, The Oast House, Plaxtol, Sevenoaks, Kent TN15
0QG, UK. Tel: 01732 810925/Fax: 01732 810632
London Media Workshops, 101 King's Drive, Gravesend, Kent DA12
5BQ, UK. (Tel: 01474 564676).
London Screenwriters' Workshop (above)
New Playwrights Trust (above)
Screenwriters' Lab, c/o Susan Benn, Performing Arts Lab, ICA, 12
Carlton House Terrace, London SW1Y 5AH (Tel: 0171-839
5677) Bi-annual residential intensive workshops
Scriptwriters Tutorials, 65 Lancaster Road, London N4 4PL (Tel:
0171-720 7047).
Richard Walter: Screenwriting – The Whole Picture (Tel: 800-755
2785 and 818-906 2785) UCLA course organiser.
Writers Boot Camp, 1525 South Sepulveda Boulevard, Suite A, Los
Angeles, Ca. 90025 (Tel: 310-470 8849)

Internet web sites

A small selection from this ever-growing sector.

(Keywords: writing, screenwriting, screenwriters, movies, television, Hollywood):

http://dspace.dial.pipex.com/town/square/gh91/lsw.htm

[London Screenwriters' Workshop site]

[E-mail to: Aten@dial.pipex.com]

[& jhobson@cix.compulink.co.uk]

http://pages.ripco.com:8080/~bbb/scripts.htm/

[complete Hollywood scripts]

http://remarque.berkeley.edu/~cohen

[Univ of Calif. at Berkeley media database]

http://uk.imdb.com/ [Movie database]

http://www.aint-it-cool-news.com [Harry Knowles' Previews site]

http://www.bfi.org.uk/ [BFI site + NFT & MOMI listing +

membership, contact info etc]

http://www.cathouse.org/pub/cathouse/movies/database

[Covers full info on 32,000 released movies]

http://www.erack.com/EMPIRE/ [Empire Film Mag]

http://www.excite.com/search.gw [good screenwriters info. site]

http://www.ftech.net/~indfilm/

[Ind. Film Wkshop/European Film Institute]

http://www.geocities.com/SoHo/Studios/8451/links.htm

[Independent film industry gateway website listing

many worldwide website film info. services]

http://www.hollywood network.com:80/hm/index.html [good]

http://www.hollywoodreporter.com [H.Rep. magazine site]

http://www.meaddata.com

[Entertainment news/info sources on the industry]

http://www.screenwriters.com/screennet.html

[Screenwriters online network]

http://www.screenwriters.com/Cox/index.html

[screenwriter Kerry Cox]

http://www.teleport.com:80/~dheemer/scriter.html

mailto:listserv@cunyvm.bitnet

[Media professionals forum exchanging ideas/info/experiences]

<mailto://movie@ibmpcug.co.uk."HELP">

[Hollywood database for directors, actors, producers, etc]

telnet://nex:meaddata.com

[Entertainment news/info on industry sources]

CompuServe have a writing forum with workshops, info and interaction with others. A useful place to be.